LOVE & WAR

LOVE & WAR

Stories of War Brides
from the Great War to Vietnam

CAROL FALLOWS

BANTAM BOOKS
SYDNEY • AUCKLAND • TORONTO • NEW YORK • LONDON

LOVE & WAR
A BANTAM BOOK

First published in Australia and New Zealand in 2002
by Bantam

National Library of Australia
Cataloguing-in-Publication Entry

Fallows, Carol.
  Love & war: stories of war brides from the Great War to
  Vietnam.

  Bibliography.
  Includes index.

  ISBN 1 86325 267 3.

  1. War brides - Australia. 2. Australia - Emigration and
  immigration - History - 20th century. I. Title.

994.0082

Transworld Publishers,
a division of Random House Australia Pty Ltd
20 Alfred Street, Milsons Point, NSW 2061
http://www.randomhouse.com.au

Random House New Zealand Limited
18 Poland Road, Glenfield, Auckland

Transworld Publishers,
a division of The Random House Group Ltd
61–63 Uxbridge Road, London W5 5SA

Random House Inc
1540 Broadway, New York, New York 10036

Typeset by Bookhouse, Sydney
Printed and bound by Griffin Press, Netley, South Australia

10 9 8 7 6 5 4 3 2 1

For mum and dad, June and Willard Fethers

Contents

Introduction

I began this book because my mother was a war bride and, as a child of the baby boom with a vivid imagination, this was like something out of the movies. My father, I imagined, was just like Errol Flynn, my mother as beautiful as Vivien Leigh, and their story as exciting as any celluloid romance.

There have been hundreds of books written about the wars of the twentieth century, Australia's role in these wars and their social, political and historical impact on this country. Yet these books pay little or no attention to the thousands of women who migrated to Australia to marry Australian servicemen after those wars. This is surprising given the number of women and that, in the view of the Department of Repatriation, they benefited Australian society: 'What better immigrants could be imagined than those who had been "hand-picked", as it were, by members of the services,' says the Annual Report of 1947–48. 'A few, it is true, were unhappily chosen, but the large majority were excellent types and an acquisition to Australia.' The Repatriation Commissioner commented: 'Australia benefits by the increment to its population, but there is a factor which is considerably more important and that is, it assists the establishment of the domestic circle which is so essential to a happy national life.'[1]

Even a quick flick through the newspapers from the end of both the world wars finds numerous stories about brides and 'stork ships' coming into Australian ports, which makes the lack of even a mention of these women in so many history books even more puzzling.

Perhaps it is *because* they were 'hand-picked' and not part of an official immigration program, that they have been largely ignored. However, it is more likely that they have been overlooked because the transporting of wives, fiancées and children to Australia was handled in an ad hoc fashion by the Australian government, unlike the United States where both a War Brides Act and Fiancées Act were passed at the end of the Second World War to establish the right of wives and fiancées to enter and live in the States.

For the purposes of this book I have defined as a 'war bride' anyone from another country who married a member of the Australian armed forces as a result of war. The war brides may have come to Australia as a wife with or without children or as a fiancée, they may have come as part of a government program or their trip may have been funded by their partner, or partner's family. They may have had to wait for a number of years before the Australian government would allow them to live in this country or before they could arrange passage. They may have stayed in their home country with their new husband and planned to live there, eventually changing their minds and coming to Australia, or they may have lived in Australia for a short while and then returned to the woman's home country.

In the 1940s thousands of Australian girls married American GIs[2] and for many Australians these are the only war brides they've heard of. The arrival of the American troops on Australian soil made an enormous impact both socially and to morale. Sent by President Roosevelt and under the command of General Douglas MacArthur, these troops not only gave Australians confidence that they could repel the enemy, they also provided a social outlet. When on leave the Yanks had money to spend and were ready to have a good time with the local girls whenever they could. In the next few years an estimated 12 000 to 15 000 Australian girls would marry Americans. Many married in Australia so that by the time they were able to join their husbands in the United States they often had little children.

These Australian women are a small percentage of the one million war brides who went to the USA after the Second World War as a consequence of around sixteen million Americans serving overseas during 1941 to 1946.[3]

Australian servicemen who were sent away from their country to fight a war were in a similar situation to those GIs who came to Australia in the early 1940s. Many left wives and lovers behind, but many more were at a time of life when they would be thinking about falling in love, settling down and starting a family. Many of these young men did – not with the girl next door or down the street, but with the women who lived in the countries where they were based or fighting, imprisoned or part of the repatriation forces.

By the end of the Great War the Australian government had already planned the demobilisation of the thousands of Australians serving overseas. They knew it would take a year at least to get everyone home and they knew too that they needed to keep the soldiers occupied while they were waiting. The official war historian, C.E.W. Bean, estimated that there were 92 000 soldiers in France, 60 000 in England and 17 000 in Egypt, Palestine and Syria, as well as personnel in Mesopotamia, Persia, Kurdistan, Salonica and India.[4] The Australian government organised training and education programs aimed at keeping these troops gainfully occupied. Officially known as Non-Military Employment the programs became known amongst the troops as 'Non-Military Enjoyment'. Bean acknowledges that of 47 000 enrolled in these courses in France, probably only 10 000 actually attended.[5] Many servicemen occupied themselves elsewhere, socialising with local people, consolidating romances that had begun during the war, playing cards and trying to contain the enormous restlessness they felt at not being speedily returned to Australia.

During and after the Great War Australian servicemen wanted to bring their wives, children and fiancées to Australia from mainly England, Belgium and France though there are reports of brides from Egypt also. Bean writes: 'Over 15 000 soldiers' wives, fiancées and children were embarked without delay'.[6] Perhaps his recollection is clouded by the fact that he wrote this twenty-eight years after the end of the war, because as you read these accounts you will find that the wives, children and fiancées waited as long as any of the soldiers to embark on their journey to Australia – originally the Australian government had not made any allowance for the transport of families with the soldiers, but it didn't take long for them to realise that this was an oversight that could have major repercussions and rectify their mistake.

History repeated itself at the end of the Second World War when wives and fiancées again waited for the government to arrange their travel to Australia where they too would start a new life. Brides in this war came from all parts of the United Kingdom – England, Wales, Scotland and Ireland; from France, Italy, Poland, Germany, Switzerland, the Middle East, Canada and Japan – anywhere Australians were stationed. Once again the Australian government forgot to plan for these immigrants and found themselves facing angry groups of women and Australian servicemen demanding family passage.

There are no official figures, but around 550 000 Australian men and women served overseas during the the Second World War so an estimate of over 25 000 war brides – and a few war husbands – would not be unreasonable. This is based on the ratio of Australians serving overseas to war brides who came to this country after the Great War. We know that over 600 brides came from Japan – and 2486 from Canada and the US in 1948 alone.

During the Korean War the men were stationed in Japan and once again had the opportunity to meet Japanese as well as Chinese and Korean women. And when Australians were stationed in Vietnam during the Vietnam War many met – and some married – Vietnamese women. However, this time around there was no government assistance in getting wives to Australia, in fact many authorities were obstructionist to those servicemen who wanted to marry or bring home a wife from this part of the world. The number of brides who arrived from Korea and Vietnam in the years 1950 to 1972 is shrouded in mystery.

No matter what country these women came from, the vast majority of them migrated to Australia for no other reason than that they loved an Australian soldier.

Over 200 war brides, their husbands or their descendants contacted me about my research for this book. Many of the women belong to associations or groups which meet regularly, with the common bond being that they are war brides, to talk about their experiences in their adopted country and to share their memories of home. Others had never really spoken about their romances until now.

There is a general expectation that couples who meet and marry during the extraordinary times of war will *not* have successful relationships. But war affects every relationship – those which were already established as well as those which grew out of war. This is borne out by statistics, which also show that after a war divorces increase.

Thousands of couples who met because of war have nonetheless had happy, long-lasting relationships. Of course during the research for this book I have found some who didn't. But it says much for most of these women that the power of romantic love and the determination to make a relationship succeed without the support of their families and friends has helped them to lead happy, fulfilled lives. Many have since visited their homelands but just as many have not.

I did not set out to write an academic text, but to put together the history of the war brides who came to Australia using their personal stories and some historical background.

In order to find war brides I advertised in newsletters and magazines of the Returned Services League (RSL) and Legacy and on radio. I did write to some brides whose names were passed to me by others, but I waited for them to tell me their stories as I wanted people to be willing to talk about this intimate part of their lives.

In trying to include a broad cross-section of accounts I have had to exclude some of the information received – I hope those whose stories are not included or those whose stories have been shortened will forgive me. Many of the real-life romances in this book are worthy of a book of their own – indeed, a few war brides have self-published accounts of their lives and these make fascinating reading. I would like to encourage many more to write down their own stories in detail, both for their families and as a historical record.

Australia is a country of great cultural diversity and it is only in recent years that we have recognised how this diversity makes us strong. The women who came to Australia as war brides have made a significant contribution.

I hope this book will go some way to redressing the lack of documentation of these important immigrants as well providing a fascinating insight into love in wartime.

A word about 'Aussie'

Using the word 'Aussie' to describe Australians came back into favour with the 2000 Sydney Olympics, but in researching this book I found that the soldiers of the Great War affectionately referred to themselves and their country as Aussie (or Ausie/Aussy – the spelling varied but the meaning stayed the same). It gave a new resonance to the word for me and so I have used it throughout the book as I feel it reflects the Australian character which so many women from all over the world fell in love with.

My Mother's Story

My mother, June Beale, met my father, Willard Fethers, in 1942.

My father, a pilot with the RAAF, was in the town of Burton-on-Trent in Staffordshire, England, with an airman friend on weekend leave. When they couldn't find a bed for the night a publican suggested they try a local household which had been billeting soldiers.

My mother and grandmother, who lived nearby, were visiting a friend, Gwen, when she received the phone call asking if she had beds for two airman. She didn't but my grandmother did, and so my father and his friend came to stay.

After their first visit they came back regularly. At the time Will was twenty-two and June sixteen.

About six months after they met Will flew with his English air crew to the Middle East via Gibraltar and Malta. They were not to see each other again for three years. In October 1942 during a raid over Tobruk the port engine of the Wellington bomber Will was flying died 50 miles out to sea. Will managed to fly it back to land on only one engine. The plane skidded during landing and the starboard engine caught fire. The crew escaped, only to find themselves in the desert with no food and little water. Ten days later they were captured trying to steal a truck from an Italian army camp and Will spent the next three years as a POW firstly in Italy and then in Germany. At the time Will was shot down, June was still a schoolgirl. When she discovered he was a POW she began to write to him, and it was during the three years of corresponding that their relationship developed. When Will was finally repatriated to Brighton after the war ended in Europe, he phoned her.

June & Will Fethers, 1947

'We took Will on a holiday to Sidmouth for at least a week,' said June, 'and he proposed under a haystack in a farmer's field.' June's initial reluctance was eventually converted to a definite 'yes', but by the time Will was due to return to Australia on a troopship they had decided to wait a year before making a final commitment. The war was still raging in the Pacific and Will was 'really worried about taking on the responsibility of a wife and not being able to support her – especially after seeing what Dad went through in the Depression,' he told me. Will's father, one of the original Anzacs, had returned from the First World War a major, but like so many diggers at that time, his family had struggled to survive for most of the Depression.

June was only nineteen and her mother was a widow. For her, leaving England would mean leaving her art studies and her mother – possibly forever.

June came to Australia as a fiancée. The rules were that her fare of £350.00 would be refunded if she married within three months of arriving. The ship she travelled on, the *Otranto*, was one of the many troopships that carried wives, fiancées and children home to Australia after the Second World War.

'Twelve bunks to a cabin and we did our own laundry,' was June's brief description of the trip to Australia via Port Said.

She arrived on New Year's Eve to a wharf strike and was welcomed to Australia by Will's family including his sister. The wharf strike meant June could not get her trunk and spent the next three days wearing clothes Will's sister had lent her. 'I got whisked off to a party,' she said, 'with no clothes except those I stood up in.'

Will and June were married in February 1946 in Melbourne.

CHAPTER 1
Sex, War and the Role of Women

Hold your hand out, naughty boy.
Hold your hand out, naughty boy.
Last night, in the pale moonlight,
I saw yer! I saw yer!
With a nice girl in the park.

You were strolling full of joy,
And you told her you'd never
   kissed a girl before:
Hold your hand out, naughty boy.

War affects the behaviour of those involved, and sexual behaviour has, throughout history, changed radically while a war is being waged. Men, it is believed, are better fighters when they are sexually aggressive. In a natural reaction to the stress and trauma of war and life in the services, which emphasises masculinity, obedience and self-discipline, soldiers will look for the comforts of female company when they are off-duty. War is also a time when emotions are heightened, and across the centuries there are many examples of the avid pursuit by women of romantic and sexual adventures during war.

War also brings social change and that, of course, affects women. There are historical examples as far back as Boadicea and beyond of women initiating change or their roles being fundamentally altered as a result of war.

For soldiers, when there are no real women around, a photo or drawing of one is a gentle, cheerful or sexy reminder of another way of life. The first pin-ups – evocative pictures or drawings of women – became popular

The refined Gibson Girl

during the Great War. The American 'Gibson Girl', created in 1870 by Charles Gibson, is considered to be the first pin-up girl. And not only did men find her appealing, she was also the model that young girls aimed to copy because she was refined and confident.

Pin-ups are also sometimes called cheesecake photos. The name supposedly came about in 1915 when picture postcards were at their height of popularity. A newspaper photographer asked Russian diva Elvira Amazar to hold up her skirt for his photo. The photographer's editor is reported to have said, 'Why this is better than cheesecake!'[1]

The postcards of the Great War, which were printed and collected by soldiers in their millions, depicted bathing beauties, peekaboo poses,

The saucy mademoiselle on page one is from a typical postcard sent by an Aussie soldier somewhere in France. The message reads:

Aug 30 1917

Dear Pal

Well Herb old man, how are you keeping? If you're as well as I am you must be pretty good. We are on the march, but away from the line this time. It is rumoured that we are going out for a long spell. We have been on the march for two days now and are still going strong. We are starting off again in the morning.

Have just been reading about Darcy's body being brought back to Sydney. He came a gutser by leaving Australia poor chap, didn't he.

Have you seen the old people lately?

What do you think of the French girls? They're not bad are they.

Regards to all,

Your old cobber

Neville

sequential love 'stories' and seduction. Some featured homilies, sentimental poems and patriotic verse as captions to staged photos of soldiers and their lovely sweethearts in numerous scenarios, from leaving to go to war to dying with angels ascending.

Cigarette cards were also popular. These postcard-sized pin-ups began as stiffening to protect cigarettes and the first illustrated card appeared in the US in 1878. These too often depicted beauties.

American star Billie Burke

During the Great War the popularity of the cinema grew. Not only were the romantic and swashbuckling adventures of the stars an escape from the reality of life for an hour or two, the cinemas also provided dark places where couples could be intimate. From the movies came the movie stars, and the postcards and cigarette cards so popular during the early part of the century were their best form of publicity. Theda Bara, Hollywood's first sex goddess who was famous for her long kisses, revealing exotic costumes and eroticism, and Annette Kellermann, the inventor of the revealing one-piece swim-

suit, were two stars whose photos became popular. Actress Billie Burke was another postcard favourite. Movie magazines followed as the ideal promotional vehicle, and the stars and would-be stars who posed provocatively in them were perfect pin-ups.

By the time the Second World War began movies were very much a part of life and many went to the cinema two or three times a week. The stars of Hollywood were acknowledged as important for boosting the morale of the men in the armed services. Stars were depicted in particular ways: Veronica Lake and

Australia's Annette Kellermann

Gloria Grahame were seen as seductresses; Esther Williams took over where Annette Kellermann left off as the beautiful water nymph; Ann Sheridan became known as 'The Oomph Girl' and Jane Russell as 'earthly, buxom – and on the wholesome side.'[2] But the most popular pin-up of all during this war was film star Betty Grable. Wearing a swimsuit and high heels and with arms akimbo she is inviting every soldier who looks at her to come this way, as she coyly smiles at him over her right shoulder. Rita Hayworth comes a close second. Flaming red hair and once again a swimsuit – in one of her most famous poses she is wearing a not particularly daring two piece, but she is lying on silk sheets with her arms in a welcoming pose and her hair spread out, just waiting for what comes next.

In the early 1940s the Varga girls appeared and these delicate watercolour paintings joined the most popular pin-ups of the Second World War. The Varga girl first appeared in *Esquire* magazine in October

*Betty Grable,
pin-up star*

The elegant, emancipated fashion of the 1920s

1940, an enticing, idealistic drawing of a girl with a 'come hither' look. Imitations of Alberto Vargas' unrealistically glamorous females were painted on the noses of just about every tank and aeroplane in the US military by the end of the Second World War.

Come the Vietnam War it was once again a redhead, Ann-Margret, who made it to the top of the pin-ups. Others whose seductive photos were plastered on walls and canvas included Raquel Welch, Marilyn Monroe and Brigitte Bardot. And the publicity shots of 1960s movies stars sat side by side with the centrefolds and photos from *Playboy* (including the popular Playmate calendars), *Penthouse* and *Men Only*.

Fashion, particularly women's fashion, is always affected by war. At the beginning of the twentieth century the dress of those with money was opulent and decorative but very restrictive, and the demimonde, whose sole aim was to enrapture wealthy and prestigious men, were the fashion leaders. But over the next decade the corset was abandoned and a more fluid dress style appeared. Young middle-class women began to use cosmetics, smoke, drive cars, dance the tango (which was considered extremely risqué) and dress as they pleased – often showing their legs. As the popularity of the cinema grew, film stars replaced the demimonde as fashion leaders.

After the Great War, fashion became even more alluring and the hems of skirts rose rapidly – and alarmingly for some, who protested against this immodesty. Flesh-coloured stockings rather than black or white became popular and more of a woman's body was exposed than ever before. Film stars wore clothes that were designed to show off their figures and women copied the styles of Lillian and Dorothy Gish, Theda Bara, Mary Pickford and Clara Bow.

With a drastic shortage of young marriageable men, particularly in Europe, many women dressed to please themselves – or their female companions. This continued during the Depression years. When war was declared in 1939, Paris was gearing up for a fashion scene which was utterly feminine. But the austerity measures of the war soon put a stop to that and fashion was based on utility until the war was over. During the war Australians saw the USA as the fashion centre but in 1945 Paris once again launched into feminine fashion and the extravagant designs of newcomer Christian Dior set the tone for the years that followed.

By the 1950s fashion had nothing to do with class and when the mini arrived on the scene in the mid-1960s everyone shortened their skirts.

Movies & Songs

The movies people watched and the songs they sang during wartime echoed their own sentiments as well as providing a way of escaping reality. Both film and song were also used as propaganda.

Popular songs of the Great War include:

Ivor Novello's 'Keep the Home Fires Burning', 'I Wonder Who's Kissing Her Now', 'Sister Susie's Sewing Shirts for Soldiers', 'Pack Up Your Troubles in Your Old Kit Bag', 'Back Home in Tennessee', 'They Didn't Believe Me', 'Take Me Back to Dear Old Blighty', 'Over There' – a George M. Cohan favourite with the Americans, 'Goodbye-ee', 'On the Good Ship "Yacki Hicki Do La"', ''Til We Meet Again', 'Mademoiselle from Armentieres (parlez-vous)' and 'I'm Going Back to Yarrawonga'.

After the Great War jazz rapidly grew in popularity. The audience for popular music expanded at a huge rate thanks to the development of recordings and the advent of the wireless (radio).

The 1930s was the era of the 'big band' and orchestras that were to provide the music for dancing, a favourite pastime during the Second World War.

Movie highlights of the Great War include:

Hollywood was born in 1914 and during the war produced many films including Cecil B. De Mille's *The Squaw Man*, Charlie Chaplin in *The Tramp*, Griffiths' *The Birth of a Nation* starring Lillian Gish, *The Coward*, Charlie Chaplin in *The Immigrant*, Mary Pickford in *Poor Little Rich Girl* and *The Great Love* (a story about a love affair between an Australian girl and an American in the British army), and *Shoulder Arms*, starring Charlie Chaplin in the trenches.

Popular songs of the Second World War include:

'There'll Always be an England', 'A Nightingale Sang in Berkeley Square', 'The Last Time I Saw Paris', 'Hang Out the Washing on the Siegfried Line', 'Somewhere In France With You', 'Swingin' Along the Road to Victory', 'Boogie Woogie Bugle Boy', 'A Pair of Silver Wings', 'Victory (Vee)' and 'The White Cliffs of Dover', 'White Christmas', 'Praise the Lord and Pass the Ammunition', a Frank Sinatra favourite called 'I'll Be Seeing You' and 'Oh What a Beautiful Morning' from the musical 'Oklahoma', 'Comin' in on a Wing and a Prayer', 'A Lovely Way to Spend an Evening', the very silly 'Mairzy Doats', 'You'll Never Know' and 'Till You Come Home'. 'Into Each Life Some Rain Must Fall', 'You Always Hurt the One You Love', 'Swinging on a Star', 'Accentuate the Positive', 'Sentimental Journey' and 'I've Got a Lovely Bunch of Coconuts', 'We'll Gather Lilacs in the Spring' (Ivor Novello), 'My Guy's Come Back'.

Movie highlights of the Second World War include:

Stage Coach starring John Wayne, *The Wizard of Oz* starring Judy Garland and Charles Laughton in *The Hunchback of Notre Dame*, Walt Disney's *Fantasia*, *The Great Dictator* with Charlie Chaplin, *Goodbye Mr Chips* starring Robert Donat, *Rebecca* with Joan Fontaine, *Tin Pan Alley* and *Pin-up Girl* starring Betty Grable and *Gone With the Wind* starring Vivien Leigh and Clark Gable (and which won five Oscars). *Road to Zanzibar* with Bob Hope, Dorothy Lamour and Bing Crosby, Humphrey Bogart in *The Maltese Falcon*, Walt Disney's *Dumbo*, *Citizen Kane* starring Orson Welles, *Forty-Ninth Parallel* (a propaganda film about Nazis being defeated), *Casablanca* starring Humphrey Bogart and Ingrid Bergman, Walt Disney's *Bambi*, *Mrs Miniver* with Greer Garson and Walter Pidgeon about London during the Blitz, *Springtime in the Rockies* with Betty Grable, *To the Shores of Tripoli*, *Desert Victory* (shot at El Alamein), and *In Which We Serve* (Noël Coward starred in this story about the sinking of a British naval destroyer). Damien Parer's *Kokoda Front Line*, *The Gang's All Here*, *For Whom the Bell Tolls* with Gary Cooper and Ingrid Bergman, Alfred Hitchcock's *Shadow of Doubt*, *Double Indemnity* with Barbara Stanwyck and Fred MacMurray, *The Purple Heart*, *Meet Me in St Louis* with Judy

Garland, *The Rats of Tobruk*, Academy Award winner *Going My Way*, *Spellbound* starring Ingrid Bergman and Gregory Peck, *The Story of GI Joe* with Robert Mitchum and Burgess Meredith, Noël Coward again in both *Brief Encounter* and *Blithe Spirit*.

Popular songs of the Vietnam War include:

'Tears', 'A Walk in the Black Forest', 'It Was a Very Good Year', The Beatles' 'Eleanor Rigby', 'Strangers in the Night', 'The Spanish Flea', 'Release Me', 'All You Need is Love' (The Beatles), 'Cinderella Rockefella', 'Wonderful World', 'Hey Jude', 'My Way', 'Gentle On My Mind', and 'Raindrops Are Falling on My Head', 'Yellow River', 'The Wonder of You', 'In the Summertime', 'Chirpy, Chirpy, Cheep, Cheep', 'My Sweet Lord', 'Maggie May', 'Amazing Graze', 'Mouldy Old Dough' and 'Puppy Love'.

Movie highlights of the Vietnam War include:

Darling starring Julie Christie, *The Sound of Music* with Julie Andrews, *The Agony and the Ecstasy*, *Morituri* and *Those Magnificent Men in Their Flying Machines*. *Dr Zhivago* with Julie Christie and Omar Sharif, *The Bible*, *The Sand Pebbles*, *Georgy Girl*, *Alfie*, *A Man for All Seasons* (which won six Oscars), *The Taming of the Shrew* starring Elizabeth Taylor and Richard Burton, *In the Heat of the Night*, *Dr Doolittle* with Rex Harrison and *The Family Way* with Hayley Mills. *Rosemary's Baby* starring Mia Farrow, *Oliver! Planet of the Apes*, *Star!*, *A Flea in Her Ear*, *Bandolero*, *Midnight Cowboy* starring Jon Voight, *Oh What a Lovely War*, about the Great War, *The Prime of Miss Jean Brodie*, *Women in Love* starring Glenda Jackson and Oliver Reed, and *Butch Cassidy and the Sundance Kid*. Andy Warhol's *Flesh*, Academy Award winner *Patton* starring George C. Scott, *True Grit*, starring John Wayne, *Ned Kelly* with Mick Jagger, *Hello Dolly* starring Barbra Steisand and *Tora! Tora! Tora!*, *The French Connection*, Stanley Kubrick's *A Clockwork Orange*, Peter Weir's *Homesdale* and *Wake in Fright*, Frances Ford Coppola's *The Godfather*, *The Poseidon Adventure*, *The Other* and *The Salzburg Connection*. And finally, two masterpieces from Japan, Kurosawa's *Red Beard* and *Tokyo Olympiad*. *The Battle of Britain* was relived with Laurence Olivier, Trevor Howard and Susannah York.

The Great War

During the Great War women were floundering in a society that was brutal, bawdy, heroic, frightening and innocent all at the same time. It was very much a man's world with double standards. Men, it was thought, were unable to control their sexual desires when faced with temptation. It was accepted that a man might 'sow a few wild oats' and have sexual relationships before or outside marriage, but a good woman never would. Women were believed to be the carriers of venereal disease and often blamed for their own infertility, a direct result of the VD carried by their husbands.

For the Australian woman it was a frustrating time socially and a frightening time emotionally. With so many men away the young women who would have been socialising in the hope of finding a husband, looking forward to a wedding as the most exciting day of their lives and settling into a life as wife and mother, had to resort to other occupations – most notably knitting socks or preparing comfort packs. In fact so many socks were knitted – and knitted badly – that at one stage an appeal was made for socks to be knitted properly or not at all. It was not that women only wanted to knit socks or to prepare comfort packs to be sent to the soldiers; many women wanted to get involved in the defence of their nation. But the Australian government would not even consider allowing women to enlist, despite numerous representations and requests from women themselves. Their work was not vital to the success of the war and was dismissed as 'women's work' in a derogatory way because it kept them busy.

The only women who were allowed to serve were nurses in the Australian Army Medical Service. This in itself posed a dilemma for the moralists. One of the problems associated with allowing women to work alongside men in factories and offices was the mixing of men and women – and the possibility that with women in the workplace, men would not be able to ignore their innate sexual drive. So when women went off to war as nurses and were placed in the position of caring for soldiers it too was seen as risky business. It has been found that women placed in that position in the Great War saw themselves as mothers and sisters and only occasionally as lovers. The authorities dealt with the perceived threat by giving the nurses austere sexless uniforms to wear at all times and by later sidelining them in the history books.[3]

Australian girls, not allowed to enlist, made themselves useful during the Great War by collecting for soldiers relief

The other role of women that the government did see as important was their support of the recruiting campaigns. Women were constantly beseeched and praised for encouraging their menfolk – sons, brothers, husbands and fathers – to go to war. The newspapers announced recruitment drives which blatantly made use of women:

A great recruiting demonstration will be held at Caulfield race-course on the afternoon of Sunday, July 8. In addition to speeches, which will be made simultaneously from 12 different platforms, 250 lady riders, each with an extra horse with an empty saddle, will make an appeal for volunteers.[4]

In contrast, in Britain women were doing 'men's work'; driving ambulances, working on public transport and in the munitions factory. They no longer worked in domestic service in such huge numbers as they had before the war; work in industry was better paid. British women also played a vital role as nurses. Finding society changing rapidly around them, women in this part of the world discovered that they now had more personal freedom before 1914. By 1917 women were able to walk through many of the streets of London unmolested and unprotected.

An Aussie wrote in The Sydney Mail, 1916, *of the tableaux made by English girls in uniform*

Young women of all classes frequented places such as cafes, which before the war had been the domain of less reputable souls.

There was a shortage of available men as they volunteered in large numbers and young British women were attracted to the camps and the men in uniform. War, history shows, always sexualises the local female population of the community and country where troops are stationed. Mrs Helena Swanwick, of the Women's International League, explained it all quite logically as 'the female complement to the male frenzy of killing...If millions of men were to be killed in early manhood, or even boyhood, it behoved every young woman to secure a mate and replenish the population while there was still time.'[5]

In fact camp followers became a real problem. Writing in 1922, English author C.E. Montague (probably unaware of his double entendre) recounts how soldiers 'kept an unwonted hold on themselves during the months when hundreds of reputable women and girls round every camp seemed to have been suddenly smitten with a Bacchantic frenzy'.[6]

The Australian soldier was sent thousands of miles from his home into a new and potentially exciting world where he was under the daily control of others, sent to face the most extraordinary hardship with the only possible escape wounding or death, and then given leave with pay in a country far away from home. It is no wonder that so many of them turned to local women as a diversion when on leave. While many found friendship and love with local women, others simply found sexual gratification.

Sergeant Major Norman Ellsworth who regularly wrote frank letters to his mother until his death in 1918, told her in May 1916:

> The women outside the Theatres are very cheeky, and put the 'hard word' on a man to take them in. If this does not come off, they pay 3/- themselves, & walk about all the night putting the 'hard word' again on a man to take them to supper, and afterwards, home in a taxi. It's the hottest thing I've seen...[7]

Writes Gunner Fred Oldfield in March of the following year:

> Dearest little mother you won't be sorry to hear that I am quite convinced you were praying hard for me all last week because I am pretty

sure nothing else would have enabled me to dodge certain things which seem to be considered the only thing for a soldier on leave to do...[8]

While a few letter-writers and others did adopt this moralistic attitude to the ready availability of female company and sex, many more took advantage of what was on offer. As the war progressed prostitutes and street women were a growing problem, but not one the English authorities knew how to deal with. At the Imperial War Conference in April 1917 General Childs is reporting as remarking, 'The point is that as a man leaves camp, the harlots are waiting outside and the soldier cannot control his situation.'[9] In 1917 it was quite acceptable to blame the women for being prostitutes and the Australians writing home were not averse to accusing the women of tempting them. At eighteen, W.D. Gallwey claimed in his letters home to have no problem identifying prostitutes and wrote self-righteous letters describing how he walked away from their propositions.[10]

H.G. Taylor wrote an account of his experiences during this war and at one point talks about going on leave with a mate:

> Fred and I had to leave the next day as our furlough had about petered out. Taking leave of our very good friends we found the parting extremely hard indeed. We both promised to return some day and we did! Then onto to the laundry [where the girls worked] to bid farewell to Lil and Dot. Lil kissed me in front of all the girls, and to put it as mildly as possible, I was indeed embarrassed. At nineteen, who wouldn't have been?
> ...I was very worried about my pal who wasn't at all well. I wasn't in any way competent to judge, but I was convinced that he had contracted venereal disease. I wanted him to report sick before he left England, but he wouldn't and persisted in returning to France.[11]

There was also a strong belief that there were many innocent victims of VD. These included those who believed that they had caught the disease from toilet seats, cutlery, towels or tea cups.

Social do-gooders saw it as their duty to prevent prostitution and eliminate 'camp following', and armies of middle-class matrons patrolled the

Were these Aussies stopped by the YMCA patrol on evening duty for a chat or a warning?

streets trying to combat what became known as 'khaki fever' – with little effect; the VD rate rose alarmingly as did the number of marriages and illegitimate births.

For many Australian soldiers this epidemic of prostitution in contrast glorified the women back home who didn't work and who were 'good' and 'pure'. And back home, because Australians were so totally out of touch with the realities of homeless soldiers having a good time on leave, many believed that 'a better spirit prevailed in their country than in Britain and France'.[12]

In Europe, as in Britain, available women were everywhere, particularly in Paris.

Health campaigner Ettie Rout wrote that 'the number of girls willing, and more than willing, to cater for their sexual desires, was abundant'. And she observed in the last year of the war, 'the battle front sways back and forth and at times refugee-women are right among the troops by the thousand'.[13] Ettie Rout's campaign was against the alarming increase of venereal diseases – a campaign which brought her into disrepute at home and made her a pariah amongst the military establishment who found it easier to ignore the problem.

Historians report little acknowledgement by the authorities of the brothels which were 'as common as heavy-drinking' and legal in France. In his extensive research on newsletters by and about the troops, historian David Kent found 'only one candid mention of a sexual encounter with a prostitute'.[14]

Sir William Orpen, an official artist during the Great War, wrote about his experiences in France:

> Amiens was a danger trap for the young officer from the line, also for the men. 'Charlie's Bar' was always full of officers, mirth ran high, also the bills for drinks – and the drink the Tommies got in the little cafés was terrible stuff and often doped.
>
> Then when darkness came on, strange women – the riff-raff from Paris, the expelled from Rouen, in fact the badly diseased from all parts of France – hovered about in the blackness with their electric torches, and led the unknowing away to blackened side-streets and up dim stairways...[15]

And the website 'In Flanders Fields' reports:

> The luckiest soldiers were quartered near to a town. There, they found food, drink, cigarettes, women and souvenirs. The Allies went to Poperinge, Bailleul and Saint-Omer, and the Germans to Roeselare, Ghent or Ostend. The soldiers tried to make the most of their meagre pay – a British infantryman earned a shilling a day, and a Belgian private had only a fraction of what a working man earned. [The Aussie soldier by comparison earned six shillings a day – so was often flush with spending money when any leave was available.] In some towns, such as Poperinge or Roeselare, there were prostitutes everywhere. As hygiene in the brothels left something to be desired, there was a real risk of venereal disease. Any infected soldier was out of circulation for at least a month. The [French and Belgian armies] tackled the problem in several ways – with punishment, contraceptive sheaths, medical inspections of the 'short arm', even setting up official brothels, called 'houses of tolerance', which were easier to keep a check on.[16]

However the English, Australian and American authorities' prudish attitudes to sexual behaviour made it impossible for them to deal with the diseases in any way other than by punishing those servicemen who were afflicted. It is hardly surprising under these circumstances that the men far from home – the Australians, New Zealanders and later the Americans – had higher rates of sexually transmitted diseases than did those soldiers who were able to go home when on leave. One in ten Aussie servicemen were affected.[17] It was a problem rarely discussed in letters home.

Historian Michael McKernan quotes from one unfortunate soldier who sent a letter to his mother in an envelope designed 'for a different pur-pose'. This young man assured his mother that he had 'never had anything to do with them or anything else of that sort and hope you will believe...there were no doubt a lot of them about as we were just going on leave and the authorities make them available, to prevent Venereal Disease.'[18] He is referring to a French Letter – a term for the envelope which became synonymous with its contents – the condom.

In the early part of the twentieth century venereal disease was euphemistically called the 'red plague', a term used to lump syphilis and gonorrhoea together, and it was an enormous health problem. The public was terrified of the diseases and of talking about them, yet one in five deaths in Britain at this time were the result of VD and in the US it was considered to be an epidemic. In Australia in 1914 it was believed that twelve to fifteen per cent of the population were affected, much the same as in London, Berlin and Paris.[19] Many deaths that were probably caused by VD were ascribed to other causes because of the social stigma.[20] The law saw VD as a woman's disease and in Britain women were jailed for infecting servicemen.

Syphilis not only killed, it affected every part of the body, causing blindness, deafness, paralysis and insanity, and it was a major cause of miscarriage and infertility.

Gonorrhoea was known as 'the clap' and mistakenly treated as triv-ial. Neither disease was curable until the advent of penicillin, though they could be prevented from being contagious by treatment with potas-sium permanganate. It was certainly preventable by the ready availability of condoms to both men and women.

The Australian servicemen brought venereal disease home with them. Early in the war men with VD were automatically sent home until the authorities realised how unrealistic this was. Every boatload of wounded men included some with VD who were disembarked separately from the other wounded because they had been dishonourably discharged. However once they were home they usually rejoined the community – without any treatment for their disease.

The Second World War

Twenty years after the Great War, when the Second World War began, Australian women were once again left at home while the men went away to fight. At first, just as in the Great War, the Australian government decided that Australia's women would be better off at home than in the fighting forces. But this time they did not have to sit anxiously knitting socks for long – though there *was* a sock knitting frenzy at the beginning of the war. They knitted: '... socks by the thousands, woollen socks that reached to the knees, although the "boys" were not in the trenches of icy Europe, but in the burning deserts surrounding Tobruk and Libya', writes Patsy Adam-Smith in her definitive work on Australian women in wartime. She describes the announcement by the Commissioner of the Australian Comforts Fund, that Australian women were wasting their time knitting socks for men overseas as 'one of the most awful setbacks women war workers received'! Cash was what the war effort needed, the commissioner said.[21]

When the Japanese entered the war, first bombing Pearl Harbor in December 1941 and then Darwin four months later, the Australian government realised that it was time to mobilise women. This time the war was much closer to home and there was a real necessity to maximise the labour force. Women were needed in the factories, not only to replace the men who had enlisted, but to build up the workforce in the munitions, shipbuilding, aircraft and defence industries. During the course of the war women also moved into other areas previously reserved for men, such as taxi drivers, railway porters and butchers.

Women were also suddenly needed in the women's auxiliary services: the Women's Australian Auxiliary Air Force (WAAAF), the Women's Royal Australian Naval Service (WRANS), the Australian Women's Army Service (AWAS) and the medical and nursing services, as well as the Land

Wartime factory workers

Army. They were given uniforms which were glamorised in the women's magazines and other media.

However this move into the work force was seen by those in power as only temporary, as it had been in Britain in the Great War. Women were helping out, even though they comprised twenty-five per cent of the work force, and once the war was over they would return to their traditional roles. There was a great deal of propaganda both encouraging women to work to help the war effort and then after the war to return to their homes and husbands. However, though in reality the war did not dramatically alter the percentage of women working, either during or afterwards, it did alter the type of women working and the sort of work they did. Middle-class women were able to join the workforce and the percentage of women in domestic service dropped dramatically. What the war also did was to improve the wages of women, without bringing them up to equal wages with men. Before the war women had not been paid anything like a man's wage even if they were working in a similar position. By the time the war drew to a close they were getting two-thirds of a man's pay.

Another very important way the Second World War differed from the Great War was that this time there were servicemen from overseas in Australia.

After the Japanese attack on Pearl Harbor and the steady Japanese expansion down into south-east Asia, the vulnerability of Australia and its meagre defence force was made glaringly apparent. The Australian prime minister, John Curtin, made it abundantly clear to the US that 'Australia looks to America' for support.[22] Following the fall of Rabaul and Singapore and the bombing of Darwin and Broome the American president, Franklin D. Roosevelt, decided to send General Douglas MacArthur to take command in Australia for a counteroffensive against the Japanese in the south-west Pacific. MacArthur's arrival boosted the morale of a nation in panic. With General MacArthur came the American troops.

Local dances were crowded with men, including servicemen from all parts of Australia who had been sent back from overseas to protect Australia from the Japanese threat. American GIs were everywhere. At one stage Queensland, with a population of 1.3 million, was the base for one million American servicemen. This of course had a great impact on the local female population who found these men romantic,

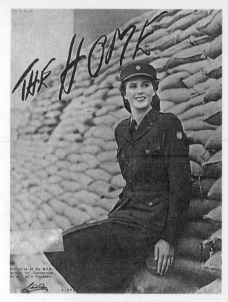

Uniforms became glamorous

generous with gifts and compliments and in need of their company. Hollywood movies also had a strong and positive impact on the image of the American GI.

So in this war it was not just the girls at home worrying about their boys overseas meeting local girls – the boys overseas also worried about their girls back home and the American 'invaders'. The insularity of Australians became apparent in the moralistic preaching which now appeared in the press and the community. People blamed the fact that women were working for all society's woes and yearned for past and 'better' times. Goods were scarce and women on a wage had money to spend and nothing to buy. The future was uncertain so many of them spent their wages on having a good time – dancing, going to the cinema and eating out.

The reaction of moralistic Australians at this time was very similar to the way the British public reacted in 1917 to the behaviour of young women with Aussies on leave. There were frequent reports of girls out of control with servicemen and it was seen as the role of parents to keep their daughters in check. The availability of condoms to the troops was seen by the Catholic community in particular as a contributing factor in this 'infamy'.[23] Lack of morals and the consumption of alcohol were also blamed. Policing of prostitution was seen as one solution and anti-venereal campaigns were also used to try to prevent the sex 'epidemic' – though spokesmen for the Roman Catholic faith objected to films on venereal diseases too. However, most of the girls were not prostitutes, they were simply girls with jobs looking for a good time.

The fact that most of Australia stuck to the pre-war policy of strictly observing the Sabbath with no drinking, dancing, eating in a restaurant or playing games such as billiards aggravated the situation, particularly among the American serviceman. They did not want to spend their free time on their base – they wanted to spend it with local women. But there was nothing to do except wander aimlessly – with or without their Australian girlfriends. Sydney was the first city to give way on the strict Sabbath rulings. Melbourne attempted to follow but the churchmen won the day and it stayed a dull city throughout the war – and beyond.

Australian cities were made even duller by the alcohol laws. As a legacy from the success of the wowsers during the Great War, pubs still closed at 6 p.m., and were not allowed to open until 10 a.m. Other restrictions were imposed too, such as a ban on the sale of schooners (16-ounce glasses of beer) on Saturdays, the idea being that people would drink less from smaller glasses![24]

Even though women were more involved in the war than they had been twenty years before, other things had not changed. Many Australian men were overseas, away from their families and in much the same position as the soldiers of the Great War. Lonely wives sought solace in the arms of an American or an Australian closer to home, or simply fell out of love with their husband and their marriage. The divorce rate from 1942 onwards increased dramatically – adultery and desertion being the main reasons. This had not been a problem during the Great War due to the shortage of men. However, then, once the men came home the divorce rate rose and continued to do so well into the 1920s as women found it difficult to live with men suffering severe trauma or found that in the years when they had been forced to manage alone they had learnt skills which enabled them to survive without having to tolerate a man who made them unhappy.

As in the earlier war, the serviceman's control of his daily life was out of his hands and once again he was being sent into battle not knowing whether he would come back at all, or come back wounded. Once again he was taking his leave in foreign countries with his pay packet in hand

Street scene in Cairo after burning of the 'Wazza'

and a need to forget about what he might face in the future. And, as in the First World War, the girls were there. Statistics reveal that wherever servicemen were based the numbers of prostitutes rose in direct proportion. So once again a part of the female population was volunteering to meet the sexual needs of the armed forces – as they had in the Great War.

Australian troops stationed in the Middle East in 1940 found themselves in Egypt, as had the soldiers a generation before them. The 'Battle of the Wazzir' in April 1915 did nothing to enhance the Australians' reputations. Precipitated by a desire for revenge for injuries they believed they had received at the hands of the brothel inhabitants of 'Wazzir' – the Haret el Wasser, a street in Cairo – Aussies ransacked houses and threw bedding and clothing into the street and set fire to it. Neither the British Military Police or the Egyptian Fire Brigade were able to stop it. A second 'battle' followed in June of the same year.[25] Venereal disease was a major problem at this time and the only solution the authorities had was to move the troops too far away for them to spend any time in Cairo.

Once again, in 1940, the Australians took advantage of the local brothels. Again the incidence of venereal disease was high and in 1941 it caused more deaths among the troops than dysentery, at that time the major disease in the Middle East.

And once again Australian servicemen met local girls there and fell in love, some marrying and eventually bringing their wives to Australia.

Occupied Japan

When the first American troops occupied Japan at the end of August 1945 it was the beginning of a long stay. The Japanese were frightened of the allies. Rumours that 'the enemy, once landed, will violate women one after the other' were rife.[26] Women were sent to the countryside away from the occupying troops and advised to wear unattractive monpe pantaloons.[27] In an attempt to spare local women the Japanese authorities even organised 'comfort facilities' (brothels) in preparation for the inevitable fraternisation between local women and allied forces. This was 'well established policy in dealing with Western barbarians' writes one historian.[28] Professional prostitutes were not as eager to join the organisation of comfort women as the authorities had hoped, partly because they were frightened of the Americans who had been demonised in the Japanese press during the war and were reputed to have enormous penises. So the authorities advertised for women to volunteer and many did, seeing their role as giving their bodies to help their countries. By the end of August there were over 1300 women enrolled in what translated into the Recreation and Amusement Association (RAA).

However this was a short-lived exercise. By January 1946 the alarming rise in VD among the troops closed the service – around ninety per cent of the women were also infected. But prostitution continued – and VD continued to be a major concern.

The authorities tried to counter relationships between the occupying allied forces and Japanese women with an anti-fraternisation policy. The VD rate shows that this policy clearly failed with the Australian forces. In December 1946 the number of VD cases was estimated at 4500 out of just 11 000 troops, and as in both the Great War and the Second World War the authorities tried sanctions and screening of local women in an attempt to reduce the rate of new cases. They had not learnt anything from the failure of this approach in the past and it did little to prevent Australians and Japanese having casual sex or forming lasting relationships.[29]

The 1960s and the Vietnam War

By the 1960s women were on the verge of becoming a political force; by the end of that decade women's issues were vote-catching. The decision of the prime minister, Robert Menzies, in 1964 to conscript twenty-year-old men into national military service has been described as having 'a critical impact on Australian social and political life', and as the one major force which unified youth.[30] It also impacted on women.

During the Great War politicians had expected little of women and only asked that they stay at home. They had used propaganda to persuade women, particularly mothers, to cajole, encourage and inveigle their men to go to war. During the Vietnam War, however, women and especially mothers used the media to promote the anti-war messages of groups such as Save Our Sons. By the end of the 1960s the Women's Liberation Movement had begun.

At the time Australian troops landed in Vietnam, there was community concern in Australia about 'free love' – the sexual revolution of the swinging sixties was gaining momentum in Australia. Sex is a word much used in connection with the sixties. It was the decade when legislation

Mothers protest against Vietnam War, Sydney, April 1969

freed up divorce, abortion, homosexuality and censorship, and the contraceptive pill freed up sexual behaviour. It was a time of easy relationships. Magazines such as *Playboy, Penthouse* and *Men Only* were readily available with the relaxation of censorship. 'Make Love Not War' was a popular slogan of the time and the morals of middle-class Australia were constantly being challenged. It was also a time of prosperity and full employment.

During the Vietnam War Australian servicemen – and servicewomen – took their rest and recreation in Thailand or in the Vietnamese cities of Vung Tau or Saigon (now Ho Chi Minh city). Vung Tau became known as 'Vungers' and was littered with bars, massage parlours, restaurants and hundreds of other places offering sex and alcohol to Aussies on 'R&R'. The Vietnamese women were seen as 'fair game' and many believed that they deliberately contracted VD in order to pass it onto Australians and Americans on leave.[31] In *Minefields and Miniskirts*, Siobhan McHugh writes that 'although Western men associated with, and indeed married, Vietnamese women', the woman she is writing about, Barbara Ferguson, did not know of any other situation like hers. Barbara was attracted to a Vietnamese man but it was a relationship which 'had to be sublimated' – there were too many forces against it. Not only was it not seen as acceptable by the Australians and Americans in Vietnam, the Vietnamese too would have seen it as the man improving his status.[32] The role of women was changing in the industrialised societies but similar changes were not occurring in south-east Asia.

After both the Great War and the Second World War Australian society was structured around building homes and educating heroes. After the Second World War the media and government worked at creating a suburban dream fashioned around the returning soldier. Women were encouraged to stay at home and have children, and magazines, movies and (by the mid-1950s) television programs espoused the happy suburban family life.

By the time the Vietnam War ended Australians were disillusioned with both the war and the government who had involved Australian servicemen and women in a war that many believed was ultimately a waste of life. The year after the last major unit of the Australian Task Force arrived back in Australia, a Labor government was voted into power and immediately abolished conscription and also recalled the Australian Army Training Team from Vietnam. The Vietnam War had led to a deep division in Australian society as it progressed. When the war was over the veterans of the campaign returned, not to a heroes' welcome, but to a country that often ignored them and their experiences.

THE
GREAT
WAR

CHAPTER 2
Meetings

Hello! Hello! Who's your lady friend?
Who's the little girlie by your side?
I've seen you with a girl or two—
Oh! oh! oh! I am surprised at you;

For all who lived during the years 1914 to 1920 the Great War was the most important event of their lives. It had enormous impact on the men away from home and the women in the countries where they were fighting, training and recuperating.

The Great War was a new experience for British society. Previously when Britain had been involved in a war those at home were largely untouched, but in this war everyone was affected. By the end of the war everyone knew someone who had been killed, many living in towns had been subjected to bombing which had killed civilians, food and basic essentials had been rationed, and thousands of refugees had arrived on British soil, beginning with the Belgians. The war industry meant many people had been forced to change their jobs and the close proximity of conflict resulted in hundreds of men in uniform from other countries becoming part of daily society. Among these were the Aussies.

In France, where the worst fighting had occurred, much of the countryside was completely destroyed. Craters of mud and slime took the place of farms and villages were completely ruined. Graveyards were full

FIRST STEPS!
Première sortie.

of hastily buried bodies. Over two million people were homeless and thousands of factories, railway lines and roads were totally destroyed. Australia was a long way away but it had not been a theatre of war and this alone would have made it attractive to a French or Belgian woman who had fallen for an Aussie.

In August 1914, when Australia declared support for the British announcement that it was at war with Germany, young Australian men (or Aussies as they soon began to call themselves) rushed to enlist. The authorities had not even called for volunteers yet nearly 40 000 men, twice as many as the army needed, had enlisted by the end of the year. The letters and diaries which remain show that many of these young men enlisted because of a spirit of adventure or a desire to see the world; others because 'the fair sex in those days mostly shunned fellows who were not prepared to shoulder arms'.[1]

Girls

Oh, London girls are sporty girls, and Cardiff girls are sweet,
And the dark-eyed girls of Charleroi are dainty and *petite*,
But now I'm on the track for home the only girl for me
Is the homespun, all-wool, dinkum girl who's waiting on the Quay.

I've had my fun, I must admit and made the money go,
For the sheelahs know the Aussie hat, from France to Scapa Flow.
There was Maisie down at Margate, there was Maggie up at Frome
But I'm forgetting all the lot, now that I'm bound for home.

'Twas 'Hullo Aussie' everywhere, and girls have saucy eyes,
And most of them have little throats just made to swallow lies
Of emu-farms in Footscray and sheep-ranches in Balmain...
But I will quit romancing when I lob back home again.

Oh London girls are sporty girls, and Glasgow girls are neat,
And the black-haired girls of Froggie land can lead you on a treat,
But now I'm on the homeward track one face comes back to me,
The dinkum girl, the only girl,
The dyed-in-the wool unshrinking girl,
The girl I never quite forgot when I went oversea.

Vance P., *The Homecoming Aussie* troopship serial,
September–October, 1919.

The young Aussie soldier – away from home for the first time, visiting places and countries he may not even have known existed before he reached them – was ready for adventure. When he was not on a battlefield or resting behind the lines, he was in training camp (most likely in southern England) or on leave.

There were plenty of girls ready to have a good time with a soldier, particularly the colonials. The Aussie men were attractive physically because they were generally taller, better built and more sunburnt than their English and French counterparts. They also had more money. The Australian soldier was paid six shillings a day, the New Zealander five shillings and the Tommy (the British soldier), one shilling.

The Australian soldiers did not have any difficulty finding girls to 'walk with' or talk with and while many of them had no intention of taking an English or French wife, others were ready to fall in love. The language was no barrier in France, the Aussies soon learnt a pidgin French which many of them used for the rest of their lives.

Writes Signalman Oliver Coleman from camp on the Salisbury plains in June 1917 to his family:

> Your reference to the girls is somewhat amusing evidently you think I am quite capable of 'getting a girl on a string' as you say. However, girls are very scarce for there is usually thousands of soldiers about but of course I got in with one just for company's sake. She was engaged to a Tommy and so I thought I was safe for a nice comfortable home. Unfortunately the Tommy was killed in the Battle of Arras. So deep was the affection that within a few weeks, there was a marked tendency to transfer her affections to me. She is a fine girl as tall as me, lovely hair down past her waist, nice brown eyes and a good lively companion.

But although Oliver finds this girl attractive, he makes the point that she has no domestic skills, saying 'she is not good to this child only for fun for company'. Oliver finds the English girls forward compared to Australian girls he has known. He tells his family that he is not ready to marry, though he adds 'though I would not be averse to a decent hard worked Pommy with a bit of common sense which seems hard to find'.

As did most of the Australian soldiers, Oliver enjoyed the attention he received from girls because he was a soldier. In one letter he mentions a French lass ('I have received a photo of my friend Laura Domerval from Vignacourt Somme') but eye problems prevented him from being sent back to the battlefields of France and possibly the arms of Laura. By September of that year he is once again writing home about an English girl and his feelings:

> I have a jolly fine English girl for a pal so goodness knows what may ultimately happen but of course knowing me you are not likely to jump to conclusions. I think 'tis up to me to make a start now Joe has made a start. I am feeling quite a love feeling now that I am the remaining single individual of the mob. You know we all want to have a few little soldiers and nurses to fight Fritz next time because he will surely come again if in 50 years time...

And by November he has clearly told the family that this girl is to be his wife:

> I wish you well father and keeping the old home squared up for my Dolly who is going to be a worthy successor of my dear mother and I'm sure you will like her. I expect someone will know my business better than my own and feel their place to say I should not marry an English girl. As it happens young folk generally please themselves in that manner and I am no exception, and can face all hostile criticism.

By 1917 the general feeling of Australians on leave towards the British had changed from the early days of the war when they had felt a kinship towards each other. Now the Australian feeling was that British women were less moral than Australian women. The British public in general no longer felt the Aussies were shining warriors – their behaviour in public had let the Aussie reputation down considerably. Letters and diaries reveal that many Aussie men did not approve of British women working in paid employment, and others felt they were being judged as possible husbands. Oliver has obviously been told some of this in letters from home.

He has also, it seems, upset one particular Aussie girl with his English fiancée, as ten days later he writes:

I was a bit upset yesterday with news from Flo Woolston for I have often thought that were some other feeling beside patriotism which prompted her constancy and as she was only one of number who wrote to me regularly and always made it plain that I was just one of five or six who she sent parcels and letters to, I thought 'twas not the thing to take advantage and find out…Her latest letter though certainly not conclusive rather makes me think she had a liking my way and I am sorry for I did not give her any reason for it so far as I know.[2]

On 22 June 1917 another Aussie soldier, Gunner Duffell, writes: 'Dad says he is going to buy the house next door & get it ready for the little French bride but you need not have any fear of that. There is not going to be any French brides for John. The good old Ausie girls will do me I guess…'[3]

Gunner Duffell (Jack) went to South Wales with a mate, another Jack, to visit an aunt and two girl cousins. It was here that Jack Duffell met Cassie. A couple of months later he was writing to ask the family whether they had organised a home for his return: 'Don't forget that I will want a home if I bring back a little Welch girl. Wouldent the Ausie girls go pop if I did.'[4]

Jack believed in keeping his options open and, although he had dismissed the French girls, he was enjoying the company of his friend's Welsh cousin and letters from girls at home. In February of the following year he tells the family that he is writing to five girls in Blighty and 'about 25' in Australia. Jack was clearly enjoying every moment of it and jokingly suggested he might even get married just for the leave.

I often wonder if I will catch one out of the lot, for you know dears I am old enough to think about those things now.

I wonder if it will be an Ausie or a Welch girl. You know we get ten days marriage leave from here, so I might be tempted to get leave that way if they won't grant it any other way…Don't think there is much chance of it happening though.[5]

Such talk worried his mother and he wrote back on 19 May 1918 to reassure her that he wasn't about to get married yet because he was still not in love: 'I've not lost my heart to any girl yet Mum so don't worry that dear old head over those matters.[6]

However Jack continued to enjoy the company of girls and later on leave in Weymouth, Dorset, on 16 June 1918 he wrote to his family about another girl:

> I've had the luck to be seeing the sights etc in company with a nice little girl in service down here…doesn't get out as much as I'd like but she is a real deacent & quiet 'Dorset' lassie. Don't let the cat out though Mum to all my 'Aussie' girls for I must catch one of that little lot if I land back.[7]

And so he did. Jack's return to Australia and a hero's welcome was made all the more exciting because he was one of a party of troops who had escaped drowning when their boat was sunk by a German torpedo. In the midst of a huge welcome parade one of the 'Ausie' girls who had written to him during the war landed in his lap – almost literally – and it was this girl he married.

Meeting nurses

As well as being wounded, gassed, suffering from trench fever or shell shock, soldiers in the First World War were susceptible to many other illnesses which today would be prevented by better hygiene, cured by antibiotics or prevented by vaccination.

A look at the statistics for non-battle casualties in France from 1916 to 1919 shows that of over 120000 illnesses in the Australian troops, 'facial and respiratory tract infection' was the greatest problem followed by pyrexia (fever), skin infestations, venereal diseases and septic pyogenic (puss-filled) infections.[8] As a result most of the men spent some time being nursed for something. From the County of London War Hospital, Epsom, where he is convalescing from a varicose vein operation, after having recovered from enteric fever[9], Sergeant Major Norman Ellsworth writes to his mother in March, 1916:

> The Nurses & Patients are still getting married or engaged in this hospital & the place has got the name of a Matrimonial Agency, and our staff nurse in our Ward has captivated a Sydney boy, who came in the same time as I did, but nearly died of his Enteric. You will no doubt be

AWM H01204

Aussie soldiers on leave in London are served tea on a YMCA outing

AWM POO516.003

Hospitalised Aussies had many opportunities to meet English nurses

The 'victory' parade for Australian troops, London, 1916

surprised to know that, our nurse told me, the Sister in charge of our ward, 'would marry Sergeant Ellsworth if he would propose.' So the sister told her, but not for this child – why, she is old enough to be my mother! But still she is awfully decent. I simply roared when the nurse told me this. The Nurses give the patients very broad hints that they want to be taken out for walks of an afternoon and a certain amount of jealousy exists between the Nurses on this account.'

Norman was to spend four months in hospital followed by six weeks' furlough and his letters to his mother with accounts of the girls he meets continue.

In April 1916 the Australian High Commission planned a march of Australian troops through London followed by a service at Westminster Abbey attended by the King and Queen. This was to be the only 'victory' parade of its type held during the war and there was enormous hype in the press and around London praising the bravery of the Anzacs.

When Norman returns to London in time for this first Anzac march on 25 April he is once again the centre of attention for English girls:

We were given the most magnificent reception from the population of London, who threw flowers & cigarettes & all that sort of thing at us &

cheered themselves hoarse at us, &, in fact we felt rather swelled headed at the way we were treated, & the way people shook us by the hand, & women embraced us, & wept over us, & all that kind of rot, & attempted to cry 'Coo-ee' & some very wonderful noises these attempts developed into, that we could only guess that it was meant for 'Coo-ee', however we really appreciated it all very much, & will never forget it as long as we live. As for the girls, well, they simply flung themselves at our boys, & they marched along in the procession too.

Later he writes again that 'the girls here have gone crazy for the Australasians, & will do anything for us'.

Norman returns to Scotland where he finishes his holiday. Back in London he stays with his relatives at Gravesend in Kent and visits many of the sights, which he describes in detail and in unique style. He also takes himself to the theatre – where he is 'disgusted' at the behaviour of the audience.

Norman is very keen to get back to the front and his enthusiasm is heightened when he meets one of his gunners in London, who says the men all want him back. But when he returns to 'Australian Intermediate Base' he writes to his mother on 21 May that he has been classified '… C2 (temporarily unfit), so how long I will be here, I do not know'. This camp is situated in Bostall Heath, Abbey Wood, and it seems that military discipline is not a top priority, the local girls providing major diversions!

'It is funny here,' he writes on 29 May:

The trumpet at 6 a.m. sounds Reveille – nobody gets up; at 6.15 he sounds a quarter call – still no appearance of anyone; then at 6.30 the 'Fall in!' sounds and nobody falls in. So at 8 a.m. the 'Cookhouse' sounds & then men begin to get up, & wash. After breakfast, at 9.30 the 'Fall in' sounds & we then report ourselves, & the officer takes our names, & tells us to 'Clear off!' & so we are off for the day.

   The girls around here all day long, come from Woolwich, Plumstead & Erith & have simply gone mad over the Australians, & there are some very fine girls, & of course, some pretty 'crook' ones, but I have managed to get hold of a very fine girl – her father is one of the Head Foremen in Woolwich Arsenal, & she has got 4 certificates for the Pianoforte, & 1 for Singing, & she also plays the Organ in the local Church, & she has several abilities, including Painting, Drawing, Cooking, etc. etc. Now Mother don't go & say ' There, I knew he would, soon or later', because there is nothing whatever in it, I assure you, only it is a treat to meet such a fine girl.

In Britain there was a labour shortage. On the home front, there was a growing need for labour in industries for war production and there was a growing need for 'cannon fodder' on the battlefront. Of the three million Britons who had enlisted in the first year of the war, 380 000 had been killed. In May 1916, King George announced conscription of British men.

Norman writes home about the situation:

There are still thousands of chaps about here in civilian attire, who will not enlist, & they don't seem to care a damn about it, either. They are awfully afraid of us lads, & always avoid us if possible, & if they have girls with them, we promptly go over & relieve them of them, much to their disgust, & we only do it for devilment.

Altho' we have got a bad name, the girls are only too glad to walk out with us in preference to the 'Tommies' or the other boys.

Maybe Norman was not as 'good' as he was painting himself to his mother!

He also sheds some light on the legendary Aussie insubordination: 'The "Tommy" officers are always complaining to our officers about us not saluting them, but our officers tell them "off" properly, & incidentally to "go to Halifax"'.

When Norman writes from the Australian Base Depot in Westham, Weymouth, Dorset on 16 June he encloses a letter from a girl (sadly it is not in the collection).

The girls over here are still madly in love with Australians, & the enclosed letter will give you a little idea what we have to put up with. The young lady who wrote me this letter, as you can see, is no dunce, & she is very talented in both Pianoforte, Singing, & Painting; . . . & altho' I knew this young lady a fortnight, she seems to have 'done her block' over me for no reason at all, & I wrote & told her so . . . I ask you to kindly destroy her epistle after you have read it, but please *do not let anyone outside of our family read, or know of it.* I have simply sent it to you to let you see how the Australian boys are being rushed in England.

As far as I am concerned, the Australian girls will always do me, but I have quite given up the idea of getting married, until the mint [Norman's civilian job] pays a living wage...

On 3 July 1916, Norman's letter to his mother tells her he has been moved to Park House Camp, Tidworth, Salisbury and he continues to keep his mother up-to-date on the local girls. 'Girls are very scarce,' he writes 'altho' a lot have followed us from Weymouth & Abbey Wood to try to catch "hubbys".'

Norman's attempts to get a posting to France continue to be frustrated and he tells his mother 'he is going to take it out of them in Leave', so on 23 July he writes from his relatives' home in Gravesend, Kent:

The new Australian Division in Salisbury (just arrived) is on leave in London (25%) & the girls are 'rushing them'. Everywhere is to be seen Australians & girls flying all over the city in taxis, etc, & dining in the best restaurants, & causing people to stare at their great physique. I myself was dining at a swagger 'eat house' in the Strand (Corner House), with a girl the other night, & I noticed 3 Australians come in with 3 girls, & amongst the Australians, was my old swimming pal (at St Kilda) Stan Martin.

It wasn't long before the image of the Aussie in England began to lose some of its gloss. Many of the English were not happy about the glamorous build up of the Aussie and the consequent lack of praise for his Tommy counterpart. Then there was the girl problem.

Norman's letters shed some light on how the Aussies got a poor reputation for leading girls astray.

The Australians here, as usual, have a bad name thro' one or two 'playing up', & so the rest of us have to suffer for it, but people who are not as narrow minded soon begin to realize that we are not all bad, & treat us very decently.

It is the young girls who frequent the camp day & night, who cause the mischief, & they have to be driven out of the mens huts at all hours of the nights, & they sneak into others then, & pull the blankets off the sleeping men, & other things like that, so you can see what we have to put up with.

There is no doubt that our physique is a great deal better than that of the 'Tommies', also I say so myself, & I am often asked by people, 'what is the secret of the Australians physique', & I tell them that it is the free life we lead in Australia & sun-worship which you people do not go in for, & I have succeeded in making scores of them envious, & they all want to go out to Australia after the war.[10]

Norman, who had finally returned to France, gets a promotion and is sent back to England. From the No. 1 Bryton Camp, Codford, Wiltshire, he writes to his mother in an undated letter of the bad behaviour of both the Aussies and the local girls. Historian Michael McKernan is unsure whether the Aussie reputation as 'amorous, dangerous, even lustful' is fair[11] – but the following account from Norman shows that it probably was!

AWM H15637

The Strand, home to the YMCA and many of London's prostitutes

The Australians have not got a very enviable name, & I must say that the conduct of the ones that I saw, was anything but good, & the class of girls they kick about with too, is enough to make one sick.

These people are nearly all reinforcements just over from Australia, & are of the larrikin type, & their conduct in general is vile.

They wear feathers in their hats, polished badges, polished buttons, & colours on their arms which they are not entitled to & on passing a Pub, one can generally hear them in a brawl inside, & using the vilest language even in the presence of women folk.

I regret very much to have told you this but believe me that I have not exaggerated it in the least, and the consequence is, that decent people have no time for Australians now, except the business people, who whip on the price of any article they wish to buy.[12]

Reading the newspapers of the times, especially papers such as *The News of the World* and the *Daily Mirror*, exposes the many stories of overseas servicemen betraying English girls. WAR MARRIAGE RISKS screamed *The News of the World* on 13 January 1918. The report reads:

A young lady...highly and justly respected, was courted with every apparent circumstance of scrupulous honour by one who had volunteered, from another part of the world to fight for the Allied cause. Her family made every inquiry that seemed possible in the case of one whose home was far away, and the engagement was recognised and had been made known, when – happily before it was too late – the fact came to light that the would-be bridegroom had a wife and child. For the guidance of parents and guardians and marriageable girls, it may be pointed out that it is not necessary to await the slow movement of the overseas post before ascertaining whether or no an overseas soldier is married. A complete record of each man is on file at the headquarters of the contingent with which he enlisted.[13]

Reports of bigamous Australians appear regularly in the British press and pressure was put on the Australian Headquarters to provide members of the AIF who wanted to marry with a certificate saying they were free to marry. The authorities refused. However for the majority of soldiers who did marry women from Great Britain and Europe it was the same kind of loving and honest relationship they would have had if they had remained at home in Australia. And it was the same from the women's point of view.

Bill Badcock has pieced together the story of his parents' meeting during World War I. Violet Chandler, her sister Louise and some of their friends were walking in Savernake Forest, Wiltshire, after church one Sunday when they met a group of Australian soldiers from the 12th Field Company stationed in Marlborough. Bill's father, William, was amongst them. Was it love at first sight or was it William only who was smitten and kept coming back to visit Violet? As none of William's surviving children know the answer, this will have to remain a mystery.

Sheila Yeatman's mother, Kate Fieldgate, lived in Brightlingsea where Australian troops were sent to train in 1916. Troops were billeted locally and this is how her mother met her father, Gordon Henderson. Sheila assumes it must have been a quick courtship because they were engaged before January 1917, when Gordon left for France, and married in August 1917.

For Rosa Seidel and Leo Baker it was a case of old neighbours meeting again. Rosa was born in Bohemia and Rosa's father, a Czechoslovakian of some importance, took his family from London where they were living to Australia at the beginning of the twentieth century. They lived in the Vice Regal Terrace in Petersham, Sydney and two doors down lived the Baker family, themselves Britons. When the Seidel family returned to London in 1908 the two daughters continued to write to the Baker sisters. So it was that when three of the Baker boys enlisted to fight for Australia and found themselves in London they contacted the Seidels. Rosa and Leo fell in love and Leo visited Rosa while he was stationed on Salisbury Plain then wrote to her from the battlefields of France for the three years he was stationed there without London

Rosa Seidel

leave. When the war ended Leo's brothers returned to Australia and Leo stayed on in London to study accountancy – and be with Rosa.

Violet Mary Apkins met Christopher Procter when she was invited to spend an evening with the neighbours he was visiting. He asked to walk her home and the romance grew from there. They were married on 9 July 1919.

On 2 February 1919 Violet wrote this reassuring letter to her parents, which has been kept by her daughter, Jean Parker:

Thank you both very much for coming – some swank isn't it buying your daughter's trousseau eh! You know you should feel very proud, pleased and happy.

Proud to think I'm worthy of a good man's admiration and attention, *pleased* to think I shall have my future assured, and that I shall not – if all's well – be condemned to an old maid's existence, which to say the least of it is not a natural life for a girl & surely not a happy one. And also feel pleased to think that I shall not have to nurse a wooden leg or lend my eyes, as may have happened to anyone less fortunate than Chris.

Last not least feel *happy* because I am very happy – only like you to be also. I know I shall not like the parting Mum and Dad dear but all the same I can't help looking forward to the time when I – Oh! Well look here Mum you love Dad so 'speck's' you understand & surely it is not such a very great hard-ship to go to a nice country & to a home of love where there is a Mum, Dad, brothers, and sisters.

I know I gain Mother & you think you lose but you don't really I shall always be just the same Vi as of old, but please, please, don't be unhappy about it or think I am very selfish: just look on the bright and right side and remember as much as some of us would like it I cannot always be a little girl.

Don't think I am not prepared for some misfortune as well as happiness, I know it will be mixed, but nevertheless I am ready.

I am afraid you will think I have grown ancient all at once but I just wanted to tell you I was happy and want you to be & that I have thought it all out & still don't want to alter things one scrap...

Roll on Friday
With fondest love
Your own
Vi XX

At 102 years of age some of Constance Turner's memories of the time she met her husband John are still quite clear. Constance Garden was from Aberdeen and it was in Scotland she met JJ, as she came to call him. He was stationed there on leave waiting for a ship to take him home to Australia. Constance remembers that it was love at first sight for JJ. It wasn't for her, she says, and her memories of his proposal and their decision to marry have disappeared with time. They married in Scotland and waited for a boat to take them to Australia. It was the *Runic*, and as it sailed a band on shore played 'Will Ye No Come Back Again?' Remembers Constance: 'It took six weeks to come to Australia. It was vile – the food was horrible and green!' The lack of refrigeration obviously took its toll on the food that was available.

Unlike the Australian government, the British government encouraged women to join the workforce to help replace the men who had gone to fight, though in many industries it was emphasised that this was only until the war was over. Queenie Soffe was one. She tells her own story beginning in 1915:

> I was employed in the office of Spiers & Pond private railway caterers at Salisbury railway station and I had to check all the invoices and accounts from fourteen railway Refreshment Bars in our district. Head office was in London, everything came from London, so we had a mail vault on the 'down' platform and we had to use the subway to get to this platform. I did my work and then sent it back to London in a Spiers & Pond box.
>
> It was in November 1917 [that I met Ted]. I had another girl [Triss] younger than myself, my assistant, and we went round to clear the London box, through the subway and up through the hall. When we got there, the wind was howling, and the London train had just pulled in which meant we had to wait for all the passengers to go through the ticket barrier. While we were waiting I noticed this big Australian in a military overcoat and I said to Triss, 'Let's get behind this Aussie.' The wind was howling. Triss went through to the mailbox and I followed her, and as we went through the stationmaster called me over. He said 'Miss Soffe, you haven't met Ted Sunderland yet have you?' So he introduced us – it was the same big Aussie. Ted was on his way to the RTO – the railway transport office – we just chatted for a second and he went

his way and I went mine. I met him several times, just casually, as he was going to his London office and I was going to mine – there was nothing between us at the time.

I was learning shorthand on a Saturday morning and I was on my way back to the railway station which I lived on. I was the assistant manager. I had been promoted because the manager had been called up and I was given his job. I had everything found for me I didn't have to do a thing not even make my bed. This particular Saturday as I was going home I met Ted. He stopped me and said 'Where is your mate?' because he talked to Triss quite a bit and I said, 'She's gone home for the weekend'. And he said, 'Would you like to go to the football match with me this afternoon – Aussie rules?' I said, 'Why not?', and my first date with Ted was an Aussie rules football match.[14]

In her autobiography Queenie recalls that there were a surprising number of chance encounters with Ted in the subway. She remembers long walks in the countryside around Salisbury and also that 'he wasn't interested in movies – movies were just coming – it was all theatre; he took me to a lot of opera'.

The relationship grew. Queenie had to work very long hours, then she developed an ulcerated throat. Told to take three weeks off by the doctor, she went home to Winchester. Ted wrote to Queenie while she was away from work and said he would love to come and visit. Queenie's aunt, who lived nearby, agreed to give Ted a room.

Queenie's grandfather sent a car to the train to meet Ted. As Aussies did not come to Winchester as a rule Ted was easy to find in the crowds at the station and so he and Queenie met again.

The next day when we were going to lunch we were looking around the garden. We had a big garden and we had a meadow down the back and a pony and just in through the gate, down the meadow, my grandfather had started building a shed for hay. Hay was difficult to get at the time, and he wanted another pony. Ted said 'What are you building here? and 'Would you like me to finish it for you?' And he set to work.

Ted finished the shed and won the approval of Queenie's grandfather. Ted arrived in Winchester on Saturday and left on Thursday, but before he left he proposed to Queenie and she accepted. 'I had never doubted Ted,' Queenie said. 'He had freely told me about his home and family, living on a property near Dubbo in New South Wales. So many girls during these war years had foolishly and indiscriminately married servicemen to their sorrow and regret.'

Queenie admitted she did have a short time where she was concerned;

> I knew lots about Australia through working at the railway station. One officer said, 'Is it serious between you and Ted?' and I said, 'Yes it is'. He said, 'Have you ever asked him to show you his pay book?' I said, 'No, why should I? I believe him'.
>
> He said, 'Well inside that pay book is his identification and his relationship to his home, parents, where he comes from – you didn't even check if he is a married man or not!' so I said 'Oh I'll give it a go'.
>
> The next time I saw Ted, I said, 'You haven't shown me your pay book with your identification'. He took his tunic off and said, 'There you are'. His number was 162, it read 'Next of kin – Mrs E Sunderland. Relationship – blank.' I nearly died and so did Ted. 'I never checked this,' he said, 'that should be Mother there.' I said, 'It could be wife' he said, 'No'. Anyway we were not engaged and he said 'I'll write home straight away and get them to answer my letter to you not to me so that you know that what I am telling you is true'. Well he did, he wrote home and it took three months to get a reply back in those days. His sister-in-law wrote and welcomed me into the Sunderland family – then I wore his ring.[15]

Meg (Margaret) Woollen lived in Yeovil, the headquarters of the Westland Aircraft Works and so, her daughter, Margaret, writes:

> In 1917 she joined the staff of Westland and worked in the Propeller Department making, mostly by hand, the propellers for the Sopwith Camel. The Camel was a small plane, only 18ft 8 ins long, and accounted for more aerial victories than any other Allied aircraft in the battles of the First World War.
>
> Meg's family regularly invited to tea the soldiers and airmen from the Front Line who were recuperating in a country house – turned hospital nearby. Meg's heart remained untouched until she met her husband-to-be at a New Year's Eve Ball at Weymouth, a seaside town south of Yeovil.

It was the beginning of 1919.

Meg lost her heart to Walter Harvie Robinson, known to his mates as Robbie. Robbie had enlisted as a private in the 4th Pioneer Battalion, Reinforcement 2, and left Australia on 12 April 1916 aboard the *Mooltan*. He was promoted to corporal during the Battle of the Somme and survived the battles around Poziéres, Ypres, Bullecourt and Villers-Bretonneux – he was gassed in 1918.

Margaret continues the story of her parents' romance:

[Robbie] was stationed at Osmington, a camp near Weymouth, and although not a dancer, accompanied his best friend, a Scotsman named Jock Bruce...to the New Year's Eve ball. His friend was a very good dancer and danced with Meg on a number of occasions. She noticed his Australian Digger friend (who kept watching her) and thought he had the most beautiful blue eyes she had ever seen – he also blew jolly good smoke rings! Eventually Robbie asked to be introduced to her and Meg sat the rest of the ball out, talking to him. In an unusual moment of complete candour (and rather shyly) [writes Margaret] my mother once told me that he was incredibly handsome...and had great charm. They exchanged addresses and promised to write to each other.

In January 1919, after writing to ask Meg if he could call, Robbie spent a weekend in Yeovil, staying at the Mermaid Hotel and getting to know Meg's family. 'My mother's youngest sister later told me that they thought he was very handsome and most kind to them all, bringing nice gifts whenever he visited,' writes Margaret.

This was a proper courtship – 'strictly monitored'. Meg's youngest sister, Hazel, '...had to accompany them whenever they went for long walks or sat in the garden or parlour'.

Meg later told Margaret that some of the visiting soldiers did not have very good reputations and her parents were only being cautious, even though they liked Robbie immensely. When it became obvious that Robbie wished to marry Meg, her mother wrote to Robbie's mother, establishing contact, and thus reassuring herself that Robbie was free to marry her daughter. Meg's younger sisters starting writing to Robbie's sisters, and so began communications that would last through their lifetimes.

Eva Rodrigues was a modern girl. Writes her daughter, Ruth Reynolds: 'Against family wishes she insisted in obtaining qualifications in short-hand and typing and after working for a while in a stockbroker's office joined the staff of Australia House in London.' (Australia House was opened in London on 3 August 1918 by the King.) 'It was while she was working at Australia House that she met an Australian who took her out for a while and then was repatriated home to Australia. They corresponded and he eventually proposed marriage.'

The young man's name was Frank Campion. Eva's family hit the roof at the thought but she accepted. (Ruth believes that Eva's decision was as much to spite them as anything else.) In 1920 she, along with other war brides, left for Australia. They were briefed in some detail (mainly erroneously) before they left. An example of what they were told was 'don't bother to take any heavy clothing, it never gets cold in Australia'.

> Give me a Blighty[16] girl
> A Blighty girl for me.
> I've been across the sea,
> I know what's good for me.
> French girls are very nice
> For Frenchmen I can see,
> But when I get back to Blighty,
> A Blighty girl for me.[17]

Europe

Early in April 1916 the 1st Anzac Corps was transported to Flanders, in northern France and a section of the front, south-east of Armentieres. Here they were issued with British steel helmets and gas masks and the first months were fairly quiet.

In July the British launched the horrendously disastrous Battle of the Somme with 60 000 casualties – 20 000 were killed on the first day alone.

Australians attacked Fromelles on 19 July and the 1st Division attacked Poziéres.

Australians suffered 30 000 casualties overall. The weather just added to the misery as the winter of 1916–17 was the hardest in France for forty years.[18]

Apart from the soldiers in billets, there were many other military personnel stationed behind the front including transport troops. Some were employed to take materials and ammunition up to the front line and others to repair roads.

There were also countless women behind the front, including foreign nurses at the many large Casualty Clearing Stations (Field Hospitals). Many were young Belgian refugees who worked as nurses, laundry-workers, uniform-delousers, or who earned a living in cafés, restaurants or brothels.[19]

The soldiers were allowed leave but it was brief, and for the soldiers in France it was not usually long enough to travel back to England. An English newspaper, the *Daily Mirror*, ran regular columns from wives and loved ones complaining about how long it had been since their soldiers had had home leave.

When the men were given a break from the battles they generally stayed in huge camps, consisting of huts or tents. Some were billeted with local people.

The men returning from the front were exhausted. The first thing they did was sleep. Then they needed to find hot water to wash in, clean clothes so they could live lice-free for a few days, and a good meal. There was little to do in the camps, apart from 'fatigue-duties' and reading what were often unsettling letters from home, and once they were rested and refreshed they began to look for entertainment and social contact with women.

The *estaminet* (local bar) was enormously attractive because it was here that young French women worked as waitresses.

In order to communicate with the local girls, particularly in the country, the soldiers needed to learn the basics. Many of the soldiers' letters and diaries include smatterings of French words or Australianised French words. This list is from the diary of one, serving in France:

Etre vous libre le dimanche?	Are you free on Sunday?
Ou demeurez vous?	Where do you live?
Combien de soeurs avez-vous?	How many sisters have you?
Serez vous libre demain soir?	Will you be here tomorrow evening?[20]

And both the Aussies and the Tommies made up songs about their experiences. Mostly they were very amateur, such as the one that follows, but they tell a story. This one was meant to be sung to the tune of 'Swanee River':

> Walking up and down the Champs Elysees
> That's what we like;
> Oh! you should see la femme – how she eyes us
> With boko[21] admiration – so says Mike
> If the war is sad and dreary,
> Nought we know of that;
> We all know a demoiselle so cherie,
> Also her charming little flat.[22]

A poem in *The Borda News*, a troop newspaper on 21 May 1919 describes how many of the Aussies felt when travelling home from the Continent:

> For one and all, at times back there:
> Lost our hearts to Yvonne or Suzanne,
>
> Le Guerre finis, and we are home once more,
> How you will think of those times, par bonne,
> But we'll never forget the girls we met,
> While on the 'Continong'.[23]

For Major Garnett Ingamells Adcock, who spoke fluent French and was therefore often sent in search of billets, life in France was interesting. His work as a tunneller was hard and dangerous and he suffered from shell shock twice, but he also made the most of his time in France. He writes home:

> There seems to be a firm impression in the French mind that the staple food of the British soldier is potato chips. Every café displays a large notice: Tea and Coffee, Eggs and Chips. If you go into a Tommies Café (there are some reserved for officers only), the first thing they say is 'You want Cheeps?' Of course Tommy, not being able to ask for anything else in French, says 'Oui!' and so the impression is fostered.
>
> There are several quite good places 'Officers Only.' I go to the 'Au Boeuf' for dinner every evening I am in the town. It is a treat to get a

French meal. It is beautifully cooked and served and licks English or Australian meals to a frazzle, while being comparatively cheap. Last night I had Hors d'Oeuvres, Soups, Poulet and an Omelette au Champignons with tiny mushrooms, was delicious. All this within 1½ miles of the front line! The French do not have sweets with their meals, neither do they drink tea, but always 'vin ordinaire'. This is extremely light, very dry, wine which can be taken by the gallon.

I have become quite friendly with the old lady who keeps the place. She can't speak English, so I have to sit at her table and talk to her and translate what the others are saying. She corrects my grammar and takes a great interest in improving my French. It is the same everywhere. The French are always delighted to go out of their way to help.

Mademoiselle from Armenteers

Mademoiselle from Armenteers
Parlez-vouz!
Mademoiselle from Armenteers
Parlez-vous!
Mademoiselle from Armenteers
She hasn't been fucked for 40 years
Inky-pinky parley-vous.[24]

He also takes the opportunity to get know a local girl and this becomes a serious relationship. Sometime in February 1917 Garnett met his future wife, who was living in Luttertap, just outside Abeele, and on 15 June 1917 he writes:

Mother asks what the French and Belgian 'demoiselles' are like. They are like the 'mesdames', only more so. Those of good family are much more strictly brought up than English girls and have them beaten to a frazzle. You never see a French girl lounge about, or be untidy. They sit primly upright and are very polite. Of course we are not away from civilization and know lots of nice people and spend many pleasant evenings. Don't be surprised if I bring a Belgian girl home as a souvenir.[25]

From then on his letters contain an occasional mention of Marguerite, though there is no actual announcement to the family of his engagement.

The attitude of the local French to the Aussies is similar to that of the English – at least in the early part of the war. Writes Garnett on 5th August 1918: 'The "Aussie" hat attracts attention. We are usually followed by a troupe of either admiring or derisive urchins who discuss my appearance... When we enter a café we are greeted with a chorus of "Ah! Les braves Australiens" and le patron insists on us having one "on the house".'[26]

Andrew Anderson, the son of a Sydney businessman, was amongst the first rush of 12 000 Australians to join the Australian Imperial Force in 1914. He was nineteen. In October of that year he sailed from Albany in Western Australia to Suez in Egypt on board the huge convoy of thirty-eight ships that was Australia's First Expeditionary Force. For these men the war began not long out of Albany when their convoy guarded by the Australian cruisers *Sydney* and *Melbourne* and the Japanese cruiser *Ibuki*, encountered and scuttled the German cruiser *Emden* near the Cocos Islands. Andrew kept a diary of his trip across half the world to fight in the Great War as did so many of those who served in this war.

The Australians disembarked at Alexandria and marched to Cairo. Here they were trained and, during their leisure time, climbed the pyramids and got into trouble in the brothels of Cairo. In April this army of Australians and New Zealanders were ordered to the Dardanelles. These straits, the gateway from the Aegean Sea to the Sea of Marmara, Istanbul (then known as Constantinople) and the Black Sea, were held by the Turks, causing major problems for their enemies. The capture of the Gallipoli peninsula, at the mouth of the Dardanelles, appeared to the British commanders of the time to be a key to winning the war.

Andrew Anderson

In 1915, Andrew Anderson, together with many of the mates he had joined up with, was one of the Australians who went ashore at Gallipoli on that first day, now known as Anzac Day – 25 April. They jumped into the waist-deep water of the Aegean Sea under the fire of the Turkish army, then scrambled up the cliffs of Anzac cove. Sometime before noon Andrew was wounded, shot through the shoulder, joining the almost four hundred men who were wounded on that day. He was eventually evacuated to Alexandria.

In Alexandria Andrew came under the protection of Lieutenant Wrigley, an employee of his father's Eagle on the Globe Steel Company, who 'made sure Andrew was well cared for and got special favours,' remembers Andrew's son Ron.

In May Andrew had recovered sufficiently to be sent back to Gallipoli. Once again he found himself in the trenches and in a contingent getting ready to go over the top. He wrote later to his mother about how his legs trembled as the trenches were peppered in sniper fire. Once again Andrew was wounded. This time he was shot in the leg and received shrapnel wounds to the head from a bullet which ricocheted off his bay-onet. He crawled back to the first-aid station and was again evacuated. This time his recovery was not as swift. His leg became badly infected and Lieutenant Wrigley decided it was time to remove Andrew from the action. By pulling a few strings, Wrigley managed to have Andrew trans-ferred to the record section and he did not return to Gallipoli.

When the Australians withdrew from the battle on the Gallipoli penin-sula in December 1915, the records section which now employed Andrew moved to Rouen in France. In Rouen the army arranged for Andrew to be billeted by a local family and this was how Andrew met the Bastide family: Gervaise, a clothing and millinery manufacturer originally from Toulouse, his wife Julie and his daughters Louise (Loulou) and Marguerite (Mimi). It seems likely from Andrew's letters that he and a mate, Will Owen, were billeted in a cottage next to, or in the garden, of the Bastide's residence.

Family records do not reveal just what month it was that Andrew moved to Rouen but by August of 1916 he was writing to his mother about Loulou:

> I must tell you that I met a very nice French girl here of very respectable family & very nearly got myself entangled in a mesh that might have

proven hard to get out of. Loulou [is] really a brilliant girl, but like all other French girls is apt to be too sentimental if not watched carefully. They are all the same & of a different temperament altogether to us...Of course it is natural for a French girl to do a good deal of 'mugging' [kissing and hugging]...& a very close friendship sprung up between us.

Despite his concerns, however, Andrew was not particularly cautious. His letter continues:

One day quite jokingly I said, 'Oh! when we are in Australia together'. Poor Loulou heaved a great sigh, & rested her head on my chest and told me how content she would be. Nothing more was said of the matter yet I could see she was becoming more & more affectionate day by day. Such little acts as sending Father down with a great bunch of roses to decorate my room began to tell, & you can imagine what a bombshell burst upon me when one Saturday afternoon I was out for a walk with the family when we drew level with a cottage which I was informed was Father's gift to us. To say I was thunderstruck would be putting it mildly. However I let things rest as they were for the time being and admired the cottage which was really beautiful. When I left them that evening it was with a sense of a pending calamity which seemed about to fall on me & and I thought to myself, well lad, you are up against it now.

Andrew decides that he must extricate himself from this romance before it is too late 'I almost felt inclined to give in and marry the girl' he wrote to his mother...

That night I sat down & wrote a letter to the girl in my best French, & told her exactly how things stood and arranged that I should get there just about half an hour after the letter. When I arrived I can assure [you] it was 'some stormy' but I managed to weather the lot and after an ocean of tears, sunshine shone on us once more.

Of course Father was 'très frackle' but I am a good deal bigger than he & I seem to possess some quality or other in humouring these French, & so did not take long in talking him over. I don't think there could be a better friendship between us now, because we know each other so well & everything is in harmony, & who knows perhaps some day I may feel that way inclined, and then she will see Australia after all.

This letter concludes with Andrew telling his family that he is going on holidays with the Bastide family and he adds a postscript which says he includes a couple of letters in French from Loulou to his family. He was not yet twenty-two years old but his misgivings did not last long.

He continues to spend a great deal of time with Bastide family, in fact his letters to his mother and sister do not mention much about army life, though we do know that he hankered to go back to the front and join his mates. Many of the letters and diaries which exist from this time reveal how much the men who

Loulou & Andrew

were not fighting at the front longed to rejoin their mates.

Loulou made up a little book for Andrew to take with him should he be sent back into action. The size of a very small address book, with a black leather jacket and the word 'Loulou' embroidered on the front in green, it contains a poem by Loulou and a number of delightful photos of the pair cuddling and talking in the garden. In two of the the photos Will Owen and Mimi also feature.

The poem which Loulou wrote to her Australian love has been translated by one of the family, it reads:

A murmur of caressing words...
A shiver of kisses...

It is a rose that is dying...
A dream that is fleeing...
A pretty ornament that is breaking...
A love that leaves a soft and painful imprint on one's heart...
A shudder that passes through your life...
But there remains these happy memories that one thumbs through with
    emotion...

While thinking of the hours lived...and spent...
And these memories I give to you, my beloved André...
In order to remind you always of me

Loulou
Rouen, 3 November, 1916

On another page of this same little book there is a photo of Andrew and Loulou sitting together on bench gazing at a flower, and the words underneath have been translated as 'She loves me...a little...a lot...caressingly...passionately'.

There is absolutely no doubt about how Loulou feels about Andrew.

By June of 1917, Andrew's letters home reveal that he is moving into the Bastide residence. The first thing he intended was to dig a vegetable patch. He writes: 'Will [Owen] and I are going to live at the Bastides' new place at the end of the month. There will be a garden, & seeing that vegetables are so dear I am going to grow a few beans & peas just to show them how we do things in Australia & at the same time economise as much as possible.'

The following month Andrew writes home: 'Loulou sends her best love & kisses along with me to you all, not forgetting the little ones...' Clearly Andrew has abandoned any feelings of uncertainty he had about his love for Loulou.

CHAPTER 3
Marriage

You made me love you
I didn't wanna to do it,
I didn't wanna to do it
You made me love you
And all the time you knew it
I guess you really knew it

Marriage during wartime could be hasty, usually because the soldier's leave was limited, or it could be postponed for that day when the war was over – or there was more time. The Australian government's offer in 1918 of a free passage to wives of Australian servicemen, provided the marriage took place prior to 1 September 1919, hastened some weddings.

Some hasty marriages were a cruel hoax played on the woman. There is one account of an English woman marrying an Australian she had only known for six hours. When she arrived in Australia she received a telegram from her husband telling her he would meet her on the steps of the Sydney General Post Office.[1] What happened to her after that is pure speculation.

Details of proposals and weddings from the time of the Great War are sketchy. For many it was a question of making do with what was available. Food and clothing rationing meant that the glamorous wedding that they would have had before the war was not possible.

When Rosa Seidel married Leo Baker, food rationing meant that coupons had to be begged from neighbours and friends to provide a wedding feast. Their daughter, Coralie Welch, writes:

Edith Kepple weds Arthur Kindred, Glasgow, 26 June 1919

The wedding vows then began with the words 'With gold and silver I thee endow'. Well the gold wedding band covered the first exigency and Dad fumbled in his tunic pockets for some silver to cover the second.

Robbie Robinson and bride Meg, 30 April 1919

'A shilling will do,' whispered the priest. 'I haven't any money,' whispered Dad! So dear Grandpa Gustave (Seidel) came good with an English shilling, which I still have tucked away to this day.

Charles Kindred had met his bride-to-be, Edith, in Scotland and records in his diary how he was looking forward to his wedding – which after one postponement took place on 26 June 1919 in a church near Glasgow. Army bureaucracy made taking leave difficult – and penalised unauthorised leave and leave extensions – but Charles took it all in his stride and made the most of his leave, often over-staying.

Meg Woollen and Walter 'Robbie' Robinson married on 30 April 1919. Meg made her own dress of white silk with silver lace inserted in floating panels and they honeymooned in London. Family history does not record how Meg came by the materials for her dress, but chances are they were part of her trousseau.

Queenie Soffe finally married her Anzac, Ted Sunderland, on 26 September 1918. Ted had proposed to Queenie early that year and they had planned a May wedding. But Ted, a gunner, had been badly gassed in France. In March he went into hospital and was there for nearly six months. Queenie recalls, 'Before he went in he was in camp in Warminster and I used to go there on weekends and lodge in the village – a lot of people with a spare bedroom would take a couple of girls in for the weekend'.

Queenie describes her wedding as a typical war wedding. Transport was by foot or public transport as motor cars were not permitted to be used for social events. Flowers were not available, nor was icing for the wedding cake as sugar was strictly rationed.

Queenie and Ted did not have a church wedding either, because Queenie was a Christadelphian ecclesiast and

Queenie weds her Ted

they were not authorised to conduct marriage services. So the bridal couple walked the three blocks to the Registry Office. She wore a navy blue suit and white blouse, a navy and white hat and a white feather boa. Ted wore his uniform.

In Britain food rationing was very strict by 1918. The shortage of shipping coupled with the dangers of submarine attacks had reduced the supply of food from overseas which Britain had been relying on to feed its population. As well, 1916 had been a year of bad weather. So Queenie and Ted did not expect a wedding breakfast. However, Queenie's uncle and aunt offered to provide a breakfast as a wedding gift. Queenie's uncle was able to get extra food from Government Food Control because of his business. Queenie and Ted were surprised and delighted by the food – they even had a wedding cake.[2]

Queenie and Ted honeymooned in Southampton and the Isle of Wight, thanks to a rail strike which meant Queenie did not have to return to work immediately.

In July 1917 Andrew Anderson writes home about marrying his Loulou and remarking that his earlier letter on the subject must have gone astray. He wrote:

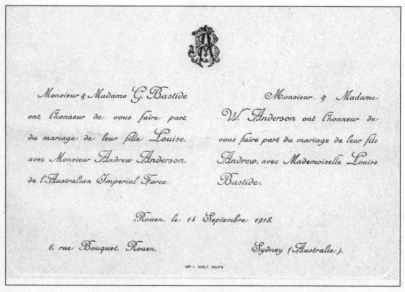

Andrew and Loulou's wedding invitation

...some six weeks ago I wrote a letter to you concerning Loulou & myself, it was a matter of 'Hearts are Trumps' & I asked you your permission to marry her. We are very much afraid that the letter is not going to reach its destination as the servant only put 1½c in stamps on it, & as they are very strict here about postage in all probability it did not get any further than the post office.

However we are anxiously awaiting your reply to please lets have it as soon as possible...
your loving son Andrew
XXXXXXXXXXXXXXX de Loulou

It was not to be until over a year later. In the meantime, correspondence reveals that Andrew and Loulou spent much time together. Loulou was an excellent seamstress and milliner and this was to stand her in good stead in years to come, Andrew wrote to his family requesting 'opossum' skins so Loulou could make them into muffs. In March 1918 he reports on an outbreak of smallpox in Rouen. Daily life was being made more and more difficult for citizens by the war which was raging in their country and the focus on keeping the occupying troops fed and cared for took precedence over the needs of the inhabitants. The Bastide family found they had to move into the town because the trams were no longer running near their house.

Loulou poses beautifully

Andrew on honeymoon

In July 1918 Andrew writes to his sister, Grace, who has also announced her engagement, that it is not easy to marry in France. By now he has obtained his father's permission but the army was another matter: 'I have been rather unlucky re my marriage...the General Officer commanding the Lines of Communication area would not allow Loulou to stay in the war zone [once we are married] which meant that she would have had to go right away from here altogether'. So the couple continued to wait.

On 14th September 1918 Loulou finally married her André in Rouen, just two months before the war in Europe ceased. They honeymooned away from the war zones in Cannes, Monte Carlo, Monaco and Nice. Andrew as a non-commissioned officer was required to travel 3rd class, but Loulou used all her persuasive charms to get them both seats in 1st class.

Major Garnett Adcock married his Belgian fiancée, Marguerite Van Coillie of the city of Roulers, in Belgium in November 1918. In 1930 Garnett added the following note to his accounts: 'The wedding took place at the Mairie (Town Hall) at Orleans on the morning of November 25th, the civil ceremony being performed by the Mayor. Subsequently the religious ceremony took place in the Eglise St Vincent. The wedding breakfast was in the Hotel Modern. The ceremonies were attended by representatives of France, Belgium, Australia and America.'

Marguerite wrote the following description of their honeymoon:

Here we are in the most beautiful place in the world, enjoying our honeymoon. Garnet says he sent you some view cards of Nice so you will be able to imagine what the place is like where we expect to spend a week.

We got married on the 25th November in Orleans. The weather was not very nice then but it is fine now. We had the wedding breakfast in the 'Hotel Moderne' and we suggested to send you the menu on which everyone present had to put his signature. We have also had our photo taken together, which we are likely to get when we come back from our trip. Our Intention has been to send it to you with the first opportunity.'

In the evening we bade farewell to our friends and went on our trip to the South. We stayed at Paris for a day. We left on the 26th at about 8 o'clock in the evening. Garnet had booked our seats on the train a long time before – and we had a very nice and comfortable place, together with three American sisters and two civilians who were very decent. We've been twenty hours on the train before getting to Nice. Needless to say that after the very little sleep we had we felt very tired at our arrival at Nice.

Garnett adds the following note:

On my way back from our honeymoon, owing to the rapid change from summer at Nice to snow at Paris, I contracted bronchial pneumonia badly. Feeling very ill in Paris I made for Orleans. I was incidentally a week over my leave. After some difficulty I was admitted to an American Hospital and was pulled through after being rather bad. By the time I was fit to return to my unit, all dates had become rather involved and the question of just when I first reported sick was not raised. It was some weeks before the British Army 'located' me!

Garnett stayed on in France, working in the education service, the Non-Military Employment program, that was established to keep the troops busy while they were waiting for passage to Australia. He enjoyed his stay there and was not in a hurry to leave.

In 1919 Garnett, at work with the Education Service, writes from Charleroi in Belgium:

Have a fine billet. The people are very nice as a matter of fact they mostly are when they hear that I have a Belgian wife.

Hope to have Marguerite here in a few weeks if she can get a visa. We are looking forward to seeing you all, but I'm not very excited about getting back to Australia. It will be hard for you to understand, but I am now more used to France and Belgium and the ways of these countries than I am to Australia. In three years of war I've led a concentrated life which has been a rapid series of great experiences of travel, and of rubbing shoulders with the world. In one year of war one sees and learns more life than in five years of peace.

On 3 March 1919 he writes from a new address in Marchienne-Au-Pont: 'Marguerite arrived here from Bruxelles yesterday and we are now installed in a little "flat" at the above address.'[3]

Garnett and Marguerite lead a cosy life in the area until it is possible to plan a return which they do via England travelling on the *Orsova*.

These are the stories of happy marriages. But the misgivings of Queenie Soffe and Meg Woollen's parents were well-founded. Some of the Aussies took no account of the hearts they broke. Reports abound in the British press on the bad behaviour of Australians. Bigamy was easy for the unscrupulous Aussie. A soldier with a wife in Australia was reasonably safe from prosecution because the law at that time required that both of his partners be present in court.[4] After the war was over, reports continued to appear in English newspapers of Aussies who had been the downfall of innocent women.

This report on 24 March 1918, from *The News of the World*, is one of many:

HAD WIFE IN AUSTRALIA

At present undergoing imprisonment as a deserter, John Lindsay Mitlard, 32, an Australian soldier, was remanded at Bow Street, yesterday, on the charge of having bigamously married Lily Cross in 1917, at St Paul's Church, Covent Garden. It was stated that in December 1916, prisoner went to stay at the Waverley Hotel Southampton-row, where he made the acquaintance of Miss Cross, who was employed there as a chambermaid. A friendship arose between them, and they went through the form of marriage in the following February. Some months later accused confessed that he had a wife and three children living in New South Wales and his military papers showed that four-fifths of his military pay had been allotted to them.

In October 1919 there is a brief report in the London *Times* of a serial bigamist! A single sentence sums up his crimes: 'A story of an Australian soldier who was married eight times during the war in France, finding a fresh bride in each sector where his unit was stationed, is told by the *Petit Journal*'.[5]

There were surely many who escaped prosecution and left their brides, and in some cases children, to fend for themselves when they returned to Australia. So it was that by 1917 the Aussie had gained a reputation which did not do him proud and many of them were treated suspiciously until their bona fides were established.

The Aussie's Farewell

We came from Australia to help to beat the Hun,
We came on business only – not expecting any fun;
But when we got to 'la belle France' we found you M'amoiselle,
Intending, if we did this work we'd have some fun as well.
You flirted, danced and sang with us – taught us to 'parley-vous';
Life would have been so rotten if it had not been for you.
But now 'la guerre' is over and we're going home again,
But tho' we're glad we're going the parting gives us pain.

So farewell, M'amoiselle, M'amoiselle adieu!
Tho' we're going home again our hearts will be with you;
When we settle down in Aussie, and have wife and kids as well,
Vous n'oubliez jamais votre chere M'amoiselle.

Now, when we came to 'Blighty' first, to spend our ten days' leave,
We didn't feel quite sure what kind of welcome we'd receive.
We'd heard that English girls were cold and froze one with a glance,
But we found you just as loving as the M'amoiselle of France.
By your barrage of beauty caught – we yielded to your charms;
The war was quite forgotten when you nestled in our arms;
But now we're off to Aussie with some of you as wives,
And the rest will be a memory to cherish all our lives.

So good-bye, Blighty girls, Blighty girls goodbye!
Altho' we're glad we're going home we leave you with a sigh;
Your winsome ways, your faces sweet, your dinky little curls,
Are twined around our hearts forever, dear old Blighty girls.

– Homeward, 1919[6]

CHAPTER 4
The Bride Ships of 1919 and 1920

Will ye no' come back again?
Will ye no' come back again?
Better lo'ed ye' canna be
Will ye no' come back again?

It was a lengthy process getting the 180 000[1] servicemen on board ships to Australia and New Zealand at the end of the Great War. The men were massed in camps in England, France and Palestine. From the front line in France and Belgium the men went to holding camps on Salisbury Plain in southern England, there to await a passage home. Resentment at this confinement and a desperate yearning to get home led to riots in the New Zealand camp on Salisbury Plain. In Paris, Australia's Prime Minister Billy Hughes, who was attending the 1919 Versailles Peace Conference, was presented with a petition from several hundred men asking for official leave – many men had gone AWOL. Leave was granted.[2] It was clear that it was going to take the best part of a year for the majority of troops to be returned to Australia. Many used this time to marry the sweethearts they had met when on leave. On 31 May 1919, the London *Times* reported that 192 Australians married English girls in a week.[3]

It was General Sir John Monash, commander of the Australian forces in Europe in 1918, who insisted that the men be given priority to return according to their length of service rather than by their units.[4] By September 1919 all but 10 000 had departed.

In the Middle East the camps were near the coast around Tripoli in Lebanon. From there the men went to Kantara in Egypt before boarding a ship. This area was mostly evacuated by May but by then a few Australians had formed relationships with European women who lived there and a handful of brides from Egypt joined the bride ships.

At first there was no government assistance offered to Australian soldiers who wanted to take their new wives or fiancées home. A report in the London newspaper, *The News of the World,* in October 1918 is headed GIRLS THEY LEFT BEHIND. The reporter estimated that between 5000 and 6000 English girls had married overseas soldiers during the war. 'As parties of Anzacs who have been in the war since the beginning have been given six months' leave to enable them to spend Christmas at home, the question arose among those who had married over here as to whether they should take their wives or leave them behind. A man may take his wife home with him if he pays the expenses of the voyage, but few have been able to afford the expense.'

However, two months later when the war was over, the same newspaper reports FREE OCEAN VOYAGE FOR FAMILIES OF OVERSEAS FIGHTERS: 'The Government's plan for sending back the wives and families of officers and other ranks in the Army, Navy and Air Force, whose homes are abroad, was published this week. All applications must be sent in as soon as possible, and in any case before Jan. 31, 1919.' The government provided 'free railway journey to the port of embarkation in the United Kingdom. Ocean passage will be provided – the usual charges will be made for messing on board ship.' The report was also quick to point out that the Government was not going to accept any liability.

Repatriation was an enormous task. Apparently the authorities had anticipated that there would be around 6000 wives and dependents and when the number rose to over 15 000 it caused huge logistical problems.[5] The only way to transport large numbers of people in 1918, as it had been in 1914, was by ship. Since the 'Kaffir War' in South Africa in the 1850s when Great Britain had mobilised passenger steamships to move large numbers of troops, passenger steamers had been called up for military service with increasing frequency. Before the war, competition between the world's leading steamship companies encouraged the construction of larger, faster and more technically advanced vessels. At the same time government subsidies for construction of commercial passenger ships, in return for guaranteed wartime use of ships, meant that when war broke out there were excellent, up-to-date ships available.

At the general outbreak of war in August 1914, most liner sailings were cancelled as governments began calling up the passenger ships. Converted passenger ships were not suited to offensive roles and their main roles were as troop transportation and hospital ships. The ships were stripped of their luxurious fittings and militarised. The *Aquitania*, for example, had carried just over 3000 passengers on her maiden voyage in 1913. In 1917, stripped of her opulent fittings, she carried 6500 troops.[6] Any ships at sea were ordered to sail for the nearest neutral port. Not all were able to find shelter and some, like the German *Kronprinzessin Cecilie*, were interned. After seeking shelter in Bar Harbor, Maine, USA, she became the troopship USS *Mount Vernon*.

Despite the use of commercial vessels there was a still huge shortage of shipping. Ships were also needed to transport freight, but because the demand for the transport of troops was so great, the shipping of freight was affected and this contributed to the food shortages in Great Britain and ultimately to the very strict rationing. Finally the British set up a central Shipping Control whose job it was to buy and build ships – and requisition them.

AWM HI5632

300 Aussie war brides take refreshment on Euston Station before their long journey

Then early in 1916 the Germans began to sink any and every enemy ship they could. By April 1917 the shipping shortage was acute. So it was that when the war ended over a year later and troops – and their European families – were to be returned to Australia, finding enough ships to carry them became a huge problem.

The soldiers generally travelled with their wives and children. It depended on the rank of the soldier what quarters were offered. For the enlisted men it was often hammocks on deck and crowded cabins for their womenfolk. Non-commissioned officers were entitled to second class accommodation and officers to first class. Generally they would have to pay to upgrade their wives' accommodation to the same standard as their own.

However many servicemen did manage to upgrade their own passage home – and that of their wives or fiancées. In other cases the authorities experienced difficulties in getting officers and men to even fill in the necessary application forms for wives and children.[7]

Some troopships were hastily made over into 'family ships' for the transport of women and children and conditions improved. General Monash regarded the business of sending wives, fiancées and children back to Australia as troublesome, believing that: 'Wives were often ignorant of basic information on how to prepare for the voyage. 'The wives of private soldiers found it difficult to comprehend the social distinctions of sea travel, although third class on the transports was generally superior to ordinary steerage and the crews mostly "kindness itself".' Monash's papers also show he was concerned about wives who suddenly found themselves travelling alone – or those without any money for the voyage.[8]

This is not borne out by first-hand accounts. Nor are the words of historian C.E.W. Bean, who wrote that 'Over 15 000 soldier's wives, fiancées and children were embarked without delay' and added that playgrounds and baby powder were provided.[9] Though playgrounds and baby powder are not mentioned in any of the accounts I have uncovered, the Australian Red Cross obviously did provide amenities for travelling families. In the annual report for 1919 it is noted that family ships had been 'carefully provisioned with infant foods, clothing and other comforts necessary to the welfare of women and children.'[10] The arrangements as noted in the *Repatriation* journal for family ships included men and women berthed separately with sleeping together being discouraged; a women's general hospital (though nurses with midwifery training were very scarce!), laundries, drying rooms and hot water for bathing babies. The aim was one bath for every thirty women 'fitted with salt-water and steam jet facilities... but showers were considered inappropriate for women'. Smoking rooms or lounges were to be converted into creches.[11]

As for 'without delay', this is wishful thinking – as the story of the *Wainama* shows.

The Times described the tale of the *Waimana* as scandalous. The passengers, consisting of 444 Warrant Officers and non-commissioned officers (NCOs)[12] and their families, were forced to wait in rain and cold before being allowed to board. Already unhappy about the long wait, they then found that the ship was not fitted out with the second-class accommodation to which they knew they were entitled.[13]

Violet and Chris Procter were among the *Waimana* passengers and Violet kept a diary of the events. Her version begins with a description of her cabin:

A small apartment, probably about 10 ft by 8 ft [3 metres by 2½ metres] which I was to share with four women and a boy of seven.

The amount of floor space was so small that it was utterly impossible for all six occupants to dress or undress at the same time. In one or two cabins there were five adults and five children and in several there two or three babies.

The only toilet appointments were one small washing basin, which was broken in such a way that water would not remain in it, and one small mirror. Nearby was an electric globe which was kept burning as the only other light in the cabin was from one small porthole. In this we were fortunate, though, as the majority of the cabins had no means of letting in the daylight.

Chris & Violet Proctor

Soon things went from basic and uncomfortable to appalling for Violet and her fellow travellers. She had embarked while Chris waited with the other men in the cold and wet:

> Soon after 6 p.m. the men were brought on board. They were fairly miserable, especially as they had been kept hanging about either on the tenders or at the wharf ever since we left them.
>
> We wives were waiting for them on deck and eagerly watched the tenders approach as when they came we knew we should have a meal, the first since our very light refreshment on the train that morning.
>
> Our dinner over, the men decided to lodge a complaint to the Colonel of the boat regarding the state of our accommodation which should have been second class [they'd all paid to be upgraded].

Things continued to get worse: Violet slept well but others did not, reporting rats running along the ceiling above their bunks.

Rationing was a fact of life in Britain and Europe so meals on board ship were eagerly anticipated. The *Waimana* did not disappoint Violet with the food that was offered, though the service was not up to scratch: 'We sat down to breakfast about 8.15 a.m. and although we managed to secure plenty of food we were not finished until 10 a.m. or after, as owing to the insufficiency of staff whole tables of people were waiting to be served for a considerable time'.

This contingent of soldiers and their brides was not going to put up with poor service on top of the sub-standard accommodation:

> At 10 a.m. [writes Violet in dainty pencil] another meeting was called at which the Colonel was again present and brought the news that he had authority to send one-third of the people ashore and to sail with the rest that day. This the men refused to agree to, for as they truly said they had one and all paid for their wives' second-class passage and it would be unfair to make some travel under present conditions.
>
> During the day there were meetings between the men and officers and before dark about 150 men with their wives and babies left our boat, the rest remained on board. But a large number of women frankly refused to sleep apart from their husbands in such bad cabins where there were rats, so that quite early in the evening beds were made up from overcoats and any bed clothing that could be obtained on the hatchways and

in spite of the bitter cold and wet some preferred to sleep on the open deck.

Violet and Chris Procter decided to take advantage of this and hunted out some decent accommodation for themselves.

The men were still not happy and after another day of meetings and protests it was decided to take their case to the top: 'General Jess fully sympathised with the men and it was finally decided to appoint delegates representing the men and women and send them ashore to interview General Monash, the head of the Australian forces in England,' wrote Violet.

The consequence of this protest was that the boat was not considered suitable as a family ship and everyone was sent ashore. Violet notes:

This meant a good deal of difficulty for several families on board as they had no homes in London.

Arrangements were finally made and the government undertook to provide accommodation for them. General Monash said he could not say how sorry he was that we had been put to such trouble and promised to do all he could for us.

Families of Aussies board the tender at Tilbury Docks

We were brought to London from Tilbury by special trains and arrived home again at Herne Hill almost 9 p.m. on Saturday 1st November 1919.

Meanwhile the shipping company, in a notice inserted in *The Times*, insisted that the re-fit of the ship was to Australian government instructions and that it was the passengers who were 'insubordinate'. A few days later the *Waimana* left Tilbury with 1000 troops bound for Australia.[14]

It was twelve weeks before Violet and Chris Procter once again set out for Australia and this time it seems the departure on the SS *Friedrichsruh* on 22 January 1919 was uneventful.

For Leo and Rosa Baker it was separate ships home. Rosa's daughter, Coralie Welch, writes: 'Mum was rushed away with her luggage and glory box for the hold of the RMS *Megantic* at the Tilbury docks and Leo in the direction of the HMS *Ypringa* from Southampton. Dad arrived in Sydney two weeks before Mother'. For Eva Campion, who also travelled separately on an unknown ship, 'It was a disaster right from the start,' writes her daughter Ruth Reynolds. 'She was mugged on the ship coming over and all her money was stolen.' Ruth knows nothing more about her mother's trip out, but says that when she arrived things did not improve.

Rosa Baker sailed without Leo on RMS Megantic

Family records do not reveal when Andrew Anderson and his bride Loulou came to Australia but we know it was sometime in 1919 and separately.

Loulou Anderson travelled to England with another French woman, Fernand, who had married an Australian emigrant living in London. Loulou stayed with Fernand's in-laws in London until it was time to board her ship.

Rather than travel directly to Australia Loulou decided to travel via America. This was not unusual – some European brides took advantage of the opportunity to see America on their way to the other side of the world. Loulou travelled on the *Balmoral Castle* to New York. On board she made friends with an English woman Elaine, a nurse who had been educated in France and therefore spoke excellent French. Loulou's son Ron recalls that Loulou nearly lost the friendship of Elaine when she took up with a group of entertainers who made a great fuss of her. Loulou was an extrovert and, as Andrew had told his family in one of his first letters, was fond of kissing and hugging. According to family history Elaine advised Loulou that these people were not suitable company and that she should choose who she was going to associate with. Loulou chose Elaine.

From New York the travellers journeyed across Canada on the Canadian Pacific train to Vancouver where they arranged to transfer to the *Niagara* for the trip to Australia. Somewhere on the way Loulou's luggage was lost. It was a huge cabin trunk about one metre square which contained all her sewing materials and worldly possessions. Elaine, Loulou's friend and protector, lost no time in taking her shopping for material so she could make clothes. Ron tells the story of how Loulou and her friend went into a department store in Vancouver where Elaine explained that Loulou was a war bride and the wife of Andrew Anderson, son of Walter Anderson, owner of the Eagle on the Globe Steel Company, in Sydney. The manager announced that he knew said Walter Anderson and gave Loulou permission to buy whatever she needed – which Loulou did, of course. When Loulou's father-in-law discovered this he was not pleased, remembers Ron; Loulou had been rather extravagant. The lost trunk went to Japan – no-one knows why – and eventually was returned to Loulou with all its contents, including a superbly gold sequinned dress and jacket that Loulou had made to bring to Australia.

Queenie and Ted Sunderland very nearly travelled separately – they received their embarkation notices for separate ships. But, writes Queenie in her life story, Ted knew he was entitled – as an Anzac – to travel on the same ship as his bride. Queenie describes a visit to Australia House which obviously involved a great deal of being passed from one person to another, but eventually they succeeded in both being listed to travel on the SS *Osterley*.[15]

Charles Arthur Kindred and his bride Edith had to bide their time before they were put on a 'boat roll'. Writes Arthur (as he preferred to be called) in his diary on 26 July 1919: 'Have not started to do any packing yet, but will have to make a start soon'.

By 12 August they knew it was to be the SS *Mahana*. However it was not until more than four weeks later that they were told it was to sail from Devonport, not Tilbury, and that it was to be on the 25 September. So on the 20 September they began their journey to Devonport – it took five days. Arthur writes, 'I was permitted to travel on a civilian train as Edith was with me', and Edith began to write her own diary.

On 25 September at about 4.30 p.m. they arrived at the SS *Mahana*. Arthur was clearly not impressed with the organisation. 'Some mix-up over luggage,' he wrote. 'Everyone had to see about travelling down to

The Kindreds and the Robinsons travelled on SS Mahana

the boat themselves. Installed on SS *Mahana* for Aussie. Everything in a muddle on this boat but expect it will get sorted out.' And he adds, 'The *Mahana* is about the same size as the boat I came over in from Aussie'. (Which his family knows was the *Port Lincoln*.)

Edith on the other hand calls it 'the long-dreaded day'. She was naturally unhappy about leaving her large family – and the only country she had known – to travel halfway round the world to 'Aussie'. Obviously a practical and intelligent young girl her misery was not enough to prevent her from planning her trip and she had the foresight to bring a deck chair. Seating on deck was not something provided on re-fitted troopships in 1919.

Robbie Robinson and his bride Meg also sailed for Australia in September 1919 on the SS *Mahana*. Meg was two months pregnant. 'Her departure saddened her a great deal,' writes her daughter Margaret, 'as in the rush to board the train to Plymouth she didn't say goodbye to her dear father, and this became one of the saddest things for her, as she never saw him again.'

Others may have been sad about leaving their family but were also excited about the adventure ahead and more concerned to record the practicalities of their departure. On 29 October 1919, Violet Procter wrote in her diary: 'We left home about 10 a.m.[16] and the whole family with May Brown and Mrs. Davies came with us as far as St Pancras where we said goodbye and left by special train for Tilbury. Light refreshment was provided and we arrived somewhere about 2 p.m. where we waited on the platform for several hours.'

All aboard

Waiting to board was part of the procedure and Edith Kindred meticulously records how she and Arthur embarked: 'After waiting for an hour, I got on board. I was on before Arthur, as he had to wait until his name was called. I merely handed my papers to a private. He called my name out to an officer. I had a labourer who carried my case and rug for me and showed me to my cabin.' Edith wrote a long and detailed diary. She notes: 'On board I believe there are 1500. Eighty are girls and wives going

Wives and babies outnumbered soldiers on the SS Osterley

out to their boys and husbands. About 70 babies under 2 years of age. Some are only about two months old.'

Queenie Sunderland remembers the SS *Osterley* as a 'small ship, only 12 129 tons, still heavily camouflaged from active war service. Only 150 men and officers on board but there are 300 Brides and 200 babies!'[17]

Queenie shared a two-berth cabin with Dot Sutherland until Dot requested to sleep on deck, partly because she was slightly crippled, and Ted quietly moved into the other bunk. 'We had never imagined we could be so fortunate – a two-berth cabin to ourselves on a troopship!' writes Queenie.[18]

Settling in

The ships bringing the troops and their wives home after the First World War were not equipped for married couples so women and men were separated. The men slept in hammocks, Edith Kindred's Arthur on the boat deck, and curfews were set.

So when Arthur came to Edith's cabin to say good night after 9 o'clock on their second day at sea, 'An officer told him it was time that he was upstairs, but he was not the only one.'

A few days later Edith writes: 'Great dispute among the men here about the rules of the ship. Some want no men allowed in women's cabins. Others want the freedom of going in and out as they like.'

The fit out of ships for families was not to the luxurious standard which people had expected of passenger travel before the war. Edith, ever the optimist, reported in her diary on the facilities on the *Mahana*: 'There is a laundry, hot water and a hot iron can be got if you tip the laundry boy. There are cold salt-water baths, cold fresh water baths if you can fill the bath with pailfuls of water. Hot baths if you tip the steward to carry up the water. Canteen on board where one can buy tinned fruit, fruit salts, biscuits, sweet drinks, chocolate, cigs, pens and pencils, note-paper and envelopes of course.'

On her second day at sea Edith, who by her own account is one of a few women who are not seasick, has a bath. After tending to her sick cabin mates she writes that she is 'glad to get upstairs and have a scrub with a pail of fresh water, then jumped into a bath of salt water. Auntie, it was great! I did not want to come out!'

Edith and Arthur continued to have salt water baths whenever they could.

On the sixth day Arthur brought hot and cold water to Edith in her cabin so she could wash her hair and a few clothes. The travellers had to do all their own washing. Edith has been on board for two weeks when she writes: 'Went around to laundry, filled sink with cold water and put in steam pipe and it was hot in about 4 minutes. Washed a dozen articles of clothes. Just ready to rinse them when the water went off. The water is off every day from 10 a.m. to 12 noon. Put clothes through the wringer, took them down to the cabin.' After dinner she returns to finish rinsing her clothes and hang them out.

The SS *Mahana* had travelled no further than the harbour mouth at Devonport and already Edith Kindred was disappointed to find there was no milk and she could not eat her porridge. Fresh milk, or its equivalent, which we take for granted today, was not readily available during the war. Her husband Arthur, whose diary entries while he was fighting were mostly only a sentence or two long, often wrote about milk. On 1 December 1918, with the war over, he wrote: 'Had fresh milk in my tea this morning for the first time in eleven months. We get a dixie[19] full every day for half a franc.'

Edith continues to note every meal in her diary. This is for the benefit of her family but it is also interesting that while the diet hardly varied from soup, boiled beef or roast, tinned fish, potatoes, jam and canned fruit and vegetables, Edith, her husband and friends always had good appetites, obviously as a consequence of the severe rationing they had lived with in Britain for the past few years. Occasionally Edith will comment on the quality of the food: '6th day Dinner; soup, potatoes, boiled beef, so-o stringy.'

Edith is delighted when they are all issued with 'two and a half ounces of tea and tin of Nestlés milk. Just the thing we wanted, so that we could have afternoon tea. We enjoyed pears [canned of course] and Nestlés milk this afternoon'. Next day Edith writes 'Arthur and I had afternoon tea at 2.30 p.m. I make it in a cup, I get boiling water from the cookhouse. Issued with 4 ounces of sugar today.' They are issued another measure of tea and sugar and a further tin of condensed milk later in the trip, on the same day that the galley catches fire!

We discover towards the end of Edith's diary that the soldiers on board were organised to help with the running of the ship. On the day they sail from Adelaide Edith writes:

'Arthur has not done any fatigue work now for 4 weeks. Today the Corporal came around and asked him if he would do about 2 hours [a day] in the cookhouse, to cut up vegetables, and he would get his meals up there. So Arthur took on the job and now the two of us get the same menu that is served up to the officers. About 1p.m. we had grilled steak, cabbage, seasoning and potatoes...'

Not all the wives were travelling with their husbands and Edith took pity on a lady travelling with a fourteen-year-old daughter, Rosa. 'I can make Rosa understand sometimes what I say,' she writes, 'but the poor mother can neither read or talk to us. She sits on the hard deck day after day gazing at the sea, sometimes for hours at a time. I gave her my chair, which she seemed grateful for and she pats Arthur on the shoulder. The other day she tried to make me understand what she was saying but I could not. After a wee while Rosa came running to me saying "Present! Scissors!" I thanked her. The scissors are very neat. They are carved in the shape of a stork and are very pretty.'

Not all the European brides were so handicapped. A Special Correspondent from the London *Times*, who travelled to Australia on an unnamed bride ship, reports that there were a number of French brides. Of one he writes: 'A most fortunate chance placed my seat at meals next to one of these brides from France. Her country could ask for no more gallant representative in the land to which she goes. In a few months she has acquired a command of English which shames our tongue-tied race. Her good spirits are a constant enjoyment. Her wit flashes but is never cruel. If there are many like her among the brides whom the Australians are taking home with them from France, then France's loss is heavy, Australia's gain beyond reckoning.'[20]

Under the weather

The first hurdle for the passengers was often storms in the Bay of Biscay which gave many their first dose of seasickness. 'Although it is not stormy, already men and women and children are sprawled all over the deck. I feel fine, but suppose my turn will come,' says Edith Kindred on her first day at sea.

Next day matters are worse. When she wakes '...about 6.30 a.m. having a good nights sleep' she finds 'the other five ladies in the cabin are hopelessly sick. Given the baby a drink of water and biscuit. I am on the top bunk, held lady's head in bunk below me, she was so sick, got her another drink of water. Still felt fine.'

Rosa Baker, in a letter to her grandson, writes about her trip out at the end of 1919 on the RMS *Megantic*: 'We had a terrific storm in the Bay of Biscay – we were battened down for 3 days. Three women died on board & were buried at sea, it cast a great gloom over everybody. The bodies were wrapped in canvas, there was a service on deck, the engines were stopped on account of the propellers & the bodies slid overboard. It's truly dreadful!'

For Queenie Sunderland, too, it was the Bay of Biscay which exerted its full force on the SS *Osterley*. She writes: 'All went reasonably well until we reached the Bay of Biscay, where we ran into a violent storm. Mountainous waves surrounded us and then plunged us rapidly down into frightening deep troughs. Heavy rain and gale force winds caused the ship to list. We were battened down until the morning when we were informed the propeller shaft had been severely damaged during the storm and we were on our way to Falmouth Harbour on the coast of Cornwall for repairs. Back to England!'[21]

Queenie and many of the other passengers would have been quite happy to disembark from the *Osterley* for good but this was not to be. Instead they stayed on board while repairs were carried out and set forth again three days later.

As they approached the tropics and the equator the heat also affected many on board the old troopships. The cabins, reported Edith, were like ovens and as the ladies were not allowed to sleep on deck they obviously suffered at night. Prickly heat – or 'tropical rash' as Edith calls it – was a problem, especially for the babies.

By Day 19 in Edith Kindred's diary she needed to see the doctor about her heat spots for which she was prescribed sulphur cream. They must have been fairly troublesome for her to bother as she clearly had a strong constitution.

Once passengers got their sea legs (or worse, discovered that they were susceptible to sea sickness) it was many days before any land or ports of call broke the journey. 'The senior troops who travelled with the young women ensured they were not too homesick,' writes Coralie Welch, whose mother, Rosa, was travelling to Australia on a separate ship from her husband Leo. 'There were points in the passages and stairs where they had to give passwords. One such was "Hoo-ja" and they had one young woman who took a long time to remember it before she blurted out "Ja-hoo".'

By 1 October 1919 it was getting really hot. 'The men are busy putting canvas over the decks to shade from the heat,' Edith reports. The heat grew more intense as the ship steamed closer to the equator. The SS *Mahana* travelled to Australia via the coast of Africa and the Cape of Good Hope. Not long after passing the Canary Islands Edith writes:

Arthur & Edith on deck

> Did not go down until 11 p.m. It is very hot, and the cabins are like ovens. Girls are sleeping in the passages and yet they

have soldiers there on guard to keep any of the soldiers from going to the married women's quarters after 8 p.m. Wish they would let us sleep on deck.

In a day or two we will have passed the equator – thank goodness! – for the heat at meal times and bed-times is terrible. While we are still on deck it is just lovely, such a gentle breeze is constantly coming from the ocean.

Violet Procter also has her first experience of tropical heat, but there was still plenty to marvel at: 'Today 5th Feb we are feeling the heat considerably and have both changed into summer clothing. We have seen hundreds of porpoises and several flying fish and when going through canal we saw several camels.'

During the passage from England to Australia, which took up to two months, the ships went through all sorts of weather and changes of season. For the Kindreds on the *Mahana* it is not long before the weather turns cold. Six days after writing about the heat Edith is enjoying sitting on the deck with her 'cosy rug' around her on her own deck chair. As the weather got colder and the sea rougher, sea sickness once again returned. The baby in Edith's cabin fell out of her cradle, but a far worse fate befell another baby, who:

> . . . died from diphtheria a day ago – was buried at sea. She was 3 months old. Although no one was allowed to the stern, some of the boys, including Arthur, saw it getting lowered. All the officials, including the Colonel and Captain were at the burial. I saw 2 sailors, one at each end carrying the stretcher with the child. It was covered with the Union Jack. Our flags are all at half-mast. It made us all very sad to think that little baby was lowered into the stormy and raging sea.

Much later she reports on another baby who died of brain fever. 'The day before he went into hospital I was speaking to his dad,' she writes. 'He told me the baby had not been eating much for a few days but had cut 2 more teeth and would soon be well again. That was ten days ago. Poor wee thing has been getting worse every day.'

Meg Robinson, who was two months pregnant when she set sail with her husband Robbie, was also very distressed by the death of babies. She talked to her daughter Margaret of 'the huge seas they experienced off Africa and how frightened most of the women were. Many were seasick and the saddest part of the voyage was the number of babies who died, their little bodies wrapped in canvas and buried at sea. My mother never forgot the devastation of the parents of these wee souls whose bodies were committed to the deep'.

Keeping busy

Occupying themselves on the six-week *Meg & Robbie on SS* Mahana
journey was a feat in itself for the pas-
sengers. The troopship newsletters, of which there are many preserved in the Australian War Memorial, give some indication of the gossip and daily shipboard life where there were none of the bars, libraries, swimming pools or other luxuries that today's travellers expect.

On their second day at sea, Edith Kindred writes that 'Tonight we had a sort of sing-song. Jean Potts plays the piano splendidly, girls volunteered to sing…We all sang quite a number of the popular songs, such as "On the Bonnie, Bonnie Banks of Loch Lomond", "Clementine" and "God Send You Back to Me". Then there was a waltz. Arthur and I got up but the boat rocked too much so gave up the waltz altogether.'

On her fourth day at sea Edith wrote: 'Enjoyed stroll around the deck for an hour before breakfast. One would think that one is at a holiday resort. Kiddies shouting, others jumping about skipping; men sprawled over the deck, some reading, others playing at house; and quite a number taking their babies for a stroll. I took baby Ellen, she is in my cabin, for a stroll around the deck.'[22]

On the fifth day things were happening: a game of whist, practice for a skipping rope race, 'started a pair of socks for him' and looking forward to a concert. Arthur taught his new bride to play draughts and they stayed up late watching the Canary Islands go by and the lighthouse of Tenerife 'signalling to us'.

'Lantern slides and a lecture on Australia' were a highlight on the sixth day of Edith's trip. But life on board ship was boring. And even a young Scotswoman embarking on a new life found it so. 'The ship has changed its course and going more easterly now, nearer the coast [of Africa]. But that does not make any difference to us for I believe if she went for miles and miles nearer the coast, we would still have sea, sea, sea, all around. Only time you do not get seeing the sea is when you are lying in your hammock and look up at the stars, but does make one feel awfully moody', wrote Edith on the tenth day at sea.

When they are level with Sierra Leone Edith recounts an amusing incident when a flying fish 'got into' their cabin. 'Some of the ladies were hanging on the rafters, but the wee brute did not appear again. I could not help laughing at one lady, she was crouched in the corner of a top bunk, with next to nothing on but a frightened look.'

Another highlight was a fancy dress parade. Arthur and Edith created a costume for her out of YMCA maps and Edith was 'feeling quite proud' when she won first prize. The photo taken of her wearing the winning outfit is part of her family's album.

Edith's winning fancy dress

Many of the ships' newsletters, as well as providing anecdotes about shipboard life and (in some cases) news updates, included poems and stories from those on board. Naturally some were about wives and lovers, such as those on pages 85 and 86, from the *Berrima News*, published on the *Berrima* at sea on 14 September 1919.[23]

On board the HMAS *Friedrichsruh* on 18 July 1919, *The Last Post* complains that it's a dry ship. A few weeks later another item reports an incident between a man who wanted to place his deck chair in a vacant space and asks permission of the lady sitting nearby. The lady's husband arrives and says, 'how dare you talk to my wife without an introduction!'. In the humdrum of life on board even such minor incidents were grist to the printer's mill.

Edith Kindred also gives an insight into the letter-writing habits of her fellow passengers when she writes in her diary that her ship has not

It was the good ship 'Berrima'
That sailed the Summer sea
And the Digger had taken his English wife
To keep him company.

Sweet she was, as the dawn of day,
As it breaks on an Aussie shore
And the Digger he thought of the days to come,
And of those that had gone before.

And he gazed on that form that won his heart,
As she nestled by his side,
And he wondered what luck they'd have in life
With the ebb and flow of the tide.

For Billjim came from way back West
Of the Cannamulla line,
And Peggie she first found Billy's heart
In the Park by the Serpentine.

And Billy couldn't quite see how
His Peg would settle down,
To the life of the good old Queensland bush,
Back of Cannamulla town.

And he scratched his head and he thought a bit,
And he looked at Peggy once more,
And then he thought of his dear old Mum,
Who had hailed from an English shore.

And he knew that there was not much fear,
When Peg got settled down,
In the great strange land that she'd got to face,
West of Cannamulla town.

                                        – E.S.H.

Dear Mister Editer
Potry like the bloke makes on the other page is easy. Ow about this:-

It was the good ship Berrimer
Wot sailed the summer see
And the Digger had bought his Blighty wife
To keep 'im company.
Blue and grey were the darlings eyes
And some had black eyes too
But they wearn't as black as the batcheler's
Who shipped in where he oughtn't to.

– 'Offis Boy'

yet left the port of Devonport, yet 'there must be hundreds of letters wait-ing to be posted as nearly everyone is writing'.

Ports of call

Edith and Arthur Kindred's boat called into Cape Town, South Africa on 16 October; they had been at sea for twenty-one days.

The people of Cape Town were welcoming and the passengers dis-embarked from the ship in alphabetical order, 'men off one gangway, women off another'.

For Edith this voyage must have been an amazing experience. Not only was this a strange country on the other side of the world, but the people were not white. She writes: 'The people we saw on the wharf were nearly all dark South Africans. We walked up to town, about one and a half miles, every shop and passer-by was interesting. The natives are dressed in European clothes, some were quite stylish in their short voile dresses and high-heeled shoes, but when I looked at their faces, I felt like laughing. However I suppose we look just as funny to them, for some of them stood still and gazed with mouths wide open and big dark eyes and wee flat noses.'

They made the most of their time in Cape Town, firstly having a meal then taking a 'buckshee[24] tram ride to Cecil Rhodes' estate. This, says

Edith was a special car organised by the YMCA. Edith makes notes of the costs of things which she knows would interest her family. 'Everything seems dear. Gloves seem to be a little cheaper than they are in Glasgow. One girl bought hat-pins with black tops, 1/6 [one shilling and six pence] each. Two pence at home for the same things.'

Edith nearly lost Arthur in Cape Town – to a lion! During a visit to the zoo she reports: 'A gust of wind blew Arthur's hat over the fence and it rested on the bars of iron. In a moment the lion pounced on it. Arthur jumped over, kicked the claws of the lion, but gave that up for the lion used his two paws and pulled the hat into the cage, tore it to shreds and seemed as if he was eating it. All this was done in a minute. The people were laughing. I could have laughed more if it had been some other person's hat.' Edith does not make it clear whether her concern was about the loss of the hat, or Arthur's close shave!

They also took the opportunity to buy fruit (including... 'apples 1/- [one shilling], 12 tangerines – 6 pence') and other supplies.

Meg and Robbie Robinson were also on the *Mahana* and explored Cape Town. 'Meg recounted how embarrassed she was at the way some of the soldiers bargained with and were rude to the poor Indian traders who came alongside the *Mahana* to sell their wares and fruit and vegetables.' writes daughter Margaret. 'She did enjoy Cape Town, with its blue table top mountain looming above the city, and the botanical gardens with friendly squirrels and the bright warm sunshine and white beaches.'

Violet and Chris Procter sailed through the Mediterranean and the Suez Canal.

Violet wrote in her diary: 'Sunday morning on board and the sea is much smoother and I have had a good breakfast and feel A1. We have passed Cape St Vincent where there is a fine lighthouse and have sailed along the coasts of Portugal, and Spain. Just at present we have mountains on either side of us, Spain and the North of Africa. The coast line leading to Gibraltar is very mountainous and the clouds seem to be resting on the tops of them.'

They reached Port Said on 1 November and Violet saw foreigners for the first time. 'We did not land but stayed at the port about sixteen hours coaling and taking water and other provisions. Egyptian people dress very quaintly and are very dark, but the majority have most lovely eyes and teeth.' As they travelled slowly down the canal through the deserts of Arabia and Egypt she wrote: 'The country around is very flat and one sees wide stretches of sand extending for miles and running along the side of the Canal is a railway. Every few miles along the canal are stations, these being pretty bungalows surrounded by palms and other native trees. The only other signs of habitation are a few mud houses and natives in their picturesque costumes. At the end of the Bitter lakes we passed Ismalia a pretty native village. Arrived at Port Suez at 8 p.m. 2nd Feb. where we took on fruit vegetables and fish. At 11 p.m. we proceeded through the Red Sea and during that night we passed Mount Sinai.'

Violet's diary concentrates on the ports of call; she was obviously not keeping a record of her daily life to send home as was Edith Kindred.

When they arrive at Colombo, the capital of Ceylon (now Sri Lanka), Violet writes of great excitement – land of any sort was always a welcome sight.

Violet and her husband spent a day in Colombo, and she gave up quite a few pages of her little diary to writing about this adventure in a foreign land:

As we left the jetty we were met by a guide who assured us he would safely conduct us anywhere and everywhere. So [we set out] with this native named Dunpowlas and dressed in native costume – a blue short jacket and a sort of skirt of blue check cotton material wrapped around him! He wore nothing on his feet and upon his right foot he had six toes. The whole time he was with us he chewed betel nuts and a green leaf something like Lilac leaf, which he informed us was nicer than chewing tobacco.

Acting upon our guide's advice we went for a two hours drive in a small cart drawn by a pony and driven by a native. We passed through some part of the town and visited the Cinnamon Gardens, Victoria Park and other pretty gardens close by where we saw rubber trees and cinnamon trees, we also picked some sensitive plant which closes up as soon as touched.

Afterwards we were taken to the museum where we saw many curios and later we visited the Buddhist Temple which we entered after first having our shoes removed by niggers. On our drive back we passed Orange trees, Cocoanut and Date and Banana palms, also Bread-fruit,

Mango and Banyan trees, the latter is very curious in that it grows a certain height and then bends over and grows again in the earth, thus forming quite a forest in itself.

On our way we did a good deal of shopping, especially in the fruit market, which was an interesting spot and buying souvenirs of various kinds proved exciting as the natives beg so hard that you will buy everything they had and it is quite difficult to make them understand that a limited income will not buy everything. 'We later had dinner at the Navy and Army Hotel where we also booked a room for the night.

We slept in a queer room very high pitched and the only day light procured was from a sky light in the centre of the ceiling, the walls were painted and the floor was of stone, with a small mat. The room contained two large beds both draped with mosquito netting, one dressing table, absolutely bare with no cloth or articles of any sort on it and an electric fan fixed in the centre of the room to the electric light.

We were waited upon by several nigger boys and it is remarkable how well trained they are and the dirty clothing they wear.

This was a climax for Violet who writes in her diary that after that 'nothing of interest happened except that we were passed by the *Osterley* on the 27th'.

Queenie Sunderland on board the SS *Osterley* described stopping at the Rock of Gibraltar.

'In 1919 the town was not very large,' Queenie writes. She tells of riding on a trolley bus to the base of the Rock, but being disappointed at not seeing any Barbary Apes. It was a brief stop and the *Osterley* was soon sailing into the Mediterranean towards the Suez Canal.

The Rock of Gibraltar from the air

Queenie describes at some length the trading boats she calls 'bum-boats' which surrounded the *Osterley* as the occupants touted their wares to the passengers: 'Fruit, jewellery, hand-crafted leather ware and souvenirs galore were manipulated by Arabs eager to sell their stock.' Ted knew some Arabic which he had learnt when he was stationed in Egypt at Mena from 1914 to 1915 and bought Queenie an ivory brooch.[25]

After what must have been a very long and tedious voyage of nearly six weeks, the ships reach the western coast of Australia. Edith Kindred describes the arrival of the SS *Mahana* into Fremantle port on 2 November 1919:

> Got into wharf about 4.30 p.m. While we were getting towed in, plea-sure boats packed with people were circling around the ship. Some of the boys recognised their friends on the pleasure motor boats. Crowds standing on the wharf waving flags, bands playing some of the favourite march tunes. We got permits to take us ashore but we had to be back by 10 p.m. Each girl felt rather excited to be standing on Australian soil, as for the boys their joy knew no bounds, some of them were actually jumping about...the Y.M. Officer directed us to the Y.M.C.A. It was a treat to see the big log fires and the big easy chairs...Plates heaped with dainty cakes and sandwiches. All buckshee. A lady was playing the piano and singing one or two of the popular songs. We then walked about the town. The shops are all dressed for Christmas and were lit up. Everything is much cheaper here...Arthur was quite delighted at the prices of things although he says they are much dearer than they were before he came away. By this time it was almost 10 p.m. so we made a bee-line for the ship. Stayed on deck for an hour, great flashes of lightning, no rain, could hardly hear the thunder.
>
> **39th Day, Monday 3rd November.** Got up in time for 8 a.m breakfast. Sun shining and very warm, about 70° in the shade. Put on blue dress and hat. Went ashore about 10 a.m. Walked around Fremantle. Quite a nice place. A lady gave Arthur a card to go around to Victoria Hall, High Street, where some of the ladies of Fremantle were waiting to entertain us. Here we got the same as the previous evening. I was also handed a bunch of flowers. Arthur bought train tickets, 1/4 for me, soldiers free.

The train took about 35 minutes, stopping at about five little stations…
We arrived at Perth about 1 p.m. After walking about the town for some
time, we went to Queens Gardens which were very pretty, from there,
two minutes walk to the river, which was just beautiful, just as we see
in the pictures. There were half a dozen little pleasure steamers at the
side of the landing stages. While we were wondering if we should go on
one (one shilling return) it started to rain. We hurried along to the car
shelter. The houses look very pretty each one with front and back verandahs and plenty of flowers in the gardens. The gardens looked as if there
was far more sand than soil. We arrived in Fremantle about 3.15 p.m.
The ship was towed out of the wharf at 8 p.m. We all got a good wave
off from the people on the wharf. The ship sailed about a mile off the
harbour, then anchored until daybreak. We went to retire to our bunks
about10.30 p.m after having a very enjoyable time. But Mother, you
would have been surprised to see how homesick the girls were, whenever we saw land. I was the same, and Arthur could not help seeing it.
Every so often while we were walking through the streets of Perth, a picture of a map of the world would come into my mind, making me realise
just how far away Scotland is.

Doris West had embarked on the SS *Zealandic* as the fiancée of an
Australian serviceman. She made many friends on the journey out, possibly because at the age of twenty-nine, she was older than most of the
other women. When she arrived in Fremantle she found the home offered
to her by her fiancé was not to her liking. 'Her disillusionment was
heightened by the fact that the house
overlooked the Fremantle gaol!' writes
her daughter Claire. 'I really wonder if
mother actually cared for her fiancée
very deeply or whether she took the
opportunity to leave England and
hoped for the best. Whatever the
reason, she decided to continue on to
Melbourne.' There she found employment in McPherson's, a large hardware
and engineering store. She met a Scot:
'He was 21 and she was 32 when they

Doris West (left), SS Zealandic

married and such discrepancy was severely frowned upon in 1923. Particularly by my paternal grandmother.'

This was not to be a happy marriage. 'Despite my father having seen service in France as an underage soldier, I can only feel that he was far too young…it was a disaster and following two miscarriages, I finally arrived. I understand my role was to strengthen their relationship. Of course, it didn't and life was extremely difficult.'

Modern Nursery Rhymes

Sing a song of happiness
The diggers and their wives,
Sailing out to Aussie land
To recommence their lives.
When the steamer reaches port
The Aussie girls will say –
'Alas we should have leg-roped
   them
Before they sailed away'.

Poor Miss de Vere
Rushed to the pier
To welcome her dear Aussie back;
But when she got there
A Wife did appear
So she came a gutzer, alack!

– *Berrima News*, 5 October 1919

CHAPTER 5
Arriving in Australia

There was I, and there were you,
Three thousand miles apart;
Who'd have bet that we
would ever have met
At the start?

What did these young women from a war-torn Europe at the beginning of the twentieth century expect when they arrived in Australia? The Department of Repatriation published a monthly journal that, in October 1919, described amazement at 'the scanty knowledge the wives must have had of Queensland when they sailed from Europe. Some bring every household effect, and it is not an uncommon sight to glance at a crate 6ft high and weighing anything up to 21/2 cwt[1] ... Some ladies bring deck chairs, arm chairs, and one even brought a piano.'[2]

None of the hopeful young brides and brides-to-be could have imagined the barrenness of the Australian countryside compared to the green fields of their European homelands, and many of them were not prepared for the basic tasks involved in taking care of themselves, let alone a husband and family. Many, too, would find themselves living in remote parts of outback Australia.

Life in wartime Australia

Although Australia had not seen any actual conflict, all Australians had been affected by the war one way or another – if not directly participating or, as in the case of the women, doing what they could such as packing Red Cross parcels or knitting socks, then working in the essential industries of manufacturing or primary production.

Life in Australia had been far from normal while thousands of men were overseas fighting and being wounded or dying in the name of their country. Industrial unrest increased during the war and in the years immediately after. In 1917 the General Strike, called to improve working conditions, was one of the worst. Wages were also the cause of many disputes. Although wages rose during the war, so did prices, and in most instances at a greater rate. In 1916 the Australian government established the Commonwealth Prices Adjustment Board to fix prices on many products, including bread.

Capping prices and wage levels were not the only restrictions imposed by Australian governments on those who stayed at home. Hotel licensing hours were reduced. (In a referendum held in New South Wales in 1916 sixty per cent of voters voted for 6 p.m. closing of public houses.) Sporting events were restricted. (The reasoning behind this was that they lured young men away from a true vision of duty, according to the Melbourne *Age* in July 1915.[3]) And those people considered to be aliens – that is, anyone born in enemy countries – were interned. News was censored – indeed, everything that was published had to be submitted to the censor to ensure that nothing appeared which would help the

Pensive brides take their first look at Sydney

enemy or hinder the war effort. As well, all mail, particularly overseas mail, was subject to checks by the censor in case sensitive information should reach the enemy.

Raising money to provide for the needs of wounded soldiers both overseas and at home was the prime occupation of thousands of women through the war. Many became involved in Red Cross work – in 1914 the Australian Division of the British Red Cross had been formed. But this was not the only active organisation; dozens of others also gave a purpose to women denied the chance to enlist in the services or be involved in the war in any other way than as nurses. These organisations, which are mentioned in many letters and diaries, included the War Patriotic Funds, the YMCA, the Victoria League, the Belgian Relief Funds and the Sandbag Fund. In 1916 many of these amalgamated under the Australian Comforts Fund.

A cool reception

In Australia there had been a drastic shortage of young marriageable men for four years. As we have seen, those 'missing' men had spent that time in the company of attractive young European women. Meanwhile 'rumours reached Australia that many of the boys had contracted hasty, foolish marriages to women with an eye to the main chance', reports historian Michael McKernan. Australian newspapers depicted the English girls as schemers out to catch the cream of Australia's manhood. The English press reacted with accounts of the hostile reception given to some English war brides.[4]

Many Australian girls had written to soldiers while they were away. Often they did not know these 'boys' before they left – they were friends of friends or relatives. Regular correspondences grew and in many cases false expectations, particularly on the part of the girls, arose. There was after all a shortage of eligible young men, and those

Thousands of postcards were sent by Aussie girls

'A happy reunion' is the caption in The Sydney Mail

who were overseas fighting and who suffered the privations of war had far more romantic appeal in the eyes of the girls at home than those men who had stayed behind. For some of the first brides to arrive the reception was not welcoming.

The Digger, a newspaper for the Australian forces based in France, ran its lead article in August 1918 headed 'The Right to Marry. Reception Accorded Anzac Brides'. The paper quotes extensively from a story in *The Age*:

> *The Age* tells how two arriving women sought in vain for a familiar face. One had travelled first class, and one had come third class, but at some point of the journey they had discovered that they were both seeking the same husband. 'And would you believe it,' a sympathiser said, 'he is not here to meet either of them!' To the mere outsider it seemed that he had chosen the only possible course in the circumstances!
>
> [There must have been hostile crowds at the pier, as *The Age* story continues:] As the boat slowly followed the tug to the berth candour compels the admission that watchers on the pier expressed themselves in unmistakeable language. Why should Australians marry such women, when far superior girls are here already? Look at that one there; see the paint and powder: isn't she a get-up? Look there, did you ever see such a fright? And the eye roved from end to end of the ship looking for some

Crowds greet a couple disembarking from an unidentified bride ship

justification for the left handed compliment the Anzacs had paid the girls they left behind them.

[But *The Age* was full of praise for the incoming wives and fiancées, saying:] The girls who landed yesterday spoke volumes for the discrimination of some Anzacs. Their complexions, guiltless of artifice, were perfect; their beauty enviable. Their taste in dress was so good that the only bit of spiteful comment possible was 'They wear short skirts as well as our girls.'

[On other occasions, the incoming girls experienced a hostile even violent reception.] 'Local factory girls with sticks and stones to avenge their wrongs upon their supplanters prepared to give this batch a true Aussie welcome. A regular fight ensued...'But the hair that could have been picked up afterwards was a caution' said a policeman. 'None of us dared to interfere, and after all weren't there plenty of good girls in Australia without going to England to look for them?'

This was not funny [said *The Digger*]. Nothing is said of the girls who sent the reinforcements white feathers when they wore civic clothes, but who got tired of waiting for them to return, and married men with even colder feet. There is an unmistakeably hostile attitude towards the soldiers' brides in many newspaper articles written. It is a thousand pities that such a foolish attempt should be made to pander to the mistaken sensibilities of the like of the Port Melbourne factory girls, who welcomed the newcomers with sticks.

Most had no claim on a soldier and if they did and he has married an English girl then they are well rid of him. And how many Australian girls would have remained true if they had met Englishmen in similar circumstances? Some Australian newspapers will do well if they adopt a higher tone towards the good English ladies who have befriended many Anzacs, and use the same 'candour' to justify the natural right of Australian soldiers to select their brides where they like![5]

This editorial produced a number of letters which *The Digger* acknowledged and published, one from a writer signing himself (for it must have been a male) Picanin, suggesting the Commonwealth pass a compulsory Bigamy Act. This would allow the Anzac to marry an Australian girl as well as the English or French girl who was kind to him. They would, writes Picanin, be known as 'married triples' and be entitled to financial assistance if the man earned under £4 per week.

Many Australians were curious to see the war brides, particularly the early arrivals. On some occasions crowds jostling to get a view prevented husbands and families from greeting the newly arrived wives. Reports one paper: 'The feelings of a blushing bride walking down the crowded aisle of a church would be a mild sensation compared with the test of courage under the scrutiny of a thousand eyes as those young married ran the gauntlet yesterday.'[6] Shipping strikes, followed by a ban on public gatherings in an attempt to stem the escalating influenza epidemic, soon meant that arriving wives did not have to endure 'running the gauntlet'.

The open animosity shown to those early arrivals was a short-lived phenomenon but there was a current of ill-feel-

Families arriving

Street urchins from Woolloomooloo greet soldiers and their brides, 1919

ing towards European wives of the original Anzacs which never went away. In 1955 Betty Roland wrote *The Touch of Silk*, a play about the French war bride of a shell-shocked Aussie. In country Australia French war brides were treated with suspicion. Most Australians knew little of England and even less of Europe before the war sent thousands of men to that part of the world. For the men it was an education in how others lived, and none returned unchanged. But for those at home, the foreigners were strangers, with strange ways not to be trusted – and this is the theme of Roland's play.

Jeanne is the French wife of a shell-shocked soldier. Together they work a vineyard at a new soldier-settlement on the Murray, but Jeanne feels alone and disliked by everyone including her mother-in-law. Jeanne is visited by a debonair travelling lingerie salesman who tempts her with silk such as she has not seen since she left Paris. Jeanne reveals her loneliness and alienation from the country and its people. The lingerie salesman sells her some expensive silk underwear she can't afford, then he takes her to a dance. Jeanne's husband, enraged by jealousy and suspicion, kills the salesman in a fight and is charged with murder. The only way Jeanne can help her husband is to admit to a non-existent affair with the salesman, to persuade the jury, already prejudiced against her as a foreigner, to consider the killing a crime of passion and impose a lighter sentence.

Jeanne is seen to have sacrificed her happiness and her husband's love. Desolate, her life destroyed, the final scene reveals her misery, and the delivery of the silk underwear at that moment is a last bitter twist.[7]

For a few wives and fiancées there was the ignominy of finding they had been betrayed and of having to fend for themselves. For these women as well as others who could not be met 'owing to the shortness of notice', there were volunteer groups such as the Victoria League 'on the wharf to give all information and if necessary arrange accommodation for those whose relations or friends may not be there to meet them'.[8] The Victoria League, established at the turn of century to help migrants, was a strong group of middle-class women volunteers whose aim was to help migrants settle in their new home country.

Meeting the new family

Some wives were not welcomed with open arms. Constance Turner, who had come from Scotland with her husband JJ, was met by her in-laws on a wet February day in 1920. When asked if they were pleased to see her all she would say was 'Oh I don't think so!'

But most seemed to have been delighted at the warmth of their welcome by their husband's families.

Edith Kindred and her Arthur had enjoyed their days in Fremantle but another four days of sailing in fog shows an unsettled Edith who does not write with the same lightheartedness as she did before.

The following Saturday the ship arrived in Adelaide. 'Some officials came on board with the land Doctor, but we were not examined after all. This is only some more red tape, as at Fremantle, we only passed by the doctor showing him our hands.'

When they arrive in Melbourne two days later they are greeted by bands playing Scottish songs including 'Will Ye No Come Back Again?' As their stay was only a couple of hours they did not have time to explore the city.

The next day, as they sail up the coast between Melbourne and Sydney, Edith writes: 'One can hardly believe that at last our long, long voyage is ending. It seems months ago that we left Devonport, and yet we have enjoyed it. Somehow I feel sorry to leave the ship, for we have had some good times. I don't blame the boys for wanting to travel around the world, and spend weeks and weeks at sea. I could enjoy the life.' But she is also anticipating their arrival in Sydney. 'Feeling very excited and wondering how I will get along tomorrow.'

And the day arrives. On their 48th day at sea, Wednesday 12 November 1919 (one year and a day after the Armistice), they sail into Sydney Harbour.

Can see the huge Heads away in the distance, the entrance to Sydney Harbour. I believe the men are more excited than the ladies. The old Mahana was soon led slowly inside the world's most famous harbour, Sydney. It really is beautiful, with all the little islands and beautiful bays, some of them can't be seen unless the boat sailed up the different bays. It would take weeks to explore the beauties of Watson's Bay, Rose Bay and Lavender Bay etc. We anchored just opposite Watson's Bay and then some officials came aboard. We were having lunch at 12:30 when word went around that we would disembark at 3 p.m, Queenslanders first. We were still having lunch when we saw a pleasure launch almost along-side. Arthur went to the ship's side and to my surprise I heard him shout 'Mother, Grace, Delta!' He then came running back to me. I was more excited than he, because although I was dressed, my hair at the front was in my usual wee way to curl. I soon made sure it was hidden and went over to the ship's side. Arthur's Mother, Father, Grace and Delta, his two sisters shouted 'Edith' and waved their hankerchiefs and called 'Welcome Home'.

We were too high up to speak but Arthur let them understand that we were going to our cabins to get everything up. We disembarked at Woolloomoloo Bay at 3 p.m, while the band played a few marches. There were 2 ladies taken off on stretchers, they had been in hospital the entire journey. Whenever they attempted to get up they were sick! Arthur and I managed to get off the gangway together. In less than a minute we got into one of the taxis that was waiting to take us to the buffet, and in two minutes it drew up. Our breath was nearly taken away for although all this time we had not seen any civilians, we were now plunged amongst thousands, who were standing at either side of the broad passage which was fenced off for the arrival. We had only walked a few yards when to our delight Dell rushed through the barricade, kissed Arthur then me and said 'Welcome to Australia Edith'. There was Arthur's mother and father, Grace, Bronie and Claud Cotton (Cot). I felt quite at home when I saw Claud for I knew he knew the merry crowd I had left behind in Glasgow and Edinburgh. We sat on a seat and in a few minutes Dell brought tea, which I was thankful to get, for I was shaking with excitement. [After getting more of their luggage together the whole family caught a train.] The trains are like our tram-cars upstairs only three times as long. The train started to whistle such loud shrill whistles. Arthur's Father had tipped the engine driver!

Edith and Arthur were continually feted on their trip home to Arthur's parents' home in Guildford. When they arrived a car was waiting: 'I was told later that a gentleman donates the use of his car for every soldier returning home to Guildford. Before we left the station the driver announced in a loud voice, "Welcome home to Sig. A. C. Kindred and to his Scottish wife Mrs A. C. Kindred".'

Arthur's family had decorated their home with flags and 'Arthur's mother took me into what she said was Arthur's and my room, until our home was ready, kissed me and hoped that I would always feel at home, and that already she had taken me in, as if I was one of her own daughters'.

A wedding feast had been prepared.

The table was beautifully decorated in white and purple, Arthur's regimental colours. Arthur's father was at the head of the table, I sat on his left-hand side and Arthur was on his right. There were over a dozen altogether dining. I was asked to cut the bride's cake (it was beautifully iced) and Arthur to cut the other one. It had orange blossom all around it, an iced Aussie soldier and a cupid with a veil and tartan bow. Supposed to be Arthur and me. This cake had on it 'Welcome to Dellwood'. The dinner was just like a wedding breakfast, fowl, roast pork, ham, jellies, fruit etc. More friends streamed in during the evening. I didn't retire until 10:30 pm and had patiently waited all that time to read my letters.

Edith settled in to Australia with the same open mind and practical outlook as she approached her long journey from home. Two months later she wrote:

I will soon love Australia and her people. Certainly everything is done differently to the way it is done at home. Even the tea-cups are not set on the table. I don't think there is any food cooked the same way as at home. I suppose I will get accustomed to everything some day. One thing I am up to date on and that is the style of clothes. Only the very up to date fashionable shops have got models in their windows of the tight skirts, and only a few ladies are to be seen wearing them.

I am very happy in Arthur's mother's home. Arthur is up at Fairfield now, rooting the huge trees in our ground, getting ready for the builders.

And so she concludes the diary which she then posted home.

Meg Robinson and husband Robbie travelled to Brisbane where they were met by Robbie's mother and the wife of Robbie's best mate, Jock Bruce. They travelled to the family farm in Lismore by car. Their daughter Margaret writes: 'Meg was overcome by shyness, as most of the family were there to greet them. Her mother-in-law made her very welcome and there was a wonderful dinner prepared with food that, having come from war-torn Europe, amazed Meg. The great cedar table was laden with foods such as she had not seen before.'

Rationing was not introduced in Australia during the Great War despite the fact that Australia had pledged to support Britian with food as well as troops. The export of food reached record heights while imports of products such as tea, coffee and luxuries such as whisky fell slightly. Foods that the war brides from Europe had not seen for four or five years were abundant, and for the English brides the type of food and cooking was very similar to the food they had eaten at home. Roast meat, boiled and stodgy puddings, vegetables with all the life cooked out of them and elaborate cakes were everyday food. The French and Belgian brides, though they would have enjoyed the easy availability of staples, must have found the non-existence of items such as garlic difficult to get used to.

For Violet Procter the passage across the Bight was rough and they arrived on Tuesday 9 March 1920.

We were driven by motor car to Sturt St. and as we passed along the streets apples and cigarettes were thrown in at us amidst hearty 'Welcome home Boys'. Here Chris was granted his final leave and given his demobilisation papers.

Mrs P. and Floss also Margaret Balding's mother in law were here to meet us and after many handshakes and congratulations we finally secured a car and rode out to North Carlton where we stayed with friends and had a great welcome feast. Spent four days in Melbourne and left at 6.30 a.m. for home. Lil and her husband met us at Wycheproof and we were driven in great style by car with flags flying to her home six miles away. Here another grand feast awaited us, and the following morning we all drove en masse to Corack East where we had yet another great welcome.

When the *Niagara*, with Loulou Anderson aboard, arrived in Sydney it was quarantined because of the influenza epidemic. Loulou, Elaine and the other passengers found themselves anchored in Sydney Harbour unable to join those who were waiting for them, for some weeks. During this time Andrew found a small boat and regularly rowed out to the ship to talk to Loulou. One day he took his father, Walter, to meet his bride. As Loulou and Elaine hung over the side talking to Andrew and his father, a woman who was standing near them suddenly called out, 'There's Walter'! This was not someone Walter was hoping to see and the explanation of his acquaintance with the anonymous woman must have surprised his son – she was the fiancée Walter had jilted many years ago, when he left England to come and live in Australia.

Eventually the quarantine was lifted and Loulou and her fellow passengers were allowed ashore. We do not know whether Walter's ex-fiancée caught up with him when he welcomed his new daughter-in-law onto

The lovely Loulou Anderson

Australian soil but it is more than likely that he avoided the ship, and didn't meet Loulou in person until she arrived at the family home in Chatswood, Sydney. Loulou had written many letters to Andrew's family and she was made very welcome. She was heavily pregnant with their first child.

Chances are that Loulou imagined she and Andrew would live nearby and that Andrew would work in his father's company.

Andrew, however, had different ideas. Before the war he had worked for the International Harvester Co. as an apprentice and had always dreamed of going on the land. He lost no time in signing up for the Soldier Settlement Scheme and they were granted land at Kulnura on what is now the Central Coast of New South Wales, north of Sydney. Here he built a solid little house for his family and established an orange orchard. Loulou tried hard to be a farmer's wife and was made very welcome by the local women who found this elegant and charming French

Loulou & her little family

woman a curiosity. They must have found French women even more interesting when about a year later Loulou's mother and sister arrived to visit.

Sad arrivals

Eva Campion's daughter, Ruth, tells how her mother:

> …arrived in Sydney to be met by a man she barely recognised. He had been gassed in the war and had TB and had only been allowed out of the hospital to meet the ship. They married anyway and he was dead within 18 months. Mum went to live for a while with his family in East Maitland, to a primitive farm with a hole-in-the-ground dunny! One can only imagine the culture shock, coming from a large home with servants and all the comforts that the monied classes enjoyed in those days. After a while she came to live in Sydney and, armed with her qualifications from London, went in search of work. It was here that she experienced the anti-British feeling that was rife at the time – advertisements for positions often ended with the words 'Pommies need not apply'.

Eva found she had to sit for an Australian course at Stott's Business College before her qualifications, which had enabled her to work in Australia House in London, were recognised.

For Queenie Sunderland, memories of the trip to Australia include travelling with:

> one girl [who] had a baby only three weeks old and she was sitting in a deck chair when I said hello. She said to me, 'I saw you walking the deck with a very tall figure'. I told her that was my husband. She said, 'How long did you know him?' So I told her that we had known each other 10 months before we married. She said, 'ten months!' Then she revealed she had only known her husband three weeks. And I said, 'Now you have the baby'. And she said, 'I don't know where he is!' When Queenie asked the young mother how she had got on board the ship the answer was that she had his father's address and the father got in touch with the military and said if they sent her out that he would find his son and he would take full responsibility for this girl. She was going to Queensland. She had no idea where he was.

Queenie also remembers: 'A very nice girl, her name was Margaret Thomas. Well educated, we had a lot in common and when we got to Sydney there was a strike on. They asked the soldiers on board to bring up luggage from the hull because of the strike. So Ted brought up the luggage. Margaret had gone to the first sitting for lunch and he came to me looking worried. I said, "Is everything OK?". "The luggage is on deck, it's ready to go on shore," he replied. "Did you get Margaret's," I asked. He said, "Yes. It's addressed to number 7, The Domain, Sydney!"'

Waiting – or abandoned?

Queenie was not to know that the Domain is a large park in the centre of Sydney and that this was a fake address until her husband Ted explained it to her. 'He said, "do we tell her or not?" I said, "No, don't tell her. She won't be the only one. Just let her go quietly to shore." We just said goodbye and that was the last time I saw her, but in *The Herald* two days later it said that abandoned brides would be returning on the next ship.'

Coralie Welch recalls her mother Rosa Baker telling her about sad cases where wives, even with a child, were not met, but left desolate in a strange land.

The Repatriation Department did not believe the stories of 'Domain girls' that were written up in the press. In their official newsletter they acknowledged that 'there are cases where the husband is not at the boat, but he comes to light sooner or later. In one extreme instance, a husband reported himself after three months, regretted the inadvertence, and collected the despairing spouse'.[9]

The Australia the brides of 1919 and 1920 came to was very, very different from the life they had known at home. Those who had married men from farming families or men who took up the government's Soldier Settlement Scheme found themselves in a landscape they could never have imagined. Those who had been used to servants at home now had to learn to cook, wash and care for their menfolk and their children, often using primitive equipment.

One of the first major crises after the end of this war was the influenza epidemic which spread worldwide in 1919 and was almost certainly expedited by the soldiers returning from the disease-ridden trenches. It cost Australia alone 11000 lives, including many returned servicemen and their families.

Australia had been changed forever by the war. Products which Australians could not buy once the war started because they had been imported were now made in Australia. Aspro is one example. It was invented by George Nicholas after the supply of painkillers from Germany dried up. Other such products included gas and kerosene engines, radiators and typewriter ribbons. Farmers prospered despite the drought of 1914–1915, with produce such as wheat, meat, dried fruit and dairy products in strong demand from Britain despite the shipping problems.

Many men were able to return to the jobs they had held before they enlisted, but many others were unemployed. Wages rose during the war and fell at the end, but the cost of living rose and life was a struggle for many a returned soldier, particularly those with families. As soon as the war ended unions renewed action over pay and conditions. Shipping was included in many of these strikes and the boats bringing soldiers – and their wives, families and fiancées were not exempt.

Schemes were organised by state and federal governments to help soldiers re-settle on their return home. One of the most notorious of these is the Soldier Settlement Scheme, which provided the men with land and equipment to farm the land at low rates of interest. As well as providing a livelihood for the returned soldiers and their families this scheme was intended to help the Australian economy. But many of the more than 36 000 farms which were set up under this scheme failed. Often the land was unsuitable for farming the way men had planned and many lacked the expertise needed to make it work, despite the basic training they had received on taking up the scheme.

A housing scheme attempted to cope with what had become an acute shortage. In 1919 the Repatriation minister announced that 100 000 houses would be built for returned servicemen at a maximum cost of £700 each to be repaid over thirty-seven years with interest at 5 per cent.

There were some changes in the role of women in Australia after the Great War, though not all were beneficial. The brides arrived in a country which in 1918, along with Britain, had given women over thirty the right to vote. It would be another ten years before this was extended to women over twenty-one. Though women had been in demand for some

A soldier settler grows cabbages, Kentucky NSW

MITCHELL LIBRARY, SLNSW

A new war service home, 1927

war work, in 1919 their total participation was the same as it was in 1911 – just 29 per cent. Some of the professions now accepted women but the main employment open to them was still domestic or factory work. The number of illegitimate babies had increased despite contraception being more widely available. Married women were expected to produce large families to populate an empty undefended country. In the ten years after the Great War 'more women died in childbirth than all the soldiers who were killed at Gallipolli'.[10]

All in all, however, Australia was in far better shape than Britain, France or Belgium – the home countries of the majority of the newly arrived war brides.

THE
SECOND
WORLD
WAR

CHAPTER 6
Meetings

Who's taking you home tonight
After the dance is through?
Who's going to hold you tight
And whisper I love you, I do?

The Great War and its death and destruction were still fresh in the minds
of those who lived through it when war was again declared in 1939.
However this war would cause more damage, kill more people and cost
more than any war in history.

In 1914 patriotic fever had caused a huge rush of young men to enlist,
but that did not happen this time. In 1939 Australia was totally unpre-
pared for war. During the Depression of the 1930s little had been spent
on defence. In 1939 the navy was ready for war with a strong force including three modern cruisers but the other two services had been neglected
because it was felt by both the government and the opposition of the
time that a strong navy was the best way to protect Australia against
invasion.

The air force (RAAF) had only 165 combat aircraft, nearly half of
these being obsolete biplanes, and the army consisted of a mere 3000
regular troops and 80 000 part-timers. So it was that in September 1939
when war was declared the Australian prime minister, Robert Menzies,
announced the formation of the Second Australian Infantry Force. Twenty

thousand volunteers were needed – the same quota as was expected in 1914 when 40 000 men enlisted – but this time the states struggled to meet their quotas.

Once more the young men of Australia were shipped off to fight a war overseas, though this time they were not as naively enthusiastic as they had been in 1914.

Once he had been sent away, the average young Aussie did not return home until the war was over in Europe. Unlike the Europeans, who were often close enough to go home on leave, the Australian on leave was a stranger in a strange country.

Canada and the USA

At the outbreak of war Australia had just one flying school and sixteen instructors, but within the first year this had expanded to thirty schools. The Empire Air Training Scheme (EATS) was set up in October 1940 at a meeting in Ottawa, Canada attended by Australia's Minister for Air, J.V. Fairbairn. It was decided that 50 000 air crew would be trained each year from Australia, New Zealand and Canada under British command. Elementary training would be in Australia or Canada and advanced training in Canada or Rhodesia. When training was complete these men were posted to both Australian (RAAF) and RAF squadrons, though less than half were to fly with the RAAF.[1]

AWM 003580

The men who joined the RAAF came from all walks of life. They stood out in the Canadian towns with their Aussie accents and their requests for ice-cold beer in the depths of what was for many their first snowbound winter. Many young Canadian girls enjoyed the company of these enthusiastic foreigners and the EATS was responsible for thousands of romances and marriages. In fact, in 1948 when the scheme for bringing wives, fiancées and children to Australian was at its peak, the largest group of wives was from the EATS, though not all those wives were

Aussies leave to join EATS

Canadian. The British government paid for 2486 passages in that year alone, including 878 fiancées, in acknowledgement of the Australian contribution.[2]

Ina Staryk met Aussie Leo Harper, who had only been in Canada for a couple of weeks, at a dance in Winnipeg in January 1944:

> Winnipeg was full of Aussies. It had a big wireless and gunnery school. We loved dancing with the Aussies, they were very good at it. I saw this boy with dark curly hair, brown eyes and a beautiful smile and that was IT! I was in seventh heaven when he asked me for a dance. We spent the entire evening together dancing and made a date for the movies for the following week.
>
> I was nineteen and he was nearly twenty-one. It was so simple in those days of movies, dancing, long walks and just talking together. Just before he left Canada he told me about the girl back home who was wanting to get married when he got back. I was completely heartbroken and cried for days, at the same time I was very angry.

Ina decided she had to forget Leo. The war ended and the Canadian boys returned home, but though Leo was no longer there he had not been forgotten. 'One day months later I got a telegram from Leo saying he had made a mistake and it was me he really loved and there was a letter following. In the letter he asked me to marry him and said he would fix up the fare and passage with the Department of Veteran Affairs. I said yes and he duly paid the fare from Winnipeg to Sydney – 125 pounds, 5 shillings, 9 pence. This was to be refunded if we married within thirty days.' It was all Ina needed.

Phyllis Westcott met the Aussie she would marry when he was stationed in Edmonton, Canada. It was at an evening for servicemen: 'I was the first girl in Edmonton Philip met, having just arrived a few days earlier'. From Edmonton Philip Bell went to eastern Canada for three months as part of training in coastal command prior to going to England in 1943. However, by the time he left Edmonton he and Phyllis had established a firm friendship. In 1944 Philip was involved in the invasion of Normandy but before then he had organised for an engagement ring to be bought by Phyllis' parents. When the war in Europe ended Philip was sent to Burma under Lord Mountbatten where once again his role was dropping supplies to Allied troops, this time those fighting the Japanese.

Meanwhile Phyllis applied to come to Australia as a fiancée. At the time she worked in a bank where many of the girls were involved with Australian and New Zealand airmen, so much of the talk was about war brides. Phyllis' parents had moved to Canada from England so they knew what emigrating involved. When it became time for Phyllis to go to Australia they accepted it philosophically.

It was 26 April 1945 and Evelyn Stephens was working for the Red Cross Blood Bank in San Francisco when Merchant Seaman John Muirhead came in to donate a pint of blood. Evelyn remembers: 'His blood pressure was too high for me to take his blood, so we talked awhile and he told me about his family and his country and how homesick he was. When the blood pressure is high through nerves, talking about family and friends usually brings it down but this was not the case.' Evelyn called the doctor in who asked John if he'd had a night on the town. The answer, yes, explained the high blood pressure.

It was Evelyn's birthday and she invited John to dinner at her aunt's that night. 'That,' says Evelyn, 'was the beginning of a whirlwind romance with us announcing our engagement on May 8 and John sailing out on May 10 – for three months.' It was 1945 and the war was over. In those three months Evelyn prepared for her wedding which would take place when John returned on 12 August. Evelyn admits that she knew nothing about John's home town of Cairns, Queensland, and says that when she asked him, 'He said he would supply me with everything I had in my home in San Francisco, when it was available in Cairns!' Those last words were the most telling. When Evelyn got to Cairns she soon realised how few mod cons were available at that time.

The English girls

Once again Australians were to be seen arm-in-arm with English girls – just as they had been a generation earlier when Aussies on leave from the trenches of France and Belgium were a common sight in England.

As in the Great War, local girls met Aussies at dances, in the street, on the train, at bars, or when they were nursing them. In the Second

World War women also played a vital role in the auxiliary services and were much closer to the action.

In the Great War women in Britain had been deployed as nurses, as kitchen staff for army canteens, as telephonists or as drivers – until 1917, when they were admitted as auxiliaries to the army and known as Women's Army Auxiliary Corps (WAAC). Within months these women had taken over administrative and communication roles, releasing thousands of men for the front line. Earlier the navy had led the way with the Women's Royal Navy Service (WRNS) and by 1918 the Women's Royal Air Force (WRAF) was also established with a strength of 9000 women. These services were disbanded at the end of the war.

In 1938 the ATS (Auxiliary Territorial Service) was established and called for female volunteers; the WRNS (Women's Royal Navy Service) were revived and became known as Wrens. The RAF formed the Women's Auxiliary Air Force (WAAF). When Germany invaded Poland in September 1939 these forces were ready to act.

Dunkirk, the fall of France and the Battle of Britain were the turning points for many women who were keen to show what they could do.

In May 1940, as the Germans advanced across Belgium and Holland and towards France they cut off 200 000 British and 139 000 French and Belgian troops, forcing them back to the coast at Dunkirk. Under fire a fleet of small craft evacuated most of these troops to England in early June 1940. Amongst the evacuees were a number of nurses – women in the front line.

When in June 1940 the Germans invaded Paris, women switchboard operators continued to staff the British army exchange in Paris as the Germans marched into the city. The fall of France signalled the start of the Battle of Britain. Now the WAAF plotters came into their own, working around the clock to keep account of the precise movement of the German bombers, homing the pilots by radio onto the enemy aircraft. When the Luftwaffe failed to reach their objective, the cities of Britain became the next target and throughout the war the ATS were vital in the operation of radar units, searchlights and anti-aircraft gun batteries to protect British cities.

In 1941 the British government gave women auxiliaries full military status and in the same year introduced compulsory mobilisation of women into the workforce. But even before then, women had begun to move into occupations previously thought to be male domains. The first occupation to be taken over by women was in the transport industry and bus conductresses had became a familiar sight by 1940. At the end of 1941 Prime Minister Churchill's Cabinet made Britain the first country to institute general conscription of women with the National Service Act No. 2, barely ten days after the Japanese attack on Pearl Harbor had brought the United States into the war.

A youthful Arvona, 1943

As soon as she turned nineteen, Arvona Small, who came from the tiny Welsh village of Loughor, joined the WAAF. A fortnight later, in January 1943, she was on her way to Gloucester. When she had finished her training she was posted to Fradley in Lichfield where she was a batwoman.[3] In order to get about, the servicewomen and men relied on passing traffic to give them a lift – 'It could be a car, lorry or even the 'Queen Mary', as the aeroplane carriers were called,' recalls Arvona. One night she and her friends hailed a covered van which, when it stopped to pick them up, also took three Aussie airmen on board. One of these men was Hedley David and soon he and Arvona were 'paired off'.

Like Arvona, Pat Warne found herself a job as soon as she was old enough. Pat worked as a teleprinter operator with the Air Ministry at Dunstable, sending weather reports to the RAF. A Londoner by birth, it was to the capital that she headed on leave, and one weekend on her way home she was approached by an Australian. 'Being an Aussie, he began to talk to me,' recalls Pat, and soon they were talking about London and Whipsnade zoo. Max Darby was the Aussie and he told Pat he was a bomber pilot and a keen photographer, hence the desire to visit the zoo. He asked Pat if she would show him around the zoo when he was next on leave. Pat admits she wasn't in the slightest bit interested in photographing birds, saying, 'I thought, he's too boring for me. Life is for living!' However she did take him to the zoo and the relationship progressed from there. 'We were just sitting in the restaurant in the zoo and he gave me the impression he wanted to be with me forever.'

Max and Pat met often after that, but 'we were very different people. I was mad on ballroom dancing and considered very good and I enjoyed life to the full because we never knew if we would live another day. Max came from a wheat farm and had led a very different life to me.'

When the war ended and just before he left England, Max once again asked Pat to come to Australia to live. She did not give him a definite answer and Max continued to ask Pat to marry him – now by letter. She finally agreed. 'I missed him very much,' she says. Pat joined the fiancée's program. 'Max sent the money because in England the pay was atrocious and mine had board taken out and a tax we were supposed to get back later, so we were always one week from the workhouse,' remembers Pat. Four days after she applied for a passage Pat found herself allotted a place on the *Stirling Castle*.

Friends Jose Carter and Sheila Hollis met in Gloucester after they had both been called up. They both came from Nottingham, and lived near each other, though they did not become friends until they found themselves together in the WAAF as meteorological observers. They did the same course and were eventually posted together to Binbrook in Lincolnshire and the Australian 460 Squadron.

Sheila met Johnnie Thomson, a rear-gunner on the Lancaster bombers, in 1944 and they married a year later in September 1945. At the time they met Johnny was getting towards the end of his second tour of operations over Germany. He had done forty-five trips, which, says Sheila, he survived by a miracle despite a plane crash on one trip. 'I well remember the night his crew celebrated the end of his second tour,' Sheila wrote. 'I was on duty in the Met. [Metrological] office – alone, because there were no operations that night, when there was a knock on the door and in walked a very sorry specimen. The celebrations had been too much! I plied him with black coffee and sympathy – my relief was nearly as great as his, to know he had survived when so many hadn't.'

Sheila asked Jose to be bridesmaid and Jose replied, 'Yes, as long as the best man is tall!' Jose fell in love with Laurie Foster, Johnnie's best friend and they too married – four weeks later. Then their husbands were sent back to Australia. 'Everything was still very uncertain,' remembers Sheila, 'and relations with Russia (our allies during the war) were becoming increasingly tense. It was a very sad and frightening "Goodbye", as we didn't know when we would see each other again. This fear and worry, I think, prevented me from realising the fact of separation from my own family, and six months later when we were told we were going, the relief and joy continued to do this.'

Jose, Sheila and many of the other brides felt that their passages to Australia were being set aside for the thousands of brides heading to the US to join their GI husbands. They joined the wives who marched to bring attention to their plight, carrying a banner saying 'BOATS FOR AUSTRALIAN BRIDES'. Finally the pair found themselves allotted bunks on the *Stirling Castle* and sailed for Australia, arriving in Melbourne in June 1946.

Mary Mowberry drove an ambulance for four and a half years with the civil defence and in early 1945 joined the Navy Army and Air Force Institute (NAAFI).

She met Bill Howard when she and another member of the ambulance crew were walking down Derby Road in Nottinghamshire and they were hailed by a couple of Aussies. This was the beginning of a relationship. When in June 1945 she was sent to Europe to drive food lorries for the army of occupation, a job which took her to France, Holland and Germany, they continued to write to each other. Like so many Aussies, Bill never actually proposed. 'I was going overseas and he was going home,' said Mary, 'and we decided to wait and see if it was the real thing.' It was, and in 1946 Mary returned to England and applied for passage to Australia under the fiancées program.

Dorothy Hunt began her wartime career in the WAAF as an ambulance driver. Later she moved to working with air crew. 'I had a tractor and I used to tow the planes,' is how Dorothy describes her role in the WAAF as a transport driver. Dorothy found the Aussies outgoing and lots of fun and admits she was not as fond of the Americans. 'I didn't like the way they accosted us on the street. I didn't see any need for that.' She said of the Aussie boys: 'They used to pull our legs and one said to me, "In Queensland it's really hot. It gets so hot you can fry an egg on the pavement". I loved working with them, they were so down to earth. Our English boys were inclined to be just a little bit reserved.'

In fact Dorothy's job was more than just towing the planes; she also towed the bombs from the bomb dump to the planes. Once the 'boys' had taken off on an operation, Dorothy and the other WAAFs would wait for them to come back and 'if they couldn't get back into the disperser properly then we had to hook on and pull them in. We probably finished at three o'clock in the morning, then would have the next day off. It was twenty-four hours on and twenty-four hours off'. Dorothy also loved the comradeship which developed between the crew and the ground staff. 'We used to be all in a big hut with a sergeant in charge, a great big stove going madly keeping us warm. The boys used to sneak extra bread and margarine from the mess and make toast for us. There were beds and they would say, 'You girls lie down. We'll wake you when the boys come back. The comradeship was wonderful and it's lasted all these years,' she says.

Dorothy met John (Edwin) Holden, who was a wireless operator on Lancaster bombers, when she was driving the tractor for the Lancaster bombers of flight 463. They gradually came to spend more and more time together until one day, about three months after they first met, John 'proposed' to Dorothy. His actual words were: 'When we go into Lincoln today we'll find a jeweller's shop and buy an engagement ring'. Dorothy agreed, and their purchase of a ring was followed by a celebratory dinner at the Lincoln Hotel.

John & Dorothy Holden

As happened in the First World War nurses were perfectly placed to meet men, though often the men were far more interested in the nurses than the nurses were in them. By the end of this war there were over 14000 nurses in the British services.[4]

Barbara Bellamy was a twenty-year-old nurse when she met Cedric Arnold. 'My introduction to my husband-to-be was when I heard the new patient down the corridor refusing to remove his pyjamas!' she writes.

> He was extremely ill and delirious and did not take kindly to orders from women – and most were younger than he. He seemed terribly old at thirty. Cedric was determined none of us would remove his pyjamas and his RAF driver was under strict instructions not to return without them. He, the driver, stood in the corridor arms folded and feet slightly apart, prepared to stay as long as it took! Up until this time I had not met this strange Australian – I'd only heard him from afar!
>
> When he was made comfortable in Royal Devon and Exeter Hospital pyjamas, I took a quart of orange juice to him announcing he had to drink it within the hour. His reply was – is it real? My reply was yes, but what you get after this will be synthetic. [He said] 'I'll drink this but nothing else.'

That was their first encounter – not very promising.

Cedric Arnold's illness grew worse and Barbara says that as time went by the staff softened to this stubborn Australian who did not make passes at the nurses, Barbara included. However when he was well enough she took him home to meet her parents – and within two months they were engaged. A month later they married because Cedric was to be sent overseas.

Dancing

The most popular leisure pastime for the young in wartime was dancing. A combination of music, dimly lit venues, the closeness of another human being and the freedom to flirt made dancing a perfect release from the tension of their daily lives. It was also an outlet for boredom – a chance to meet new, interesting people from faraway places. Teenagers, married women escaping from lonely nights and servicewomen on leave all dressed up and headed for dances and 'hops' whenever they could. Most English towns and cities had at least three or four dance halls and often dancing continued even through the air raids.

'My girlfriend Anne and I loved to dance on the Pier,' Betty Cooper told me. 'Two bands played non-stop. The best song of all was "Who's taking you home tonight?".' Though dancing on the Pier and other coastal locations came to an end with the bombing of Plymouth in 1940, it didn't end the girls' love of dancing and they soon found other locations – and other distractions. Betty and her friends found the air force provided

Betty wearing RAAF brooch

some interesting company, particularly the men in the number 10 Squadron which flew Sunderland flying boats. Conrad (Con) Gehrig was flying a Sunderland when he and Betty met in 1941. 'Courting was very difficult,' remembers Betty. 'Double daylight saving was introduced so we went to work under the stars and it was daylight until 11 p.m. – not

many darkened doorways for a good-night kiss!' Conrad was a member of the RAAF when war broke out and his overseas contract was for two years, so he would shortly return to Australia. Before he did so he asked Betty to marry him – if he could arrange her passage to Australia.

Beryl Barnes met Trevior Boyd at a dance and they continued to write to each other and meet up whenever possible, but when the war was over Beryl said goodbye to Trevior as he sailed on *The Australia*, thinking that was the end of the relationship. 'During the war we met

Trevior Boyd at Windsor Castle

so many,' she writes, 'and had to say goodbye so often, I do not remember feeling devastated about that particular farewell. Life goes on!' And so it did, but not as Beryl had planned. She and Trevior were to go through a courtship and marriage which had many highs and lows before they finally made it to Australia – and more adventure.

Estelle Mydat met her husband on a blind date. 'I was home in London on a weekend pass and was looking forward to spending it quietly with my sister, Doreen, also on leave from her nursing duties. We had envisaged lolling around – feet up and catching up on all the news. Our intentions were shattered when our mother informed us she had accepted an invitation on our behalf to accompany two Australian pilots who our cousins Bobbie and Henri were entertaining at the Grosvenor House Hotel.' Estelle is direct: 'I was in the WAAF and frankly didn't relish the idea of meeting "Two blue orchids" whom I did not like anyway from my dealings with them.' Try as she might, Estelle could not find an excuse to avoid the date her mother had set up and finally she and her sister went to the Grosvenor '...vowing and declaring we would leave the party no later than midnight for home'. The evening did not get off to a good start. Estelle and Doreen arrived at eight, but the 'blue orchids' did not arrive until 9.15 p.m. 'We had spent the waiting time repelling Yanks trying to pick us up.

Estelle Mydat, 1943

'From the outset Keith attached himself to me while I endeavoured to be as difficult as possible. He made sure he sat next to me at dinner and approximately one hour later he turned to me and said "I am going to marry you". I laughed and told him to back off and not be so stupid. He didn't back off and persisted in talking about me as his future wife.' The dinner finished too late for Estelle and Doreen to leave by midnight and the next stop was the Embassy night club where they stayed until 4.30 a.m. The next day Estelle found herself meeting Keith for dinner. 'He extracted that promise from me before we could get him to return to his hotel after the Embassy.' Estelle was beginning to soften. 'I met Keith and enjoyed the dinner very much' with Keith continuing to declare his love. Estelle says 'I felt nothing except amusement'.

Keith Bridgford continued to court Estelle and they met frequently in London. 'In hindsight I suppose he grew on me like a wart,' says Estelle, 'but I didn't fall in love with him (or admit it) until he was posted to the Middle East and I was sent on a course to Windermere.' Keith managed to visit Estelle before he left for the Middle East and it was then that he 'extracted' a promise that Estelle would marry him on his return. 'I caved in,' is how Estelle describes it.

This was in May 1943. In October, when Keith returned to England, Estelle told her family that she was going to marry an Australian. 'My father hit the roof and said I was mad because I knew nothing about him or his background and proceeded to tell me all about the Aussies in World War I who married English girls and then went home to their wives and children. Father wouldn't even meet Keith until he produced a certificate from his Commanding Officer advising he had permission to marry and he was not married or supporting a de facto wife.'

Estelle and Keith Bridgford married in England 1943 and by September 1944 Estelle had resigned from the service because she was pregnant. But all did not go smoothly. 'In October 1944 I was jolted into reality when Keith was shot down near Holland and I didn't know for four days whether he was alive or dead. Another pilot phoned my parents and told them, I was out shopping. The other plane followed Keith's down as far as they could and it appeared they had landed on a grassy field. Keith passed out and was rescued by local resistance fighters. He spent a few nights behind the lines.' A week later he returned 'shaken but in reasonable health'. Estelle said 'I didn't worry because they said they thought he'd got down quite safely. My father was quite distraught when he told me though.' Their daughter Vivienne was born in April 1945, 'one week before the war in Europe ended'.

Joan Cooke was a post-controller with the Royal Observer Corps which was located underground on York Racecourse. Her job was to plot the aircraft in 4 and 6 Group Bomber Command in Yorkshire and Lincolnshire. Joan liaised with outside posts to collect numbers and details of aircraft leaving and returning. Both their own and enemy craft were plotted.

It was at a dance in the city of York that Joan first met Russell Crane and the others in his crew who were stationed at Marston-Moor and Snaith. 'I liked all the crew,' recalls Joan, 'and invited them to my grand-mother's home at Pontefract, which was the nearest big town to Snaith airfield and where I used to spend my weekend leaves. My grandmother and three spinster aunts made them all very welcome, and invited them home whenever they could get away. Russell and his skipper, Gil Hodgson from New Zealand, bought an old car from our family doctor and so I saw a lot more of Russell and we became close.' But then fate intervened. Russell and his crew were shot down over Holland and Russell bailed out over Germany. Three of the crew were killed, including Gil, and Russell was taken prisoner. That was in 1944. When Russell was released from Stalag Luft I, a camp which experienced long cold winters on the border of Russia and Germany, he went to Joan's grandmother's place to recuperate. It was while he was there that they became engaged.

Mary Hill's mother had a large country house not far from Bournemouth in the south of England. She had joined the Lady Frances Ryder scheme, the purpose of which was to provide home hospitality for servicemen from overseas while they were in England. They took six or seven ser-vicemen into their home at any one time and provided a home away from home. Mary remembers the main problem being food rationing though she also remembers local shopkeepers being helpful and her mother bidding for poultry at the local markets. Mary's mother was a widow and she and Mary provided this accommodation for servicemen throughout the war. 'I entertained the air force,' said Mary, when asked what she did!

Mary met John Adams when her mother sent her to meet him from the bus that was bringing him to stay at her house. 'I was smitten when he got off the bus,' she admitted, 'but there were many other good-look-ing young blokes around.'

Sadness and loneliness
There were 7116 Australians captured by the Italians or Germans during the Second World War and by far the greatest number were captured on

Crete.[5] Crete was where the first airborne invasion took place. It happened on 20 May 1941 when Hitler's troops, even though vastly outnumbered, drove the Allied troops from the island, at enormous cost to themselves.[6]

Daisy Ward's romance with Frederick Bruton began when he was taken POW by the Germans on Crete. Daisy had a friend whose brother was captured with Frederick and she asked Daisy to write to Frederick because both his parents were no longer alive. Daisy wrote to Frederick when he was in Uflag VIIB through the Red Cross club. They wrote for eighteen months until in September 1944 Frederick was repatriated because he was very ill. Sent by ship via Sweden Frederick arrived in England weighing only seven stone (about 46 kilograms). 'I was contacted by telephone,' said Daisy, 'and we arranged to meet at the Strand Palace Hotel in London.' London was Daisy's home town. 'He came to my home in Winchmore Hill to meet my family and was asked by a small boy on the bus if he was a cowboy because he was wearing his Aussie hat. We had five days together.' But Frederick was advised not to hang around for the English winter and went home to Australia before they could marry. 'We wrote regularly and an engagement ring reached me in 1945,' Daisy said.

The Germans developed V-weapons[7] and one of these was the doodle bug. Also known as a buzz bomb, it was a self-steering aerial bomb that was powered by a pulse-jet engine. Launched by the Germans from land-based platforms in Europe the bombs would fly low over the heavily populated London suburbs. When the engine noise stopped abruptly people below knew the bomb would dive and explode. The first of these was launched on London in June 1944. Doodle bugs killed many Londoners.

For Olive Johnson, meeting her Johnny happened at a time when she was mourning the loss of her best friend who had just been killed in a doodle bug attack. Both Olive's brother and a boyfriend had also been killed. 'It seemed at the time that everyone I loved was going to die. I was a very unhappy girl,' wrote Olive.

At the local dance Olive was approached by a golden-headed airman who asked 'Will you dance with me pretty lady?' When Olive told him

Johnny Fitzgerald, 1944

he had been drinking he replied, 'I have been to a wedding, but all Aussies look and sound like this'. He made Olive laugh – and she fell in love. Johnny Fitzgerald took Olive home on the last bus, which meant he had to walk five miles back to town. When Johnny asked to see Olive again she invited him to tea: 'In those days one didn't go out with young foreigners without taking them home to meet the family.' Johnny arrived with tea, coffee, jam and chocolate and won everyone's hearts.

'We saw each other quite a lot in the next few months. I worked for the Law Courts in London and he was able to meet me quite often. We would have sandwiches on the Embankment. He loved London and England and wanted to be married there but that wasn't to be.' Olive sailed to Australia as a fiancée and she and Johnny married in Sydney.

CHAPTER 7
Getting Married

Love is the sweetest thing
What else on earth could ever bring
Such happiness to everything,
As Love's old story.

In Britain the rationing of clothing began in June 1941 a year before Australia. It was worked out on a points system and in theory allowed each person to buy one new outfit per year. So, unless there was a wedding dress hidden in a family cupboard, war brides had to make do with whatever was available.

Food rationing began in Britain in 1940, starting with butter, sugar and bacon. Meat and tea followed, then cooking fats, sweets, conserves and eggs. Official food rationing did not begin in Australia until 1943, with butter the first item, followed by meat in 1944. However, rations could be supplemented with home-grown produce, and when a wedding was about to take place it was surprising what could be found, even without resorting to the black market.

Many brides simply did not have time to plan a wedding because the decision to marry was speeded up by the knowledge that one partner, usually the man, would be either going back into combat, or returning to Australia.

This meant that a white wedding with all the trimmings including a wedding breakfast was often not possible. As rationing extended into the

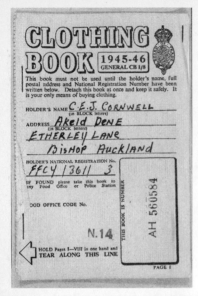

Clothing was rationed in the UK

post-war years, weddings which took place then were affected too. Under the circumstances it was an achievement to have a ceremony at all. A look at the wedding pictures shows that long white dresses were still possible for some, while others married either in uniform or a smart suit.

For those who waited until they got to Australia before they married, a traditional white wedding was more likely as rationing was lifted much sooner and was less strict.

Betty Cooper married Con Gehrig in 1941. Con was returning to Australia and Betty rushed her mother into giving her consent. In hindsight Betty regrets that she did it this way as her father was in the navy and unable to attend. 'He never forgave my mother for consenting to my marriage and depriving him of the dream of walking down the aisle with his only daughter,' wrote Betty. 'I saw him briefly at Paddington station before leaving for Liverpool – he gave us his blessing but I never saw him again.' Betty's parents separated shortly after.

Her wedding dress was 'practical pink dusky crepe' due to the shortage of clothing coupons; her reception was at home with a chocolate cake. 'Pink or white icing was banned by Mr Denman the minister,' Betty recalls. 'Goodness knows why!'

Dorothy Hunt and John Holden married in the same parish church Dorothy had been christened and confirmed in, and by the same vicar, in June 1945. The wedding dress of Nottingham lace belonged to the WAAF. It had an elastic waist so it would fit all sizes and, says Dorothy, 'the sleeves came to a point. I turned the point back which made it sit nicely'. Dorothy also borrowed a veil and bought her own headdress. When she returned the outfit to the WAAF Dorothy recalls paying five shillings to have it cleaned. 'I was the second bride to borrow it,' she said. Her bridesmaids wore pink – because they both owned pink dresses.

John left England in November and Dorothy followed on the bride ship *Stirling Castle* in June 1946.

Arvona Small and Hedley David arranged their wedding in a matter of days. They decided to get married, though Arvona admits: 'I can't remember when he actually proposed; it was definitely not a down-on-the-knees proposal.' Arvona needed her parents' permission to marry and when this was given the pair married soon after – they were both twenty-one years old. In fact, as with so many weddings during the war, it was all done with amazing speed

Dorothy in the WAAF dress

and efficiency. On 5 November 1944, Arvona who was back in camp at Fradley, received a telegram from Hedley which read:

ARRANGE LEAVE FOR AFTER DUTY ON MONDAY 6TH. TO BE MARRIED WEDNESDAY
AFTERNOON. PLEASE WIRE IMMEDIATELY IF LEAVE IS GRANTED. HAVE WIRED YOUR
MOTHER. LOVE HEDLEY.

Arvona's leave was granted and when she arrived home on that Monday night she found 'the page-boy, flower girls and bridesmaids all had their clothes, the family had been busy shopping and sewing. I borrowed a wedding gown from a friend.'

Arvona had three older brothers in a band and they arranged a wedding cake from one of the band members who was a baker. The reception was at the 'Cross Keys', a local hotel. 'It was wonderful how everything was arranged in a day, family and relations all turned up.

Arvona & Hedley David

It went so well that we missed a train to Ebbw Vale where we were going to honeymoon.' However it was to be a very short honeymoon. The next day a telegram arrived telling them that Arvona's mother had collapsed and the pair returned to the small Welsh village where her family lived. Arvona never returned to her base because during the three months she spent nursing her mother she became pregnant and she was demobbed in March 1945.

John & Mary's wedding day

John Adams arrived back at Mary Hill's house as soon as he reached England in May 1945. He had been a POW for a year and half in Stalag Luft I, close to Germany's border with Russia. He was captured by the Germans when his plane was in a collision following a bombing raid over Berlin in 1943. Mary had spent six anxious weeks wondering whether he was still alive and in the ensuing eighteen months they had written to each other. They married just three weeks after his return in a little church in West Purley. It was ten months later that Mary boarded the *Athlone Castle* to come to Australia, John having left England earlier on the troop ship *Stratheden*.

Few of the brides admit to second thoughts or even reservations about getting married. Beryl Barnes is one who does. Having farewelled her friend Trevior Boyd she was then surprised when Trevior returned:

> Instead of being demobilised on his return to Australia he was signed on to the crew of *The Shropshire* which was going to England with a complement of the three Australian services which were to take part in a victory parade through London. I received a cable which simply stated: MAKE WEDDING PREPARATIONS, WILL BE RETURNING MAY/JUNE.
>
> Why did I go along with these instructions! Maybe because there was no way for me to contact him and speak to him. Maybe because my

mother seemed to go along with the idea, so much so in fact, that she borrowed a wedding dress for me to use, and I was in a state of numb euphoria.

Then all of a sudden there was a change of heart apparently – maybe my mother began to realise the enormity of it all. Anyway, unbeknownst to me a plot was hatched with one of her sisters, one who had always been very close to me.

Beryl was invited to make up the number at a dinner dance with her aunt and uncle and a couple of their friends. There was also her aunt's brother, Ernie, who had just returned from overseas to find that the girl he hoped to marry had married someone else. 'Ernie asked me questions about myself and my oncoming marriage, and I started to own up to the fact that I was not ready to marry, and was just getting carried along with the arrangement,' admitted Beryl. 'So I decided that I would write Trevior a letter for him to receive upon his arrival in England, telling him how I felt, and that I was being rushed into something I was not sure about.'

Beryl asked her brother to deliver the letter to Trevior. Meanwhile Ernie continued to ask Beryl for a date and finally she accepted an invitation to go to a show in London. On the day of this date Beryl received a phone call from Trevior who said he had received the letter but wanted to talk to her and Beryl agreed to talk with him after she came home from her date.

'However my workmates had other ideas,' said Beryl. 'They told me that I had to cancel my date with Ernie and go home to Trevior. They said that if I did not they would not relieve me from duty.' Beryl took her workmates' threats seriously and phoned Trevior, who met her at work and took her home.

I must admit that when I saw him, my heart missed a beat, he had a lovely golden tan and he wasted no time in asking me to marry him and had an argument for any reason I gave for not agreeing.

He spent days with me, as much as my work would allow, and continued asking me to marry him. He was starting to sway me, when one day my mother received a letter from one of his aunts in Melbourne. She stressed that my mother should not allow the wedding to take place and gave several reasons for this. I cannot remember what those reasons were now, but I know it made me very angry that someone could interfere in this way, and so it made me determined to go through with it.

My mother, however, had other ideas, and for whatever reason, had decided that she would not allow a marriage to take place. As I was under legal age I had to have her written consent.

By now Beryl and Trevior were united in their determination to get married. Trevior who had been living with them, moved elsewhere and Beryl's mother continued to refuse permission. Beryl's father, who was separated from her mother, gave his permission, but this just made her mother more adamant.

Time was running out: Trevior had to return to Australia on *The Shropshire* so they made a booking at a registry office and arranged a place to stay on the night of the wedding.

'The night before, I arrived home and my mother said to me, "Give me that paper you want me to sign, and I want you to leave this house and never come back". I gave her the paper and I don't know if she realised that arrangements were made for the following day...She signed the paper and as I took it from her I knew that the price I was paying was heavy one.'

Then another obstacle arose. Trevior too was underage and needed the permission of the captain of his ship and this had not arrived.

'Action stations! We took a taxi to Australia House, told them our plight, the captain was contacted by phone and all was made possible. Another taxi back to the Registry Office – we were almost 15 minutes late – the following couple had not arrived and so they were able to marry us. All I can say about that experience was that it was dreadful, in a dreary office, and words quoted parrot fashion. We had to tip a couple of workers to sign our wedding certificate.'

Beryl was devastated also that she was not wearing gloves – or her wedding dress. She refused photographs and then they arrived late at the house they had organised to stay at.

'We arrived to see the entire family...finishing off a meal that had been prepared for us as a wedding breakfast. Mrs Drew had raided her pantry for hoarded goodies from the severe rationing at the time, there was even a sponge cake with a bride and groom on top. They had presumed we were not able to marry and were not going to waste the feast.

We had to prove to them that we were indeed married and then they left the table and we had the scraps!'

Beryl and Trevior stayed with these friends, Beryl helping her friend Eileen with the cleaning and Trevior helping Eileen's husband with the shopping – and visiting the pub each day.

Says Beryl, 'I wonder how many others have had a wedding and honeymoon such as I?'

Trevior had to leave earlier and without Beryl. After he left she phoned her mother, hoping

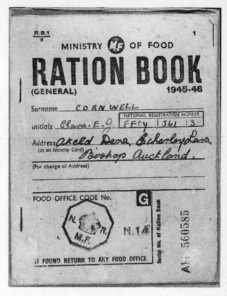

UK food ration book

for a reconciliation. When she met her mother, 'there was never any mention of my married state, the only giveaway was a wedding ring – that is, until I found that I was pregnant'. Beryl's mother was very upset and wanted her to have an abortion, but Beryl refused.

'The Australian authorities made every effort to get pregnant girls over as soon as possible so that they could be with their husbands, failing this one had to wait until the baby was three months old, so in no time I was given my ship's sailing date.'

Beryl was not the only girl whose parents objected to her marrying an Aussie. Joan Cooke found that her parents were not at all delighted at the prospect of her marriage to Russell Crane. They had never met Russell. 'Being very Victorian,' recalls Joan, 'they couldn't believe that I would want to leave my "good home" to go and live over 12 000 miles away, especially as I knew little about Australia, or Russell's family'. Joan had made up her mind. 'I didn't care or even think about the future, I just wanted to get married.' Joan had something else in common with Beryl – she was underage. Joan stood her ground and it became a matter of urgency when Russell was given his orders to sail. 'Very reluctantly my parents signed the form for a Special Licence for us to marry on 12 July 1945,' said Joan.

'Our wedding at the Central Hall Methodist Chapel was a very quiet affair. My CO and his wife came from York to support me and two or three cousins, one school friend and an aunt attended with my parents, but there was no reception. My CO had arranged for us to stay in a hotel for one night in York after the ceremony and then we went back to Russell's RAAF headquarters in Brighton.'

It wasn't just the British parents who could be disapproving. For some Australian families it was difficult to accept that their son had brought a fiancée from another country and they made their feelings known by not attending the wedding. When Ina Staryk from Canada married Leo Harper it was in Kempsey, New South Wales. They travelled to Kempsey from Sydney the day after Ina landed in Sydney on the notoriously dirty US ship the *Marine Falcon*. She was made to feel very welcome by her sister's Australian family – Ina's sister had also married an Aussie a year previously. None of Leo's family came to the wedding, though and Ina and Leo spent the week after the wedding in Kempsey.

CHAPTER 8
The Bride Ships

Wish me luck as you wave me goodbye
Cheerio! Here I go on my way
Give me a smile I can keep all the while
In my heart while I'm away.

At the close of the Second World War, Australia was still a long way away from Europe and the northern hemisphere, though not as far as at the end of the Great War, when it could take up to two months to reach Australian shores, depending on the route taken and stopovers. During the Second World War, war brides were transported to Australia during wartime, unlike the Great War when government-funded passages were not even considered, let alone organised, until after the war was over. In 1941 the Australian government gave free passage to wives, widows and children of servicemen who had married outside the country. In fact in the early part of the Second World War dependants of Australian servicemen sailed when the war was at its height even though enemy action was at its most likely and there were few ships considered suitable for families. Beryl Gehrig, who sailed in 1941, was not happy about sailing to Australia at this time: 'it was such a thoughtless and selfish thing to do – and for the powers that be – to send us off under such dangerous conditions. Just afterwards, regulations were relaxed and any personnel who were engaged or married could stay in England if they so chose to do so.' Few brides travelled to Australia while the war was in progress, probably for a number of reasons. Once Japan entered the war the Pacific Ocean was particularly unsafe; if they moved to Australia the women would have had far less chance of seeing their new husbands than if they stayed in the place where they met and married, and many of the women were themselves in the services. Later the Repatriation Department acknowledged that bringing young wives to Australia while their husbands were still serving overseas was probably not a wise move as in some cases living with their in-laws was not successful.[1] Once this war was over, there were enormous queues for passage to Australia, just as there had been in 1918 and 1919.

Betty Gehrig believes she must be one of the first war brides of the Second World War. Then Betty Cooper, in 1941 she married Con, a pilot with the Sunderland flying boats who was returning to Australia. The difficulty was to also organise a passage for Betty. By making the most of his contacts and paying the sum of £106, which was later refunded, a passage was found for Betty on the MV *Amerika*, a Swedish cargo and passenger ship taking men back to Batavia and also to the rubber plantations in New Guinea.

Betty waited in Liverpool for a week with strict instructions to tell no-one why she was there. 'We left Liverpool in the dead of night in November with another couple from the same squadron. The men travelled as civilians as we were aboard a neutral ship.'

Despite Sweden's neutrality there was the constant threat of being torpedoed or bombed and the voyage was not a pleasant one. 'It was a bad time to cross the Atlantic,' Betty recalls, 'the seas were mountainous.' She also remembers being part of a convoy and standing on the deck at night watching 'ships attacked and blazing from direct hits by U-boats – but never even considering that we could also meet the same fate'. Once the *Amerika* reached the coast of North America things quietened down and life became more enjoyable. Betty and Con relished the food, after the strict rationing in England, and sunbaking. The *Amerika* was forced to call into the Panama Canal for some repairs – it was around the time that the Japanese were attacking the Americans at Pearl Harbor in Hawaii. The *Amerika* still had to cross the Pacific, and Hawaii was to be the next port of call. American troops boarded the ship for its passage through the canal but the ship broke down again and an enforced week in Curaçao followed. Betty, Con and their fellow travellers enjoyed a week of dancing and being entertained by the army unit that was stationed there.

When the *Amerika* eventually set sail it travelled south to avoid Japanese submarines and arrived in Melbourne three weeks later without sighting land again.

While Betty was amongst the first war brides to arrive in Australia, Sheila Howes, was among the last. Sheila met her husband Vic Henderson at the end of the war. Vic was with the RAAF and was waiting to return to Australia, Sheila, a dental nurse in the WAAF, was on embarkation leave before going to Blankenberg, Belgium with the Air Force of Occupation. Sheila and Vic kept in touch for almost six years and in 1951 Sheila sailed for Australia on the SS *New Australia* as a fiancée: 'It was, I believe, the last free passage ship to Australia for ex-service personnel', says Sheila.

With the exception of special cases (such as POWs), Australian servicemen and women were demobilised after the Second World War using the same priority system that General Monash had employed after the Great War. Length of service, age at enlistment, and family responsibilities are the main criteria, and 'the higher the score, the earlier the release,' states the Demobilisation of the Australian Defence Forces Act of 1945. Transport availability was an important consideration.

As in the Great War, passenger liners had been requisitioned for military service with larger vessels being used as troop transports and hospital ships. Once again this was their premier role which meant that families and fiancées had to wait their turn – indeed, families and fiancées are not even mentioned in the Demobilisation Act.

Flying to Australia was so unusual that when two brides did take to the air it was reported in the newspaper. BRIDES FLEW FROM UK IN LESS THAN THREE DAYS, said the headline in the *Sydney Morning Herald* on 12 July 1946.

Two English brides who arrived at Mascot yesterday made the fastest trip of any bride to come to Australia. They travelled from England in a new Qantas Lancastrian on its delivery trip. The two brides, Mrs Betty Locke and Mrs Patricia Mullins, met their husbands, Squadron Leader Harry

Locke, D.S.O., D.F.C. and Bar, and Flight Lieutenant Reg Mullins, D.F.C. and Bar, while they were stationed in England with the RAAF. Squadron Leader Locke and Flight Lieutenant Mullins joined Qantas as pilots while they were in England and became engaged before they returned to Australia in February 1945. Qantas gave both men leave in April this year and they flew to England to marry their fiancées.

But for most, the process of getting wives and fiancées to Australia did not proceed quickly enough. Throughout the first six months of 1946 there were daily newspaper reports about the delays, with the Australian Leader of the Opposition, Robert Menzies, claiming it was a political ploy on the part of Prime Minister Chifley's government.

In February it was reported that many English wives were in 'desperate straits':

> In Australia a man earning £5 or £6 a week can support a wife in reasonable fashion, but with the actual buying power of the Australian pound at about 5/- [shillings] he cannot afford to send his English wife a living allowance as well as maintaining a separate home for himself.
>
> Many wives of demobilised men have young children or are unable to work. Some have been waiting more than six months for transport. Their situation is becoming desperate.'[2]

'Delay in arranging transport for wives and children of Australian servicemen from England to their new homes in Australia was entirely due to the failure of the Commonwealth Government's efforts to persuade the British Government to provide the necessary shipping,' Arthur Calwell, the Australian Minister for Migration, is reported as telling a group of servicemen's wives in England. Calwell told the group that the Australian government was doing all it could to obtain shipping particularly the *Queen Mary*, *Queen Elizabeth* and other big liners.[3]

The *Queen Mary* spent the early part of the war sheltering in New York harbour where she had been painted grey, which together with her incredible speed, was to later enable her to avoid Nazi U-boats. In early March 1940 she slipped out of New York harbour and headed for Sydney, Australia, where she was stripped of her luxurious fittings and converted into a troopship capable of transporting 5000 troops.[4] Together with the

Aquitania, *Mauretania*, *Empress of Japan*, *Empress of Canada* and *Empress of Britain*, the *Queen Mary* sailed for Britain as part of an Australian troop convoy on 4 May 1940. The liner spent the next year transporting troops, returning to Sydney at the end of 1941, making it her home port. So it is understandable that when it was time for Australian troops to return home, bringing wives, families and fiancées, it was hoped the *Queen Mary* would be made available. However, after the attack at Pearl Harbor the *Queen* had been turned over to American military commanders based in Sydney. When the war ended she was busy ferrying Australian war brides and children of American and Canadian soldiers across the Atlantic. In all she carried 22 000 women and children in thirteen trips.[5]

In March 1946 an order of priority was announced for wives and fiancées: 'first, expectant mothers; second, strong compassionate cases; and third, cases of long separation from the husband, but nothing happened.'[6] The women waiting for passage to Australia formed groups to march and protest about the delays. Meanwhile their husbands in Australia also campaigned. In Brighton, England in April 1946 members of the Kangaroo Club, a group of women waiting to embark, were told they would have no hope of leaving before June. The leader, Mrs Barbara Jungwirth, called on the women to volunteer for a protest march in London from Australia House to the home of the Australian Resident Minister, J.A. Beasley, in Kensington.[7] A few days later Mrs J. Maloney is reported as saying that 'she was going to the airport with a banner to meet Mr Chifley' on 19 April. At least thirty brides had volunteered to picket Australia House every day. It was decided that pickets should buttonhole all prominent persons whenever they entered or left. They would walk round and round Australia House to keep passing the migration inquiry branch.'[8] And also possibly to help pass the long waiting time. It would not have helped the husbands and fiancés waiting at home to see headlines such as LUXURY SHIP FOR CANADIAN BRIDES. With the exception of the wealthy few who paid their own way, the brides had to take what shipping there was. However this particular group of Canadian wives and children were fortunate enough to travel on the *Letitia*, which in wartime was a luxurious hospital ship. Said *The Argus*: 'The Exchange Telegraph describes *Letitia* as the best equipped bride ship yet to leave England. Four doctors and thirteen nurses have been retained from the hospital staff to attend the passengers.'[9]

Boarding the Indefatigable

When the women were finally allocated a ship it could be anything from a converted troopship to an aircraft carrier. In April 1946 the aircraft carrier *Indefatigable* carried many brides and a few children to Australia. When they have been at sea for four days Brenda Smith writes in her diary: 'Several garments hanging on a line including nappies. I wonder what the Navy thinks. We have only two babies on board, because of the Flight Deck – no children.' Brenda had married Stewart Smith, a navigator in the RAAF, in 1945. As an aircraft carrier first and a bride ship second naval traditions were observed throughout the journey. Brenda remembers loudspeakers which issued instructions throughout the day and how the men lined up on the decks as the ship entered and left a port.

Leaving

Leaving home, family and friends and not knowing if you will ever return is an enormously traumatic experience. And the trauma of parting was often worsened by the privations of the journey itself.

The first entry in Brenda Smith's diary describes how she arrived in London and found she was to spend the night in an air-raid shelter sleeping in bunks – not in a hostel as she had expected.

Next day she was to write: 'A dreadful night, an awful breakfast, then onto the buses.' These took the women to Waterloo for a day spent finding the *Indefatigable*, getting on board and orientating themselves.

For Estelle Bridgford, whose daughter Vivienne had been born in April 1945, the departure was emotionally fraught. Her husband Keith left England in September of that year to return to Australia because his father was dying. Estelle was given four days notice that she would be leaving on the RMS *Rangitata*. While she was rushing about organising baby food and clothes her mother was ill in hospital and her father was devastated at the departure of his daughter and his only grandchild. 'I never saw Dad again,' said Estelle. 'He died two years later.'

For Beryl Boyd, whose marriage and honeymoon had been such a disaster and who had gone through a painful reconciliation with her mother (who was opposed to the marriage), leaving was very painful. When she boarded the *Asturias*, she noticed many girls in tears, 'but I was determined not to break down myself and I managed that until I had my back to my mother, sister and aunt, and was walking up the gangplank. I went to the upper deck to wave my goodbye so that they could not see that I was in tears.'

Olive Johnson boarded the *Strathmore* along with other fiancées in September 1946. Many of them were young women who had never before left home. Feelings of loneliness and fear of the unknown were common. 'I was very lonely,' admits Olive. 'If it hadn't been for the girls in my cabin I really do not know what I would have done. I think they were all feeling very much like me. We were after all going thousands of miles away to a strange country. None of us knew what was waiting for us at the end of the journey.' Olive remembers the *Strathmore* passing a troopship in the Suez Canal. 'As we passed the soldiers

Olive Johnson

flicked their cigarettes in the air, all at the same time, and shouted, 'You are going the wrong way!' It was night-time and very dark. I prayed that they were wrong,' admits Olive, whose happy marriage to Johnny Fitzgerald was to last forty-eight years.

Betty Cornwell found she was to share her cabin with eleven other wives and a baby. She writes in her diary that her cabin on the *Orbita* was 'nicely fitted out with six wardrobes, dressing table, table, eight chairs,

Elizabeth Cornwell

two armchairs, green cushions and carpet, also gay curtains over a make-believe window, as we had no port-holes on "E" deck which is below the sea.'

However by the time the *Orbita* reached Australia descriptions of the conditions aboard were far from glowing.

Like Brenda Smith, Hilary Bradley set off as a fiancée on the aircraft carrier HMS *Indefatigable* in April 1946. She was to marry Flight Officer Earle Butterfield in June. When she received a letter telling her of her transport she admits she was not overly pleased, but she says, 'It turned out to be a wonderful cruise. I occupied a Fleet Air Arm Officers' cabin right above the poop deck with another bride.'

Brenda Smith writes in her diary of some of the other facilities on board the *Indefatigable*:

When we had been on the ship for a few days extra ablution [facilities] were made for us. We had an extra bathroom made available in the ships quarters. A sentry was placed at the entrance, as they were at the entrance of our quarters at all times. The Captain wanted no "hanky panky" on his ship! We also had some funny toilets, in one of the gun turrets (guns taken out). You had to be careful not to be in there when the ablutions detail arrived – they called out "any ladies in there?" The toilets were only Elsans [portable chemical toilets] and had to be emptied daily.

The *Stirling Castle* was the ship Pat Warne found herself travelling to Australia on after her last-minute decision to join the fiancée's program. 'Also on board was the first English cricket team to travel to Australia after the war. I found that I was on the top deck and in one of the best suites, with two others of course. The ship was still pretty basic, but on the first evening going in to dinner I noticed a small piece of white bread on my plate. I nearly burst into tears. Our bread had become dark brown

The Stirling Castle *carried brides – and the English Cricket Team!*

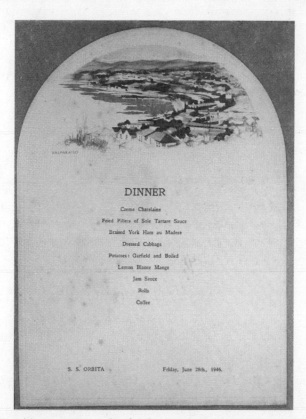

For many women, the food served on board was a treat

Please read carefully

EMBARKATION INSTRUCTIONS FOR PASSENGERS

H.M.T. " ORBITA "

1. The following embarkation instructions are for the help and guidance of passengers.

Particulars as to the date of embarkation and time of the Special Train will be sent as soon as they are known. It is expected that the steamer will embark her passengers at Liverpool about the 20th of June, 1946.

2. It is regretted that under existing conditions, relatives and friends cannot be given access to the berth from which the ship sails, nor can they be allowed on board the ship.

3. **BAGGAGE.** Passengers **must** take their baggage with them when they embark, and are reminded that every package is liable to examination by H.M. Customs. They, therefore, should have their keys available. If passengers are in any doubt as to whether there are articles in their baggage the export of which would be contrary to Board of Trade regulations, they are recommended to enquire from the Board of Trade at Stafford House, King William Street, London, E.C.4.

H.M. Government's Regulations governing the quantity of baggage allowed to each passenger are :—

(a) Each adult if unaccompanied by husband or wife   4 cwt.
(b) Married couple (3 cwt. each)   6 cwt.
(c) Each child of over three years of age and under twelve years   2 cwt.
(d) One child of twelve years of age and over, paying full fare   4 cwt.
(e) Two children of twelve years of age and over, paying full fare (3 cwt. each)   6 cwt.
(f) No allowance for children under three years of age.

Rules about what could and could not be taken on board

and not nice, I had completely forgotten that bread could be white and taste good.' For Pat the voyage was 'boring' – apart from the time a child 'tried to set fire to the ship'. There was also a measles epidemic.

Travelling with a baby

The facilities on board the bride ships were crowded and basic. Estelle Bridgford was assigned a two-berth cabin with five other war brides.[11] 'My baby had a hammock attached to my bunk. The facilities for washing bottles and nappies were practically non existent and the cramped conditions of the cabin unbearable. Fortunately my baby was a model child, however she did come out in a dreadful heat rash as we sailed through the tropics.' Estelle decided she had to escape particularly when it was hot. 'I was granted permission to take Vivienne up on deck at night where it was cooler – but there were conditions. I couldn't go on

Embarkation instructions

Pasted into Betty Cornwell's scrapbook are the 'Embarkation Instructions for Passengers'. She sailed on the *Orbita*.

The authorities are not making any promises. 'It is expected that the steamer will embark her passengers at Liverpool about the 20th of June, 1946' it announces. Porters and baggage handling were not available and passengers are instructed that they '**must** take their baggage with them when they embark.' The weight was also restricted. Single women were allowed 'four cwt' [hundredweight]. Married couples were allowed three cwt each and each child over three years of age and under twelve was allowed two cwt – children under three years of age had no baggage allowance. This would have meant that wives with babies would have had to include nappies and other baby needs in their own meagre allowance.

Bicycles, 'strongly crated or cased' could be taken for an additional charge of 67/6 [67 shillings and 6 pence].

Passengers were required to produce their 'Travel Permit Cards or passports, Identity Cards and Food Ration Books'.

There were also tight restrictions on how much money the women could take with them. '£1 or 10s notes, or Foreign Currency up to a total value of £15'.[10] Jewellery was a prohibited export: 'Passengers are reminded of the Board of Trade Order prohibiting the export without licence of jewellery, postage stamps and other valuable articles.'

deck until 12 a.m. and had to leave the deck by 5 a.m.' Estelle believes this was because the captain did not want any trouble with the New Zealand servicemen on board. 'I was exhausted because of lack of sleep – deck chairs are not made to sleep in'. Help was at hand. 'One day a very nice Sergeant pilot, seeing me so distressed, offered to look after Vivienne while I had a sleep in my cabin. His name was Rangi and he was a godsend! He played with Viv and nursed her and fed her cool drinks, even changed her nappy. He had two small children of his own. He probably never knew how grateful I was.'

Children on board the Athlone Castle

Estelle was not the only mother travelling on the RMS *Rangitata*. The press christened it 'the Stork Ship' because there were seventy-six children on board.

Arvona David and her nine-month-old daughter Noeleen sailed on the *Largs Bay* from Tilbury in August 1946. Noeleen also slept in a hammock which hung on the side of Arvona's bunk in a six-berth cabin.

As well as those with their babies many of the women were pregnant. One story has it that on one trip the *Dominion Monarch* carried many women who were six months pregnant when they embarked. Says bride Phyllis Webster, 'The rule was that if you were that far gone you couldn't travel till three months after the birth so they all declared they were only four months. As they were all embarking the ship's doctor was heard to say "Bloody hell, if I'd known this was what it was going to be like I'd never have signed on!"'

Sea sickness

After the Great War the voyage out was hazardous for many. Medical science had not learnt how to cope with many of the childhood illnesses and the severe living conditions of Europe meant that many of the passengers were not in good health, so there were deaths and illness as well as sea sickness.

Twenty-five years later medical science was more advanced and, though once again many of the passengers were undernourished, there were better facilities for caring for those who became ill on the voyage. Nonetheless sea sickness was a problem which still had to be dealt with.

Audrey Neely followed her father's advice. 'I was terrified of getting seasick,' recalls Audrey, who had travelled a good deal between Dover and Calais and was familiar with how awful it could be. 'My father suggested if I was feeling unwell to have a brandy, lime and soda, but only the one. He also told me not to eat chocolate and food my stomach was not accustomed to.' Audrey believes this is what saved her as during the rough crossing of the Bay of Biscay she was the only female at the breakfast sitting.

A washbasin marked 'For sickness and no other purpose' was one of the first things Brenda Smith found on her second day at sea. Despite her queasiness she staggered up to breakfast and proudly writes that she was never to feel seasick again though many of her fellow travellers were sick.

Lifelong friendships were made, such as Enid Dover's (back, second left) with Joyce Berrill (bottom right) on the SS Atlantis

The heat was another problem for folk who had only ever lived in Europe and not encountered the sweltering temperatures of the tropics and the equator. On a navy ship that was not built for comfort the heat was unbearable for many of the female passengers. Brenda notes that on a day in May the temperature in the mess deck, which was situated just under the iron flight deck, was 110 degrees Fahrenheit, and that the heat made her feel ill.

On Thursday 4 July 1946, Betty Cornwell writes in her diary:

'Hotter than yesterday. Six men fainted in the engine room. We change our clothes three times a day, the sea is perfectly calm, women faint all over the place. We hardly know where to put ourselves. Slept on deck again.' And the next day: 'Heat dreadful, the temperature of the sea is 110 deg. And the engine-room got to 145 deg. Imagine men working in such heat.' On the Friday she wrote, 'Thank goodness we are at the end of the Red Sea.'

The overwhelming heat was followed by a storm the next day: 'Everyone seasick, sheer will power kept me OK. I just dashed down to eat which was an awful effort, and had a bigger dash back on deck where I just lived. The waves came right over forward and down the main deck, Marjorie and I got wet sleeping out so we changed our sleeping quarters to one of the lifeboats.'

The American ships

The ships which carried brides from the United States and Canada to Australia were also troopships and many were no more equipped to carry women and children than the boats coming from England.

In September 1945, with war barely ended the arrival of an aircraft carrier into Sydney Harbour with Canadian and American brides aboard was enough for a full page story in the *Australian Women's Weekly*. BRIDES AND BABIES ARRIVE IN AIRCRAFT-CARRIER is the headline to a story written by Betty Nesbit.

Ms Nesbit describes the women's trip as 'de-luxe' – 'thanks to the co-operative efforts of the Royal Navy, The Australian Legation in Washington and the Repatriation Department in Australia'. The attitudes of the day are very clearly expressed in the language in this article written for women readers. The women are described as 'girls', and as 'charming' and 'pretty', the sailors as 'brawny'; the fashion of the day and the incongruity of women on an aircraft carrier is made much of: 'As the carrier came up to its buoy in midstream observant ferry passengers might have seen a dozen or so pretty girls standing on the bow of the flight deck, silhouetted against the planes, the skirts of their frocks blowing in the breeze.'[12]

These were certainly not the first brides to arrive in Australia from the Americas, nor would they be the last. And if the brides on this ship travelled 'de-luxe' style, then others were not so lucky.

Ina Staryk left Canada well prepared for her life in Australia:

My parents were sad to see me go but knew they could not stop me – I had turned twenty-one and knew what I wanted. They were happy that I would be near my sister [who had also married an Aussie and left a year earlier]. My friends thought all this very exciting but a few of them had met boys from distant places and were getting married too so I guess it was a very romantic and exciting time for us all.

The Australian embassy in Ottawa advised me of the procedures I had to go through and also to be ready at short notice to sail on whatever was available. They also sent a list of things that were in short supply and what we were allowed to take. I packed a large cabin trunk with towels, sheets and dress materials as I did like to sew. I also took a good stock of nylons – oh yes, and my wedding gown and veil.

I was sent rail tickets with sleeping berth also meal tickets for the four day trip to San Francisco. The train picked up the girls across Canada as we travelled along and we all stayed in the same carriage. There was a man from the Veterans Affairs who was in charge until we boarded the ship.

We sailed from San Francisco via Honolulu, Samoa and Auckland to Sydney – a long trip about 22–23 days, especially the way things were. The ship carried US troops to the war zones and was still in the same dirty condition, very sparse in its fittings and bad food.

Notorious ships

This particular ship, the *Marine Falcon*, made headlines and the lead story on the front page of *The Sun* of 23 August 1946 announces:

Crammed with 550 angry passengers and with a large calico sign draped over the side, SS FLOATING FLOPHOUSE, the US Army transport *Marine*

The Marine Falcon *makes the front page of Sydney's* Sun

Falcon arrived in Sydney from USA today after what passengers described as a nightmare voyage.

Passengers complained that they were herded into dormitories, sometimes in filthy conditions, that a large section of the crew behaved badly, that medical attention was poor.

They claimed that girl passengers were accosted by white and negro members of the crew, and that the only real attempt to clean up the vessel was made as it neared Sydney.

Another newspaper story includes a photo of an Australian behind bars. It does not explain why, but it does say that 'his brother, who was being deported with him, hanged himself in the brig while the ship was at Auckland.'[13]

Ina's photo featured in most of the newspaper reports because she could not get treatment for a foot infection. 'I could not get medical attention for five days,' she is quoted as saying. 'Unable to leave my bunk because of the pain, I cried in my cabin for two days. I had to crawl on my hands and knees to the lavatory and washrooms. A passenger heard my cries on the second day and sent five times for a doctor but no doctor was on duty.'[14]

She said, 'When the boat finally got to Sydney and I was carried off and interviewed by the various officials I was surprised to see Leo coming towards me with a big grin. He had been notified of the problem and was allowed to come into the area where I had been taken. Needless to say it was a wonderful moment.'

And the *Orbita* too was criticised in the press for poor conditions. 'Some of the brides were packed 30 to a cabin with no shelves or drawers provided for their clothes,' writes the reporter in Melbourne's *The Argus* in July 1946. One bride told how there were only four wash basins, one of which did not work, and that when they reached the Red Sea 'conditions were intolerable'.[15]

The *Marine Falcon* was not the only ship carrying brides to offer less than luxury accommodation. A number of ships were described as providing really unpleasant conditions for their passengers. The *Dominion Monarch* on a trip from the UK was also criticised for providing 'appalling' conditions. The Minister for Repatriation, Mr Frost, received a telegram from an irate father, Squadron Leader Doudy, who demanded 'the removal of any menace' to the health of his seven-month-old daughter who was on board with his wife.[16]

Ina, carried off the Marine Falcon

The most unruly bride ship ever to sail

By the time the *Orbita* reached Sydney more trouble had broken out. Although neither the crew nor passengers are implicated in the report of a fire deliberately lit under a pile of chairs, tables and newspapers, this report makes much of the dissatisfaction among passengers and crew. 'The fire,' reports the newspaper, 'occurred before dawn yesterday, as the liner was steaming up the coast from Melbourne... The fire was put out with buckets of water before much damage was done'. The passengers blamed the crew: 'Passengers declared that the stewards' service was dreadful and the ship filthy', and the crew blamed the passengers: 'The majority of the passengers have been quite happy. One or two always have a grouch.' Perhaps it was more that the behaviour of some of the passengers did not meet with the approval of others: 'Some passengers alleged that a small minority of wives fraternised with the crew, and that beds on deck were not entirely due to tropical conditions.'

'The difficulty was keeping the passengers from the crew not the crew from the passengers,' said the captain in an interview.[17]

When the *Rangitata* docked in Melbourne on August 4 1946, brides were reported as complaining of 'insufficient medical attention, rudeness from the ship's staff and lack of organisation on board'.

Flight Lieutenant Stanley Taylor who was travelling with his wife, Margery, had something to tell of activities on board as well as bad conditions:

Conditions on board were worse than those on a troopship. In the tropics the men slept on deck, but could not get any sleep because of the brides flirting with the ship's stewards and the crew of a merchant ship who were travelling in *Rangitata*. There seemed to be no discipline among the stewards at all.

Some of the brides took exception to another's bride's conduct with a steward that one night they sent a message to the stewards' quarters which the bride was visiting and said she was wanted on deck. When she came on deck they jumped on her and gave her a good thrashing.

My wife was ill for 14 days and the only time a stewardess came to see her was on the last day, when one came for a tip.

One girl (an Irish nurse, travelling to England, but not as a bride) died on the ship, and a man who jumped overboard at Port Said is still there. A baby was taken to Tilbury Hospital seriously ill as soon as the vessel arrived in England.[18]

John & Evelyn Muirhead

Evelyn and John Muirhead left San Francisco on the *Matsonia* in October 1945 headed for Brisbane. 'It was still a troopship, John was in one end of the ship on E deck and I at the other end on C deck. We were in cabins of six to eight bunks.' On board the *Matsonia* there were also Dutch repatriates, nuns going to Indonesia and 'about 200 rejected Australian fiancées' of American GIs. The rest of the passengers had little time for these girls, according to Evelyn. The general feeling among the other passengers was that they were 'mostly tarts who just thought they would get a free trip to America'. Though there could have been a few innocent girls who found they had made a mistake, 'they made life miserable for the nuns on board and the rest of us', said Evelyn.

Evelyn has strong memories of the only port of call, Pago Pago in Samoa, and of her first sighting of Australia in October 1945: 'The purple flowers of the jacaranda and the red of the poinciana trees. It was a sight I will never forget,' she says.

Sight-seeing

For many of the women it was the first time they had left the shores of their home country. For others who had served overseas it was not such a new experience.

Brides collect mail on SS Atlantis

Comparisons with home are natural and the abundance of food in some of the ports they visited was overwhelming for some after the strict rationing they were used to.

Beryl Boyd was astounded by the amount of fruit available when they docked at Las Palmas in the Canary Islands. She also remembers being 'amazed at what some of the Air Force boys wanted more than anything else, a BIG steak and salad, and I was even more amazed to see them eating it all on the same plate – hot and cold together!'

Colombo as it appears in a brochure belonging to Betty Cornwell

It was also the first time many of them had come in contact with other nationalities. Beryl Boyd's memory of the South African wives of Australian servicemen is the way they dealt with their laundry. 'Many of them were in a panic trying to wash some of their husband's clothes. These girls had not done any domestic work before as they had all had servants. Many an article of clothing was thrown overboard because it was in the too hard basket.'

Betty Cornwell writes in her diary of the visit of the *Orbita* to Port Said on 1 July 1946 (Note: the use of the term 'wogs' for people of North Africa and the Middle East was common at this time – it now has numerous connotations, not all derogatory.):

'Port Said seemed quite modern, "Johnny Walker" whisky sign made it look like home...Saw my first Arab on his camel trotting along these banks...We had taken aboard some "wogs" with four of their small craft to tie us to the banks while other ships passed along the other way... Half way down the canal we came to the "Bitter Lakes!" it was really beautiful to watch the sun go down.' Betty also writes in her diary that day how she haggled for a bag with one of the locals and is clearly proud that she succeeded in getting what she thought was a fair price. Betty's daughter still has the bag which is in almost pristine condition.

The SS *Orbita* stopped in Colombo a few days later and shore leave was granted. Betty writes of her excitement at being rowed a mile and a half across the harbour from their ship to shore by 'a couple of blacks'; of exchanging money and buying cheap shoes, fruit and tea; of meeting up with a couple of RAF boys who took Betty and her friends on a sightseeing trip and who 'piled our arms full of oranges, pineapples and coconuts', and of rowing back to the boat. 'Many of the girls got drunk and the sights coming back to the ship were disgusting'.

For Hilary Bradley it was ' a wonderful cruise'. 'We had a short sojourn in Aden where we were chased by natives. Fortunately we were rescued by Air Force personnel who were returning on the same ship. At our next port of call, Colombo, we had an excellent meal at the Galle Luce Hotel, had a paddle in the ocean and visited Mt Lavinia.'

Betty Smith also enjoyed hotel life in Colombo when she stayed at the Grand Oriental Hotel with an aunt and uncle who lived in the city. 'Fans in all the rooms,' she writes after the heat of the cabin on the aircraft carrier *Indefatigable*. 'Aunt took me shopping with Andrew her head boy coming with her to carry the parcels.'

Her other impressions of Colombo were of 'rows and rows of native shops and streams of people. Women in coloured saris and the Eurasian girls in modern dress. There were even double decker buses. All the houses and streets were drab and dirty, but the beautiful trees made up for it, with the vivid red of the flowers.'

Happy reunions?

Having second thoughts about the husband or fiancée they had last seen in uniform and at home – and in many cases barely knew – must have been common. Beryl Boyd admits to her misgivings when the *Asturias* docked in Melbourne. 'Many people were on the dock and many of the passengers were lined up against the railings looking for a familiar face. I spied Trevior, but I did not let him see me. Suddenly I was afraid about what was ahead for me. I don't know what I thought I could do at that late stage, but I was reluctant to leave the ship.' Her friend Pam advised her to think of Trevior who was anxiously awaiting her arrival, and she nervously let herself be seen.

And after a long time apart there was the odd case of mistaken identity. A husband who had not seen his English bride for twenty months 'waved frantically to the wrong girl for twenty minutes as HMS *Indefatigable* drew alongside no. 3 Woolloomooloo Wharf this morning with 110 British wives of Australian servicemen on board,' reports the Melbourne newspaper *The Argus*.

'A shout of recognition from another girl farther along the flight deck, which was lined with excited brides, soon corrected this mistake.' Did she realise? The report does not tell us any more![19]

Sheila Thomson was playing cards with her best friend Jose Foster when the *Stirling Castle* docked in Melbourne in June 1946. Told that they had to wait for customs to do the paperwork before they docked, they were filling in time. Then says Sheila, 'Suddenly I looked up and saw Johnnie's face looking through the window. I let out a loud shriek, knocked over my chair and flew to the door – everyone thought I'd gone mad! We met at the doorway in a gigantic hug and I didn't know whether to laugh or cry.' Johnnie had managed to have himself smuggled aboard by a friend in customs and had shinnied up a rope in the dark!

Olive Johnson vividly remembers her arrival in Fremantle in October of 1946 on board the *Strathmore* with other fiancées – and how suddenly their handsome lovers were not as they remembered them.

> One has to remember that the boys they were engaged to were all in uni-
> form away from home; handsome and young and as far as we can
> remember, always laughing, no real responsibilities. There all of a sudden
> we had young men in striped de-mob suits, not fitting too well. Half of
> them had no work to come home to, they were so very young when they
> were sent away.
>
> One of our cabin friends was leaving the ship in Fremantle. She was
> confronted with a pinstripe de-mob not-fitting-too-well suit. She also
> learnt that he was living in a bedsitter, his
> landlady had kindly made room for her
> in the lodging house until she got mar-
> ried and then she would move in with
> him. She was crying and said she would
> not get off the ship. Finally after a lot of
> coaxing she did go with him and the next
> day she seemed to have come to terms
> with it all.

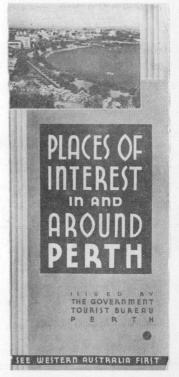

Arriving in Australia and setting foot on Australian soil was made more difficult when the welcome was not happy. Apart from relatives, or soon-to-be relatives, who did not feel welcoming to the Aussie boys' brides, the local girls were sometimes not pleased to see the newcomers either. Having comforted their cabin mate and encouraged her to go with her fiancé, Olive and her friends set off to explore Fremantle. 'The first

Most brides saw Perth first

Olive & Johnny kiss for the Sun

Australian girls we met were waiting on the dockside,' she recalled. 'As we walked by them they shouted "Go back, you pommy cows". I think that the bottom fell out of my world with those words: I was horrified.' A decision to go to the movies did not fare any better. 'We were all sitting down ready to enjoy the movie when we were told to leave. None of us knew why until we were told that one was not allowed to smoke in the cinema. By the time we got back to the ship we were all ready to go home.'

By the time the *Strathmore* reached Sydney Olive was feeling very nervous, though the arrival of two Australian women in their cabin in Melbourne had cheered the group considerably. 'We were all peeping out of the portholes trying to see if we could see a face in the crowd that we knew. I could not see him anywhere. I did not want to leave my friends and go out into a world that I was not sure of, people I had never met, people that might not like me. I was just twenty years old. When finally I was walking down the gangplank my legs had turned to jelly, I was shaking all over. Then I saw my golden headed boy, complete with pinstripe suit and an enormous bunch of flowers.

'He was smiling and so very shy. A photographer from the *Sun* newspaper came over and said "Go on then, kiss her". He gave me a little peck on the cheek. So the photographer said "Not like that! Kiss her properly". So he did and the photo appeared in the newspaper the next day.'

But Olive's adventure was not over. She had yet to meet Johnny's family.

CHAPTER 9
Arriving in Australia in the 1940s

Que sera sera
Whatever will be, will be
The future's not ours to see
Que sera sera

The docking of the ship was the end of the voyage and it was also the beginning of a new life for the war brides of the 1940s. For the brides from Britain, Canada and the United States there were similarities with home, but for brides from other countries these were few. Canadian and American brides found Australia behind the times in many ways. The climate was different for nearly all the brides, and the seasons were topsy-turvy.

Many had come from places devastated by war and from a danger-ous life where each moment was a bonus. Though Australia had been threatened and Darwin had been bombed, there was none of the devas-tation of the cities of Britain and Europe.

Like the Great War, this war had also influenced the production and export of food. Enemy action once affected the import of food to Britain, and Australia, in order to keep its pledge to send food to Britain, also had to impose rationing. However, in comparison food in Australia was still abundant.

Many Europeans arrived in Australia as immigrants as well as war brides but it would take almost a decade before food and cooking styles would begin to influence the foods most people ate. In the meantime brides from Europe and the Middle East missed many favourite foods.

The aftermath of the Second World War brought prosperity – not depression, as followed the previous war. Industry began to expand and more people were wealthy. The arrival of immigrants from Britain and Europe increased the general prosperity.

Meeting and greeting

Many women were met when they arrived, but others needed overnight accommodation after they had disembarked and before they could set off on overland journey. Organisations such as the Red Cross came to the rescue, often arranging overnight billets in private homes. The voluntary aides (VAs) of the Red Cross were given the task of helping the new immigrants to settle in.

In NSW the Red Cross established a Reception Canteen and Rest Unit at Pyrmont Wharf at the request of the American Red Cross. Initially to help the thousands of Australian women who were married or engaged to American servicemen and on their way to America, it was also a place to welcome women coming into Australia. It was run by the VAs on a roster system and divided into areas including reception, a nursery, and a place for vaccinations (or inoculations as they were commonly known at the time).[1]

Voluntary Aids to the rescue!

Perhaps one of the most hectic days for the VAs involved with war brides was on 24 October 1946 when VAs met the *Strathmore* which came from England and had fiancées and wives of Australian servicemen on board. The ship arrived at 7.15 a.m., and the passengers were fed and assisted in the normal way. Simultaneously, however, the *Monterey* was embarking for America with Australian brides and babies. To cap it off, there was, once again, a wharf labourers' strike, so the VAs on duty ended up doing much more than usual, providing city tours and lunches for the delayed passengers.[2]

The Victoria League for Commonwealth Friendship was founded initially in England at the beginning of the century with the aims of providing hospitality for migrants, refugees and visitors. It was established in Tasmania in 1903 and in NSW in 1917. The work of the Victoria League has not made much of a mark on Australian history written thus far and there is very little published information about it. Anecdotal evidence has it that members of the Victoria League also welcomed the brides on the ships arriving after the First World War.

As well as the Red Cross, women's organisations such as the YWCA provided rooms for the women who were waiting to leave the country, and others, such as the Victoria League, also made arrangements to welcome newcomers.

The war brides were mostly full of praise for the work these volunteers did to ensure they had food and accommodation before they continued on the long journey to their husbands and fiancées. The *Argus* reported: "'I cannot praise Red Cross enough," Miss Cornfield, a Canadian fiancée, said on arriving in Sydney in February 1946. "All the way from Vancouver

AWM 080985

Wives and children of Australian servicemen disembarking from HMT
Euripides

to San Francisco and on to Sydney they did everything possible to make the journey a comfortable and happy one for us all.'"[3]

Some wives had very high expectations. A group of women bound for New Zealand voiced the disappointment they, and the women who disembarked in Melbourne, felt when there wasn't 'a band and some bunting on the pier' to welcome the *Athlone Castle* brides into port. 'After the welcome given to Australian [servicemen and women] in Britain they had expected that their wives would receive a similar welcome in Australia', five women told the press. They went on to voice disappointment with the Red Cross, expecting them to:

> . . . have boarded the ship with fruit and similar comforts for the women and children. The arrangements were so faulty that wives whose husbands could not meet the ship had to remain on board.
>
> Newly arrived brides should be given every possible consideration, for they had to adjust themselves to a new environment. Australian customs often irritated a girl freshly arrived from England because she did not understand them. In England, for instance, women could go into public bars and take their places with men. Here they were herded into parlours.

'Much disappointment was undoubtedly caused by Australian soldiers in England over-advertising Australia,' the report concludes. How much of this report is actually what the women said and how much the reporter's interpretation is open to speculation, but such a news item would not have done the public perception of the brides much good.[4]

The SS *Orbita,* whose trip to Australia in mid-1946 has been varyingly described by brides and the press as 'intolerable', 'filthy' and 'the most unruly bride-ship ever to sail' was welcomed in Sydney by the Red Cross. In her history of the VADs, Melanie Oppenheimer includes an account of the trip nineteen Scottish, four babies, one child and two husbands from this ship had to make from Sydney to Brisbane one winter's night:

> It had not been possible to reserve accommodation as a group, so seating was scattered throughout the train. After the train left Central at 7.40 p.m., thirty-six blankets, pillows and hot water bottles were distributed.

Wives and children often had to continue their travels by train

The babies' bottles were filled and supper, consisting of tea, biscuits and sandwiches, was served. It was a far from simple operation, and owing to the length of the swaying train, took three hours...and involved stepping over sleeping bodies and avoiding suitcases while balancing tea pots and bottles of milk. Brides were visited again at 1.30 a.m. and 4.00 a.m. As it was very cold, several hot water bottles were refilled. At 2 a.m. Mrs Ross [a VA] was washing napkins.[5]

This group was kept supplied with food by VAs along the way and when they arrived in Brisbane they were met by the Queensland Scottish Pipe Band.

Joan Crane arrived in Melbourne on the *Athlone Castle* and was met by members of the Victoria League who made sure she was on a train to Sydney and again from Sydney to Brisbane where she met her husband Russell. From there they travelled to Kingaroy and Joan sums up her life in Queensland by saying: 'My twenty-three years in Kingaroy, Maryborough and Brisbane were without doubt, the happiest time of my life. We had very little money or possessions but the people of Queensland were so very very kind to me and I loved the life.'

Meeting the in-laws

Having reached Australia the women then had to face meeting their new in-laws – and for many this was the most difficult and most feared prospect. Not all had corresponded with their new families before they arrived, and they had no idea what sort of reception lay ahead – they could only hope that this first meeting would be a happy one.

For Ina Harper from Canada, married for only a week to Leo, the meeting with her mother-in-law was uncomfortable.

> I met my mother-in-law in a taxi cab in Townsville. We had just flown in and were heading for [home] when Leo spied his mother walking down the street. He stopped the cab driver and called out to her. She stepped into the cab and the introductions were made. She had been working at the hospital, having just left her second husband. She was polite, rather distant and not happy. She said she was sorry she couldn't come to the wedding.

Later, when Ina almost miscarried during a near flood in the steamy weather of Townsville, her mother-in law said that 'she did not expect the marriage to last. She said her son always liked to be different and that was why he had married me and not an Australian girl.' Not long after Ina and Leo moved back to Kempsey. 'Leo's mother mellowed over the years,' writes Ina. 'She could see we really loved each other in spite of all the hassles.'

Patricia Heath arrived in Australia in the last trimester of her pregnancy to be met by a mother-in-law who hated Poms and let her know it. Her baby was born a few weeks after her arrival but died within minutes and Patricia felt 'deep deep down' that she should never have left England and her family. For Patricia, life with her in-laws did not improve and when it came time to vote she once again faced her mother-in-law's dislike. She says, 'We had always voted Liberal in England and at the first election I did the same, not realising they were the conservatives. My mother-in-law, a fervent Labor voter, nearly had a fit.' Finally, when her doctor advised her to leave the home of her in-laws, she and her husband Athol moved to a shared house.

Kathleen W. did not fare any better. She arrived on the *Orbita* in 1946 with her twelve-month-old son. Her husband had promised his family he would not marry while he was overseas so when his bride and son arrived the welcome was a cold one. Kathleen also found that her husband was suffering from what we now know as post-traumatic stress syndrome, a condition which has affected the rest of their lives. She found her relatives watching every move she made, so eventually she took control and moved her family to an isolated farmhouse, away from the family farm in outback Queensland where they had all been living.

Beryl Boyd from England encountered one of the urban myths about 'dirty Poms' when she met her mother-in-law:

> She did not like me at all. I was constantly asked how often I bathed, how often I washed my hair and as she kept asking I can only presume that she was trying to catch me out in some way. She was a rather ignorant lady and was looking for an argument all the time. I soon felt very frustrated so I gave up and tried to ignore her. This made her angry so she refused to let me touch anything of hers and would not sit at the same table as me. One day she was particularly nasty and Trevior grabbed and pushed her against the door. I know that he has always regretted

Beryl Boyd meets her husband's family, November 1946

this, after all she was his mother. She had been corresponding with an old girlfriend of Trevior's in Sydney and obviously was hoping that she would be her daughter-in-law.

Jose Foster's first impression of her father-in-law has stayed with her for over fifty years. 'He took me to the room we were to have and said, "It isn't the pounds and shillings you have to save – it's the pennies!" I was astounded. He was kind but oh so parsimonious and religious.' Jose also remembers her first Christmas church service when the Christmas hymn made her break down with homesickness – she had to leave the church.

Phyllis Webster dressed in her latest fashionable outfit to meet her mother-in-law. 'Up the gangplank strode my mother-in-law, greeted her son, turned to me, took one look and her first three words were "Drop your skirt"! Australia was a bit behind England in fashion and we had been wearing our skirts above our knees practically all through the war. And there I had been, out buying a new wardrobe with which to impress and it went down like a lead balloon.' Phyllis found that two of her husband's friends were also hostile towards 'Poms' and reduced her to tears. Another of her friends was told by her in-laws to go back where she came from, that she wasn't wanted. For these women the antagonism on top of the loneliness made their new life in Australia miserable. 'I'm sure if a lot of the war brides had had the money they'd have been back in England pretty smartly,' says Phyllis.

Olive Johnson discovered that her fiancé's mother and sisters were not at all pleased about her arrival: 'I'm afraid that his family hated me on sight, my only friend was his father. I never found out what they were jealous of. I think it boiled down to having the wrong religion and the wrong nationality.' Olive and Johnny Fitzgerald married amongst Johnny's friends but then returned to Johnny's family home after the honeymoon. When Christmas came a couple of months later Olive was once again ostracised. 'Neither Johnny's sisters nor his mother spoke to me. I had brought them all presents which to my knowledge were never opened, except by my father-in-law, who made a big fuss – and that made things worse. We stayed there for five weeks and I did all the cooking as everyone was working except the mother who was never home. Things finally came to head one Saturday morning. We packed our bags and left. My husband said "I will never forgive them", and I don't think he ever did.'

Now Olive and Johnny were faced with Sydney's extreme housing shortage. They found a room in Kings Cross while they looked elsewhere, and finally found a room in a house in Kensington, a more respectable suburb, where there were already five families. Every man was a returned serviceman and the only stipulation was 'no more children'. But Olive was not feeling well and she soon discovered she was pregnant. 'When I told Johnny he said, "Things can't get worse – they must start improving soon".' The landlady allowed them to stay in the house.

In the final stages of pregnancy Olive's doctor sent her for an x-ray. Two days later she received a telegram asking her to go to the surgery. 'The doctor's wife came out and asked everyone to leave, then looking at me she said, "Not you dear, I have a prescription for you". We were taken in to the doctor and he informed us that we wouldn't have a live baby. We both thought our world was coming to an end. That was one of the only times I saw my husband cry. I was sent to a specialist and put into a hospital where I met a woman who is still my friend to this day – we both had mothers-in-law from hell. After a lot of trouble I did produce a small beautiful little girl. We were both very ill for quite a long time.'

When the baby was fourteen months old Olive took her back to England where she stayed until Johnny had bought a house for his young family.

Olive remembers her return to Australia fondly. 'The few friends I had made were waiting on the docks for me and there was my golden-haired boy with his large bunch of flowers, no photographer this time but oh so much love and joy.'

Olive & baby Helen

Finding a home

One of the greatest problems for ex-servicemen and their wives was accommodation. Many newly-arrived wives and fiancées found themselves living in the crowded homes of their in-laws. For some this was a happy experience, for others a painful one, and for some a disaster.

Although both a Land Settlement program and War Service Homes were part of the government's program[6] there was still an acute housing shortage. The story of Soldier Settlement after the First World War was not a happy one, nevertheless it was once again offered to ex-servicemen after the Second World War. This time servicemen were discharged earlier and in great numbers and their presence exacerbated an already drastic housing shortage. The War Service Homes Act offered financial assistance to purchase an existing house, to discharge a mortgage or to build a house – but this did not help the housing shortage. Housing construction had been at a low level since the 1920s because of both the Depression and the war. Despite the government's attempts to control the massive shortage, including rent-pegging, tenant protection, limiting the size of new houses and controlling house prices, building materials were in short supply and houses could not be built fast enough.

The arrival of thousands of immigrants – at the time called 'New Australians' – who had been recruited from Europe increased the pressure, as did the baby boom which followed the return of Australia's

Arvona David's first home is typical of many

servicemen. Many young couples actually built their own homes, often living on the land in tents, sheds or caravans while they did so.

Once landed, Ina Staryk and her fiancé Leo Harper did not stay in Sydney for more than a night because accommodation was so difficult to find. 'My first night in Sydney was spent sharing a small room with my sister in a private hotel, while the men shared another.' The next day they left for Kempsey and Leo's family.

Beryl and Trevior Boyd had taken a room in Melbourne. Beryl was pregnant and found that the landlady was quite excited at having an English girl in her lodgings. She writes:

> The novelty was to wear off. After our baby was born, the retired naval officer and his wife who had a room beside ours, decided they wanted our room and started ganging up on us, accusing us of things we could not have done, such as dropping razor blades in the toilet – Trevior did not use razor blades because I had brought him a Rolls Razor from England.
>
> It became very uncomfortable living there and Trevior hated leaving me to cope each day when he went to work, as the landlady had forbidden anyone working for her to talk to me, so he arranged for me to spend the days with some people he knew living nearby. Every morning we would pack up the pram with our baby, food for him and myself, all our washing, baby's nappies, wood for the wood copper for washing, and walk to the friends' house where Trevior would leave me and go off to work himself.

This was not an easy or comfortable situation and eventually Beryl decided she would stay at home and cope. But the landlady's nastiness continued and finally Beryl and Trevior answered an advertisement for a young couple with a three-month-old baby to share a home with another couple.

'We should have been aware that it was all very strange at that time, but . . . we fitted the bill. So we moved in. We found out that the idea was that they wanted to share our baby as they had lost one that would have been three months old at the time. The sharing, however, often entailed our baby being taken out of his pram and taken into their room with the door closed between us. We did not like this at all.' It was not long before Beryl, Trevior and baby moved again to another share arrangement in a happier situation.

For Marie Perry, home was the outback. Her husband Ray tried to ease the culture shock he knew his young wife would face. When she arrived in Perth they stayed for a few days in the Royal Hotel, where Marie was delighted at the quality and quantity of the food after the rationing in England. Then towards dusk one day Ray drove Marie to their new home – a drive which took four hours and ended at the family homestead, 165 miles east of Perth. Here they shared a house with Ray's brother and sister-in-law for two years.

'From being a rather "happy-go-lucky townie" where I worked in my father's retail business on a busy main road, a trolley bus stop outside the door, ballroom dancing, cycling and watching soccer my favourite activities, to being a farmer's wife was quite a transformation,' recalls Marie. 'At times I felt very inadequate but I survived with the help of a very patient and kind husband.' Snakes and spiders frightened her, but she learnt to deal with them.

Nineteen-year-old Molly Ashdown had a similar experience. After arriving on the *Asturias* in Fremantle in December 1946 Molly went to live in the outback gold town of Wiluna, over 760 kilometres north of Perth in Western Australia. Formerly a thriving community with a population of over 50 000, by the time Molly arrived the population had dwindled to around 8000. 'We stayed for a few days in Perth,' Molly remembers, 'to soften the blow of what was awaiting me up North!' They travelled by train and Molly remembers huge water bags hung at each end of the carriage, not to provide cool drinking water for the passengers but for the men to keep their beer cool.

Molly had travelled from the green countryside of Surrey in England and she was about to be initiated into the real Australian outback. 'There was nothing but red stony earth dotted with dry-looking bushes,' she recalls. The average height of these bushes was about half a metre with the occasional two-metre-high mulga tree. 'I had never laid eyes on such a desolate scene, or on such a brilliant blue sky with a blistering hot sun burning down on my sensitive English skin,' wrote Molly. 'I saw wide dusty stony streets, queer little houses made of asbestos with a chimney outside from the ground up to the roof. There were rusty roofs, rusty corrugated iron everywhere, and rickety fences of wire and posts. All of the houses had verandahs and many of them had pepper or tamarisk trees for shade.' Molly's husband Brian was finishing his apprenticeship as a fitter and turner and so they stayed in a company-owned house at Wiluna Gold Mine.

An outside toilet in the Australian outback was even more primitive than those many of the women encountered in the cities. Molly describes her introduction to the Australian bush dunny: 'It consisted of a wooden seat, a bottomless hole with a lid, and a piece of string holding cut up newspaper which was our toilet paper. I used to like reading in the toilet, but not in this one! Huge flies buzzed around and creepy crawlies were everywhere. The heat was insufferable.'

As for so many women new to the Australian bush, the insects were a force to be reckoned with. Cockroaches, beetles and centipedes were just as frightening as spiders and snakes. And Molly met with another fright when a group of Aboriginal tribesmen arrived at the gate with spears. She recalls locking the doors and hiding inside the house because she thought she was going to be killed. It wasn't until a neighbour arrived and rescued her that her visitors left; they had only wanted food.

Few of the women had any idea of the society in which they were about to make their home and it seems few had even thought about it before they arrived. These interviews with Canadian and English war brides appeared in *The Sydney Morning Herald* on 23 October 1946 and show some of the reactions to their new life:

> Mrs C. B. Best, from Canada, president of the [Overseas Brides' Club], said that the only real complaints by members were about the housing shortage, but it was realised Australia was in a similar position to that in the countries they left.
>
> 'Some of the Canadian girls find the warm weather very trying,' said Mrs Best. 'We miss the snow and the cold winters, but on the whole we like Australia. I have been very amused at the little telephone boxes out

in the street. At home they are always in drugstores or shops, never in the open.'

'We find ourselves living in Australia under conditions which were old-fashioned in our own countries years ago,' is the opinion of many overseas wives. They say they are unaccustomed to women doing their own laundry without the help of washing machines (which are cheap and easily obtained in Canada); to living in weatherboard houses instead of two-storey brick or stone structures; to attending church in tin or board buildings when 'the parish church back in Surrey was twelfth century'; to living as close as ten miles to the city and yet not being serviced by main sewerage; to not being able to buy utility clothes of a good cut for a reasonable price (such as £4 for a coat); to being deprived of the social pleasure of drinking a glass of beer with their husbands or friends at the 'local' (which, in England, is an institution).

For most overseas wives the climate and the food compensate for these discomforts and differences, but they all would like to know why we have no community life.

'People just don't get together for inexpensive entertainment,' they say. Young people in Australia have no organised night amusements; 'night-clubbing' is out of the reach of the average pocket and the local dance in the local draughty hall is to be deplored. The value of repertory theatres, bowling alleys, table tennis clubs operating on a side radius throughout suburbs is known to these girls and they can appreciate the difference they would make to the social activity of younger people.[7]

Phyllis Bell, coming from Edmonton in Canada, found the first thing missed was central heating. 'I found the first winter very cold, I was just about frozen,' she says of her first home in Chatswood, New South Wales. By the next year she had learnt about singlets and putting on more clothing – and she was pregnant. Phyllis also remembers having to learn about pounds, shillings and pence instead of dollars and cents.

Beryl Boyd remembers her first kookaburra call. 'It was so loud I could only think that some ducks were trapped in the garage.'

Dorothy Baulch was overwhelmed by the space. She arrived in Australia in 1946 on the *Dominion Monarch* and says 'I never realised Australia was so large – even Victoria was huge, much larger than England.

Travelling to my husband's home though only seventeen miles from Melbourne, was the longest drive I'd ever experienced.'

'No houses!' she also remembers surprised her. 'Just wooden bungalows with wire netting at the windows. Was that to keep me out or keep me in...?' She continues:

> A long verandah spread the width of the house, all the windows had blinds on them. Why isn't the sun allowed in? I thought. Well I soon learnt the answer to that.
>
> No bathroom or toilet inside. The toilet was at the bottom of the garden – not really a garden; one went out the back door through a wire door, passed an apple tree and what looked like a railway carriage, through a garden gate then threaded ones way between chickens (which were called chooks) and finally reached the toilet. The bathroom was in the old railway carriage and inside was this monstrosity that you had to light with kindling wood to obtain hot water. I never quite managed to control it and got very used to tepid baths.
>
> At the end of the carriage was the wash house, and another fire-eating contraption used to boil the clothes.
>
> Inside the house was a kitchen with a huge black stove, which seemed to fill one wall of the kitchen. It went from early morning until after the last meal in the evening. It never seemed to go out, and – phew – it was so hot in that kitchen!
>
> The milkman came but not with bottles. He ladled the milk from a can into a 'billy'. I wondered if I had regressed to the middle ages. Where were all the parks and trees? What had I come to?
>
> Would I ever reconcile myself to living in this land, when the thoughts of even a war-ravaged England still filled my heart?

Arvona David also found the toilet 'half way down the backyard' and the lack of hot water a surprise; at home in the little Welsh village of Loughor her family had an indoor toilet and hot water on tap from the coal fires.

For Evelyn Muirhead, coming from the relative sophistication of San Francisco, the way of life in Cairns, Queensland, was also an eye-opener. Not only was the toilet not in the house, but its contents were collected by the nightcart which came early every day. In fact there were five outhouses behind the block of flats where they first lived.

War brides meet in Perth, 1946. Arvona David with baby Noeleen, far left

Home delivery using carts and horses was a normal part of life in Australia in the 1940s and '50s in both country towns and the suburbs, and Evelyn, who was used to supermarkets at home, soon became accustomed to the daily deliveries of milk, fruit and vegetables and eggs and chicken. She did miss the 'mod cons' of her American home and found doing the family washing in a copper instead of a washing machine an experience she could do without. So when the first washing machine arrived in Cairns, Evelyn was the one to buy it. Even little things like saucepans and china were unavailable. Evelyn bought her first dinner service after she had been interviewed by its original owner to find the most suitable purchaser!

Evelyn's fashion was years ahead of the local fashion in Cairns. Whenever she went out she found herself the talk of the town. 'My attire was always in the news,' she remembered.

Pat Warne noticed the flies. Her future husband's parents met her at Fremantle dock and suggested they go for a cup of tea. 'I noticed in horror my father-in-law-to-be's coat back: it was literally covered in flies.

It was the beginning of a long association with flies and I quickly learned the Australian wave.'

Max Darby's family looked after Pat, and made her feel at home from the beginning. A full white wedding was organised and the only thing missing was Pat's family, 'but they sent lots of telegrams. We honeymooned in Yanchep, then a tiny place with one hotel and a lovely beach'.

Estelle Bridgford had a very different experience:

> I realised as soon as I arrived at my new flat that I was extremely lucky. The flat had been the previous home of Keith's parents but as Keith's father had died my mother-in-law decided she didn't want to live there any more and so handed it over furnished from top to bottom to Keith. I had everything you could possibly ask for, and while Keith was waiting for Viv and me to arrive, he refurbished the second bedroom as a nursery equipped with absolutely everything.

However, one of Estelle's first memories of Australians is not so happy:

> I had only been in Australia about two weeks when my next-door neighbour asked me where I bought my groceries. I told her it was a small shop nearby that also housed a post office. She looked surprised and said, "You don't want to shop there, they are Catholics". I was nonplussed to say the least, so I asked her "did that mean they had horns on their heads?" She didn't like my reply. I was to learn quickly after that. There was deep rooted anti-Catholic feeling in Australia that was abhorrent to me coming from England where we had been shattered by the revelations of the holocaust.

Estelle also found her mother-in-law was anti-Catholic and denigrating towards migrants – including the English.

Food

Food in Australia was one of the first things most war brides were impressed by. In comparison to what had been available at home, fruit, vegetables and meat in Australia were abundant and varied. Only tea, coffee and sugar were still rationed, though meat had been rationed during the war.

In every part of the world except the USA living standards declined during the Second World War. In the US they had actually improved, which made arriving in Australia a backwards step for the Yankee brides.

In Europe both food and clothing were strictly rationed. Generally everyone was hungry, coal and wood were impossible to get in winter and soap to wash with was in short supply. The black market flourished.

In Asia the Japanese had been forced to open public feeding centres in 1944 due to the American blockade of Japanese shipping.

Mary Johnson wrote back to her family in Macclesfield, England, telling them of the first meal she had when she arrived in Perth on the *Atlantis* in June 1946. Her parents passed her letter to the local paper which commented that it 'made Australia sound like the promised land to rationed Britishers'.

Mary wrote: 'We kicked off with chicken broth and then had roast duck, green peas, cauliflower, creamed and baked potatoes. There was more than one week's meat ration on each plate and none of us finished it. As for the sweet, we just gazed at the menu and ordered coffee. I won't tell you what the sweets were, but they were unheard of or forgotten in England.' Mary also tells her family how she, and her fellow brides, were overwhelmed at the fruit that was available.

Mary had married Harold Johnson, a sergeant in the RAAF, and was heading for Mittagong in NSW where she was made to feel very welcome by the local community who sent her flowers and fruit.

For Pat Darby the food was also a pleasure. 'Every morning we had eggs and Max's mother took me shopping in Perth thinking I would buy clothes but she couldn't get me away from the butchers' windows! I had never seen so much wonderful steak! – The clothes I could do without.'

Audrey Neely recounts a delightful story of being sent with a friend to buy passionfruit for a fresh fruit salad when they arrived in Port Adelaide. In those days few British had encountered this exotic fruit. Passionfruit were not in season and that made the hunt particularly difficult but they finally found a greengrocers which had them. Says Audrey, 'We were handed a bag of very uninteresting things and we thought we would taste them. We had a small fruit knife so we cut one in half, threw away the seeds and ate the skin – it was dreadful! When we arrived back at the ship we didn't say a word – we weren't going to be called stupid Pommies!'

Some of the wives formed clubs and associations to help them cope with living in this new country. For many of them it wasn't just the different way of doing things that was the problem, it was also homesickness.

They held meetings with guest speakers such as a Walter Bunning, who in July 1946 is reported as giving a series of talks on 'Australian Homes' to seventy women in Sydney.[8]

Brides who went home

Some brides and fiancées did not stay and many who did remain have stories of women who didn't like what they saw when they got here – or even changed their minds before they arrived. Some of the brides I interviewed said they would have returned to their home country if they had been able to afford it.

Audrey S met an Australian in Canada in 1943. She was a switch-board operator at the Number 2 Wireless School Royal Canadian Air Force in Calgary, Alberta. He was a Flying Officer with the RAAF. They first met when he wandered into the room where she was working look-ing for a medical officer. They did not see each other again for weeks, until Audrey was stationed at Shepherd Flying Base and he turned up again. This time he asked her out. He was persistent and after a few

War brides meet, Cairns, October 1946. Evelyn Muirhead is on the left

rejections Audrey accepted his invitation and he met her parents – who liked him. At Christmas time 1943 he asked Audrey to marry him and she agreed.

For the rest of the time that her husband was in Canada the couple lived with Audrey's parents and by the time he left in July 1944, Audrey was pregnant.

Audrey's new in-laws sent clothes for the baby, who was born in January 1945. In December of that year, after receiving a letter from her husband, Audrey and her son prepared to go to Australia. After a train trip from Calgary to San Francisco they boarded the SS *Monterey* for Australia. Audrey's memories of the ship are not pleasant. 'It smelt terrible,' she remembers and 'the crossing was tedious, often stormy.' However, she enjoyed the company of the other brides, many of whom had children. The ship stopped briefly in Suva, Fiji and overnight in New Zealand before reaching Sydney in April.

The group that met Audrey and her son at the wharf was not friendly. 'The mother,' she remembers, 'was a large woman, nearly six foot, the father was tiny and ill looking. They made a fuss over my son and never spoke to me. I was rushed to their car and next thing I knew we were at their house.' Audrey was very disappointed that she did not have time to say goodbye to any of her shipmates or to get any addresses.

Audrey's next disappointment was the accommodation. She found that they were to share a bedroom, the three of them, in her in-laws' house. 'I was not going to get a place of my own, the excuse being he would inherit the house when they died. I could not believe I was stuck with parents who obviously did not like me. I was informed I was to do as his mother said.' Things went from bad to worse. There was no telephone and the house was only heated by a fireplace in the front room, which was out of bounds to Audrey. She was told she was not to eat with the family but to serve the meals and eat in the kitchen. She was never taken out, nor did she meet anyone, though her son was taken on outings on Saturday and Sunday. Then Audrey found she was pregnant again.

The last straw was a letter from an English girl addressed to Audrey and asking for money because she was pregnant to Audrey's husband. When she showed her husband the letter he threw it in the fire, hit her and told her it was none of her business. Says Audrey, 'I'm afraid at that point I lost it and hit him with a chair, knocking him out. I refused to do any more work and planned to leave.' However Audrey, who had saved five hundred dollars from her husband's pay which she had been allotted while she was living in Canada, did not breathe a word of her plans. One day she went to Canada House in Sydney and after telling them her story, paid her fare home. She crept out of the house not long after on a Sunday while the family was eating their dinner. She took her son, some of his clothes and the clothes she stood up in. 'The ship MV *Wanganella* sailed and I never saw them again,' she writes.'As you can imagine, I have no fond memories of Sydney nor of Australia as I never got a chance to see any of it.'

Marjorie and Robert Roseneder also returned to Canada, but their reasons were very different. Marjorie and Bob had also met in Calgary where Bob was training. They met when they were both part of a group going to visit a friend in hospital. They went by taxi but Marjorie remembers that 'the taxi was so small I had to sit on Bob's lap on the way there'. Not long after that Bob asked Marjorie for a date and they went for a streetcar ride. 'We held hands and later we went for a waffle supper. We just grew together after that,' she said. The time was July and August 1943. They saw each other a couple more times before Bob was told he would be leaving for England in March of 1944 and this triggered his proposal.

Though Bob had proposed there was no ring. Bob posted it when he got to Brighton, England and wrote to Marjorie telling her it was coming. When it arrived it gave Marjorie quite a shock because the packaging was similar to that used by the services when returning the effects of a serviceman killed in action.

Marjorie's dad thought she was crazy to marry an Australian and go to live so far away. Her mother said she was sorry she was going so far away, but she too had been a war bride, being an English girl who met a Canadian serviceman

Marjorie & Bob

The Roseneders' wedding day

during the First World War and coming to live in Canada.

Once the war was over Marjorie had to wait for a passage. Marjorie travelled on the same ship as Audrey S, the SS *Monterey* departing from San Francisco. She remembers the accommodation as being very basic.

Marjorie was met in Sydney by Bob. They stayed for a couple of days with Bob's aunt, though 'after they found I was Catholic they didn't talk to me the last day', she says. Then they took the train to Brisbane. By this time Marjorie was feeling very homesick. They were not met and caught a taxi to Bob's home 'where they more or less just said "Oh hello"'. Marjorie was surprised by their casual welcome. As did so many brides, she found the lack of indoor plumbing and the spiders very hard to get used to.

In 1948 Marjorie and Bob had their first child, and in 1951 they were told their daughter, Jan, was suffering from asthma. When Marjorie and Bob were advised Jan would be better off in a high dry climate they moved to Alberta, Canada, where they have lived happily ever since.

CHAPTER 10
Against the Odds

*Somewhere the sun is shining
So honey, don't you cry,
We'll find a silver lining,
The clouds will soon roll by*

Couples who met and fell in love in an English-speaking country, and who shared customs and social behaviour had a difficult enough time when it came to getting married – and getting to Australia. But couples who met in countries where English was not the first language, or couples whose countries were wartime enemies, often had enormous bureaucratic and social hurdles to overcome before they could be married or be together in Australia.

An escaped POW in Italy

Vittorina (Vicki) Pellegrini was one of two daughters of Seconda and Angela Pellegrini. The Pellegrini family owned a farm in Vercelli, between Turin and Milan in northern Italy, not far from France.

In September 1943, Italy was in turmoil. When the Fascist Grand Council passed a vote of no confidence against the dictator Benito Mussolini and King Victor Emmanuel handed power to Marshal Pietro Badoglio, the Italians decided to surrender and changed sides. In the ensuing turmoil the Germans took over and set up a military administration. For the rest of the war Italy was in a state of civil war as countrymen who supported Mussolini fought against fellow countrymen who sided with the allies. All the time the German army maintained a strong presence, particularly in the north.

The Pellegrinis helped a number of escaped POWs, hiding them on their farm and helping them to reach nearby Switzerland over the Italian Alps (sometimes diguised as women), with enormous risk to their own wellbeing. One incident which could have been the family's undoing has stayed strongly in Vicki's memory. It concerned a young POW her parents harboured and fed for about two weeks. On the escape route to the Swiss border he was re-captured. The Pellegrinis learnt later that he had been tortured in an attempt to find out who had hidden him. His body was found with teeth and fingernails and half his tongue cut out.

George McDonald was an Australian soldier stationed in the Middle East. In April 1941 he was captured by the Germans. The German army handed their prisoners over to the Italians who interned them in POW camps in Italy and George was interned in Camp 106, Carpanetto, not far from Vercelli. He escaped in September 1943 and was hidden from the Germans by the Pellegrini family. Vicki described how George stayed with the Pellegrinis until the war was over. 'He was 22 or 23 when he had just joined the army and we fell in love. We let all the rest go but I wouldn't let him go,' she said. At the time Vicki was only seventeen. Vicki's brother, Egidio, had come home because the Germans came to search for the escaped POWs 'They knew we were helping them.'

'Two or three times they came to our farm,' she recalls, 'and they kept hitting my father and putting a gun to my head.' The Germans took her brother Egidio captive and Vicki was never to see him again.

George hid on the Pellegrini farm for eighteen months. Every few weeks the Germans would search the farm, but they never found George. 'We had a big farm and we had an idea when they were coming,' says Vicki. 'We would send George into the paddock and they couldn't find him.' The Pellegrinis hid many escapees in the same way, but George was special – and he and Vicki were in love.

In 1944 Vicki became pregnant and the baby was due to be born in March 1945. Vicki made her way to the main hospital which was occupied by the Germans. 'I was so frightened because I was having an Australian baby,' she said. 'I was very lucky when she was born because

she was very blonde with blue eyes –
which is very German.' The officer in
charge came to inspect the baby. Vicki
remembers this as a terrifying experience because the Germans were known
to kill babies that did not fit their notion
of the perfect Aryan. 'When they saw she
was blonde with blue eyes they said
"Good girl,"' and baby Margherita was
safe.

But Vicki's troubles were not over.
The next day the British bombed the
hospital and half of it was destroyed.
The war was close to its end in Europe
– 8 May was VE day. In June 1945 Vicki
and George were married.

Vicki & baby, Italy, 1945

It was only a matter of weeks later that George was liberated and the
little family moved to Naples. From there George was flown to England.
Vicki and Margherita were taken by the air force to Heathrow in England
a couple of weeks later and the family was reunited in Southampton. But
the reunion was short-lived. In December 1945 George left for Australia.
Vicki and Margherita were to travel separately.

On 1 December they boarded the MV
Rangitata with 250 other war brides.
Vicki mostly enjoyed the trip, particu-
larly the company of a Polish bride, Pola
Lumby, and a Russian bride. 'The
English wives did not mix much with
the European women and called us
"dagos",'[1] remembers Vicki. By the time
the ship berthed in Melbourne in
January 1946 Vicki was six months preg-
nant. From Melbourne Vicki and
Margherita had to make their way to
Brisbane.

When they arrived in Brisbane
George was there to meet them, and so

George & Vicki, 1946

Yvonne & George Chard

was Vicki's mother-in-law. This was not to be a happy relationship and it began with George's mother making Vicki feel most unwelcome. Vicki and her mother-in-law never got on, George was her only son and his marriage to an Italian never ceased to be a disappointment to her.

From Brisbane they went on to Inglewood in inland Queensland where George had found work as a rouseabout and Vicki set about learning to live in a hot dry land with strange animals, where no-one spoke Italian and there was still some resentment towards Italy's role in the war.

A girl from Alexandria

Yvonne Athanassiades was born in Alexandria, Egypt on May 25, 1924, to Greek- and Cypriot-born parents who emigrated to Egypt in their youth. Yvonne's story is told by her daughter Marcia and granddaughter Genevieve.

Living and growing up in Egypt was carefree and exciting for people with a good income. In the 1940s Alexandria was a multicultural society with a distinct French and British influence.

Yvonne's father managed a stylish cinema and Yvonne had the opportunity to watch all the latest American, English, and French films. Actually, she said this is how she first began to learn English and French, because she could learn from the subtitles in Greek.

She attended a small variety of schools including a Greek primary school, as well as the German school and later The British Academy of Alexandria. She spoke five languages fluently: Greek, English, French, Italian and German, and a smattering of Arabic.

During the War, British women (usually wives of British servicemen) would host tea dances at the Red Cross. The dances were known as the 'Under 20 Club' and local young ladies were encouraged to meet young British Forces servicemen stationed in 'Alex', as everyone called it.

Because Yvonne was always a very sociable person who loved to dance, she and her friends went to these dances often.

George Chard was a six-foot-tall, blond, blue-eyed, good-looking Australian serving in the RAAF. Whereas Yvonne's friends were swooning, and making 'ooohs' and 'ahhhs' over him, Yvonne thought he seemed too conceited. She used to say, 'He looked like he loved himself'. To her surprise, George singled Yvonne out of the group and asked her to dance. Later on, when he asked to kiss her goodnight after taking her home, she said, 'You may kiss my hand'.

George was based in Egypt for about four years and Yvonne and George corresponded daily. George had discovered a sort of new-found home in Yvonne's family. When on leave, he was always invited to dinner with the family and extended relatives. As George's own parents were divorced, he had never experienced such a warm and affectionate family life. Yvonne encouraged George to improve his mind and suggested books for him to read, and taught him some French language and songs.

George Chard proposed to Yvonne Athanassiades in 1943 – but Yvonne insisted George ask her father first. Yvonne's daughter continues the story:

My grandfather asked my mother how she felt about marrying George. Yvonne felt hesitant about it at first because she would be marrying a foreigner. At the time she never thought she would leave Egypt, because she had a very comfortable and happy life there. But she liked George's relaxed and outgoing nature, typical of Australians, which had made an impression on her and was a refreshing change from the usual English types that she had met. Also, George and Yvonne were very much in love. George would tell her how he couldn't live without her. He was very romantic towards her, which is evident in the years-worth of love letters Yvonne kept all her life.

My grandfather was also swayed by George and was instantly charmed by him and gave his blessing. They married on 9 June 1943 (three days after George's 22nd birthday on 6 June).

The couple had a baby girl, Frances Jean, while living in Egypt, but unfortunately due to birth complications, the child died after two days. Yvonne and George were devastated.'

Yvonne and George travelled to Australia separately and Yvonne arrived in Melbourne on the *Strathaird* late in 1945.

For Yvonne, the steel-making town of Newcastle on the coast of New South Wales was an enormous culture shock. 'She was baffled to learn that lunchtime consisted of one of her in-laws picking up some corned beef, ham or "savs" from the corner shop, washed down with tea and followed by fruitcake,' writes her granddaughter, Genevieve, 'being used to her mother's fine cooking and to the fact that lunch was the main event of the day.'

Yvonne found the food in Australia very unexciting and the discovery of a Greek who owned a café gave her the opportunity to once again enjoy delicacies from home, such as grilled fish, Greek-style, with lemon juice. Yvonne was also a good cook and would 'whip up a variety of delicious meals, and the beautiful cooking aromas would permeate the stuffy old terrace house'.

A concentration camp in Poland

In 1941 a young Polish Jewess, Pola Brafman, was taken from her bed in the early hours of the morning and sent to work in a German factory in Sudetenland, the border area of Czechoslovakia's two western provinces, Bohemia and Moravia. She was twenty-one at the time and the eldest of five children. Her occupation, together with another 350 women, was spinning cotton. The women worked in the factory from 5 a.m. to 5 p.m. Helen Leperere, who was in the same camp as Pola, wrote a short piece about their experiences: 'They, of course, do not look glamorous, not pretty, not even in the slightest bit feminine. In fact they hardly look human. I am one of those women.'

The Germans needed men to do the heavy work and for this they used prisoners of war who had a reputation for escaping. Noel Lumby was an Australian who had been captured by the Germans on Crete after being stationed in Palestine and Greece. On the trip from Greece to Germany by train Noel and a number of fellow prisoners escaped and were hidden by the Greeks until they were betrayed to the Gestapo. From there Noel was sent to a camp in Germany and once again he escaped. The next time he was captured he was sent to a punishment camp and from there he joined a handful of POWs assigned to work in the factory, which by now had become the concentration camp known as Gabersdorf.

The men and women were forbidden to talk to each other: 'If a girl was caught talking to the prisoners they shaved her hair off,' remembers Pola. They could also be publicly beaten or sent to Auschwitz, one of the most notorious concentration camps. However, this did not prevent communication – and attractions began to form. The men attempted to cheer the women up with winks, smiles and encouragement. Writes Pola's friend Helen Leperere, '"Keep your chin up" is a sentence I learnt from one of them, an Aussie who seems particularly kind. He is always smiling encouragingly. It takes me a while to understand this sentence, although of all the women, I have a little schoolgirl English.' Helen remembers that the POWs were treated in a more humane way than the Jewish women workers, but that their very presence was enough to encourage the survival instinct in the women.

In the mornings the men delivered empty spools to the factory. It was the task of the women to spin the cotton onto the spools and fill the boxes, which were then taken to another part of the factory for the next part of the processing. The workers were closely supervised by German guards. After a while, notes from the men began to appear in the boxes, asking the women their names or making comments. The men also passed across little things, such as a piece of chocolate or items from their Red Cross food parcels. The women were starving as well as frightened and exhausted, and these little gestures helped their morale enormously, even though they knew the punishments for being caught were extreme.

Two romances developed: one between Noel Lumby and Pola Brafman and another between a young girl, Guta, and a Scotsman, Alex. At first Noel wrote to Pola in English and she wrote to him in German; they each had to ask fellow prisoners to translate their letters. 'Then,' said Pola, 'the girl who translated my letters, after a few months she made a joke about the mushy letters and I said from now on I am writing my own.

Pola & Noel after release

I could read and write in English before I could speak it.' Helen, who was the girl who did the translating, remembers that as well as talking about their emotions the men wrote about their homes and their families. 'It seemed so very strange to us.'

Noel was particularly concerned about the welfare of the women in the camp. He learnt to hide much-needed medicines as well as food in the boxes which were passing between the men and women. It wasn't long before he was taking advantage of every lapse in the guard's supervision to talk or be with Pola. He soon found, too, that he could sneak out of his camp at night and get to the women's compound via a tunnel which went under the factory. By cutting the barbed wire at the entrance to the compound he was able to meet with Pola secretly – until one night they were caught. The guard's name was Frieda and fortunately, says Pola, 'she was humane, but she had to do her job and she said, "Pola, don't do it again please. I will get into trouble". I said "No, I promise", but of course the next week I went again. The Germans had told us that if they won the war we would stay in the factory for the rest of our lives and if they lost the war they would kill us – that was Hitler's orders.' So Pola felt she had little to lose.

When the war ended in Europe in 1945 the prisoners were liberated by the Russian army. Transport arrived but it was only for the servicemen. However, Noel refused to go without Pola and finally she was allowed to leave with him. Meanwhile Alex left for Scotland, promising to send for Guta, and eventually she did make the still-hazardous journey across Europe to Scotland and to marry her Scotsman in Dundee.

Noel and Pola went to Prague in Czechoslovakia which was held in part by the Russians and part by the Americans. There they married in a registry office on 1 June 1945. Then they went to Pilsen (Pizen) in the American-occupied sector, to a refugee camp which included many French people. From there, Noel managed to organise seats on a plane to Lyons in France and then to Paris, where they were given accommodation in a beautiful hotel on the Champs Elysee – a far cry from Gabersdorf. The next part of their journey took them to Eastbourne, in England – Noel by boat and Pola by plane – where Noel was stationed with the army and Pola found accommodation with an English family. It was here that Pola learned to speak English. She was to stay in Eastbourne for six months until she was given a passage on a ship to

Australia in December 1945. Meanwhile Noel returned to Australia in September.

Pola came on the *Rangitata* – the same ship as Vicki McDonald. She well remembers the day the ship docked in Melbourne, 5 January 1946.

Her next trip was to take a train from Melbourne to Sydney where Noel was waiting. 'It was the biggest heat wave in fifty years in January '46 – so hot the railway lines were buckling and we had to stop. The English girls were saying, "How will we get around in this heat?" It was a terrific culture shock.'

Noel met Pola in Sydney and took her by train to his family in Newcastle, who welcomed her with open arms. Not long after, Pola learnt that her entire family had perished in concentration camps: her four siblings, both her parents and her many uncles and aunts and cousins – 100 people in her immediate family. Pola has never returned to Poland and regards Australia as home. Helen Leperere eventually settled in Australia and has remained very close to both Pola and Noel.

The Australian military police in Palestine

Eva Tuckfield was born in February 1919 to Hans Isaac and Regina Pagel in Beuthen, Upper Silesia, Germany. Writes Eva, 'We were a devout Jewish but modern living family. My parents were highly respected and very active members of the Jewish community and the Zionist Movement.'[2] The family ran a fashion business and were comfortably off.

Eva had a happy childhood but as early as 1931 she recalls, 'There was a tense feeling around the city [which] affected even me. I did not understand what was going on, but saw youths dressed in brown uniforms marching around in flaming torch processions and singing very loudly.' She also recalls her parents speaking quietly to each other and her father suddenly going away.

When Eva was thirteen, in 1932, the family made the decision to leave Germany for Palestine. Eva went to stay with a beloved aunt and uncle – for the last time. Her father tried to persuade them to join his family in Palestine but they stayed behind and perished in the Holocaust.

The family settled in Tel Aviv and took Hebrew names – Eva became Hava. Eva has some fascinating stories to tell of growing up in the young city of Tel Aviv and in that time grew away from her family's strict religious observances.

Little Eva Pagel outside her parents; shop in Beuthen, Germany, early 1920s

In 1941, when Eva was twenty-two, the Australian forces arrived in Palestine. Writes Eva: 'They were repatriated from Syria and the North African Desert, El Alamein and Tobruk, after heavy fighting. The Australians were very much liked by the whole population, first of all because they fought the hated Germans and because they were happy and likeable young men. We tried to make them feel at home, which they appreciated.'

About this time Eva's mother fell ill and Eva was needed at home. Because she could speak English, a friend got her a part-time job in a restaurant called 'Danieli'. The Australian military police, who were quartered nearby, had their meals at this restaurant. Eva described meeting her future husband: 'One morning a new soldier walked in, his name was Jim, he was tall, very good looking and quietly spoken. I liked him straight away and started to flirt a little. A girlfriend of mine liked him too and asked him to the pictures. The next day she complained to me that he fell asleep and was very boring. No wonder – she could not speak English very well. Well, I said, I'll ask him out and see if he'll go to sleep in my company!'

Jim was 'Corporal Milton James Tuckfield, twenty-five years old, born in Gawler, South Australia', writes Eva, who admits she had no idea where Gawler was. 'I had only heard of the Melbourne Races.' Jim had been repatriated to Palestine from the Western Desert (Tobruk) to recuperate from sand in the lungs.

It was not long before Eva invited Jim home to meet her family, who welcomed him. This was apparently not uncommon. 'Australian soldiers were very much liked by the people of Palestine,' writes Eva, 'who often invited them to their homes.' When Eva got a full-time job, she and Jim continued to meet 'every night at 7 o'clock closing and in the strict blackout. I just saw the glowing tip of his cigarette and knew he was there. It gave me such a warm and satisfying feeling.'

The love affair flourished even though Jim was transferred to Jerusalem. Thinking back, Eva says it never entered her mother's head that something might happen between Jim and herself: 'He wasn't Jewish.'

'Just after he was transferred I became very sick with the flu and was feeling very sorry for myself. Suddenly Jim arrived from Jerusalem to visit me, and to make me feel better gave me a lovely bracelet with matching brooch. Both made of silver filigree with blue stones. That was the first time in my life that I had received a piece of jewellery and coming from Jim I knew then that he loved me too. He stayed with me for about two hours and then had to return to Jerusalem. A two-hour bus ride on a road called The Seven Sisters as there were seven dangerous curves along that road.'

When she was well Eva went to visit Jim in Jerusalem: 'We had already decided to get married'. However Eva knew this was going to cause problems, though not from the army. 'As I came from a strict Jewish family and Jim was not Jewish I knew there would be a great upheaval. I decided not say anything for the time being.'

Nor did she. Eva and Jim married without her family's knowledge in the office of the British District Commissioner in Jaffa on 7 April 1942. 'Of course my family was very upset and for some time my parents and [sister] Miriam did not speak to me. But I was very happy and we had three wonderful honeymoon days in a little beach hotel in Bayit Ve Gan. On our return to Tel Aviv we were invited by Hanna [another of Eva's siblings] to wish us luck which Jim and I appreciated and remembered for ever.' Eva's nephew Ami was delighted to have an Australian uncle.

'I can still see him in my mind as he marched up and down the street with Jim's army slouch hat on his head.' Then the young couple returned to Jerusalem where Eva had to look for accommodation.

Eva makes friends easily and the next day found another Jewish girl, Esther Dowell, also married to an Australian, and she also found herself a room. 'Jim had to live in the garrison and could only stay with me on his days off.' She enjoyed her life in the 'German Colony' of Jerusalem and during this time became pregnant with her first child. Her friend Esther was pregnant at the same time. The birth of Eva's first child is described in her memoirs:

'It has been a thirty-hour-long difficult labour. Jim had been called from the township of Rehovot and my mother had also arrived from Tel Aviv to be with me. In those days no one was allowed in the labour ward so they just waved to me through a little window to let me know they were there. They were allowed to do that only because my husband was an Australian soldier. We called our son Raymond Gil (Ray, my little ray of sunshine and Gil translated from Hebrew means joyful). As soon as he was born and before he was washed the nurse took him outside so that Jim could hold him for a few minutes. Jim visited me that night in the ward but had to leave the next night to go back to Rehovot.'

Before she gave birth, Eva had paid the hospital three pounds for an eight-day stay, however this was not enough!

'Because of the difficult birth I stayed two extra days. Then I went to the nursery to pick up my baby. They wanted extra money for those two days which at the time I did not have. I had no opportunity to pick up my army allowance, which was due while I was in hospital. At first they would not give me my baby. I became most upset, [and] I had to leave them my ration card just to be able to take my son home.'

Eva's problems were not over. Her landlady did not want a baby in the house so she found herself looking for new accommodation.

In January 1943 Eva and Jim were separated. 'All Australian troops were recalled to Australia to defend the country against the Japanese.' Eva was devastated, but her natural optimism won the day when 'the night after Jim left, snow fell in Jerusalem. It was the first time for many years that the city was deeply covered in snow, and what a beautiful sight it was. It would be many years before it snowed again, so I was happy I was there to experience it.' Eva settled into life in Jerusalem with the

Jim, Eva and baby Raymond Tuckfield

company of her friend Esther and Esther's son Maxi. Writes Eva, 'If it had not been for Esther and Maxi I would have gone back to live in Tel Aviv. And who knows, I might have never left.'

In 1944 Jim wrote from England where he had been sent to assist in the repatriation of Australian prisoners of war in Europe, to Eva in Palestine. A few months later she was to receive another surprise. She was advised by the authorities, with only a day's notice, that she was to leave for Australia. Her mother hurried over to help her pack and Eva and her friend Esther who was also going, hurriedly prepared for their journey to Australia.

They left from Jerusalem railway station for Egypt the next day. As Eva boarded the train she realised just what her departure meant. Leaving her family, her friends and her home of many years, where she had been happily raising her son, Ray.

Because of time constraints she had to leave without saying goodbye to many of her family. It was 22 November 1944 and the war with the Japanese continued in the Pacific. Eva writes: 'I had set out with a child into an unknown country and an unknown future not knowing when I would see my husband again and not knowing how his family would receive me. But I was determined and had the courage to work at making this new country my new home and make the best of it. If only for my child's sake.' For Eva and Esther it was the start of an extraordinary journey.

Eva had promised her mother she would be back in three years, but she notes sadly that she did not return until 1970 – twenty-five years later. For many war brides from this war and from the Great War it was the same. Travelling home to see family and friends was not easy. Until air travel became more accessible in the 1960s most international travel remained by ship. War brides from this war who made the journey home not only had the problem of getting there, but most also either had to travel with their young families or wait until their children had grown up beyond childhood.

Eva and Esther were part of a group of five war brides travelling to Australia, but Eva notes that they did not have much in common with the others, who did not have children.

With one stop in Gaza for a meal in the British Army base, they continued to travel on the train through the night and through the next morning. At Ismailia they changed to another train for Port Said and their ship. 'It had been a long and very tiring train trip for us,' notes Eva. They had spent the nights sleeping sitting up while the children slept on long benches in the compartment.

The five war brides were told that the ship had been waiting for their arrival, and sure enough, no sooner were they on board than the ship departed. 'We were taken to a large cabin,' writes Eva, 'which had four double bunks on each side facing each other. Already in the cabin were three Egyptian war brides with children, so we felt a bit better that our children had company.' Despite the fact that Eva was exhausted she unpacked her damp clothes hastily taken from the washing line days before and hung them over the rails in the ship's corridors to dry.

Their ship was the *Changi* and besides the war brides it was packed with Australian and New Zealand soldiers going home, most of them repatriated from prisoner of war camps in Europe. 'They loved playing with Ray and Maxi and made swings for them out of their lifesaving vests. The Army nurses looked after the children while we went down for our meals, but the children always ate first.'

The war with Japan continued and the *Changi* was part of a convoy. Eva notes that the ships were always zigzagging but that she felt safe.

They stopped for a day outside Aden then sailed onto Bombay, India, arriving on 4 December, 1944.

'An American troopship was there ready to sail to Australia but the captain refused to take children and only took women without children. The reason was firstly the danger and secondly [that] they would only have two meals a day and were not prepared for children.'

The war brides spent a few hours wandering round Bombay before being taken to the railway station and 'put into first-class compartments: 'I had never seen such luxury before, every compartment had its own door to the outside with comfortable easy chairs, its own toilet and did not look like a train compartment – just like an ordinary nice room.' Eva and Esther travelled together.

Obviously the difficulty of transporting the wives and children of Australian servicemen over the Indian Ocean was not going to be solved overnight and Eva and Esther now found themselves sent on to the city of Poona where they were billeted inside a British Army Engineers camp until January 1945.

'The camp was very large,' writes Eva, 'and we had Indian soldiers on duty around our billet day and night. It was a very safe place for us and the children who could play on the big lawns in front of our rooms. The Indian soldiers loved the boys and could not do enough for them.'

Money was a problem however. Eva and Esther had left Jerusalem with little time to spare and 'In between two army pays. We were lucky that the Red Cross came to our help and lent us enough money.' This was to last them until they reached Australia.

Eva and Esther made the most of their enforced holiday in Poona. They hired push bikes, and, leaving their sons in the care of the Indian sergeants, went into Poona, bought fabric and organised new clothes for themselves. They rode in rickshaws as well as on their bikes and spent their evenings in the officers' club playing housie. The Egyptian mothers who were also billeted in the camp did not join them: they never left the camp, nor did they socialise.

Eva sent her family a cable from Poona explaining why they were there, but it was never received. 'Apparently,' she writes, 'the censor did not let it through for our own safety as we still had a long sea trip ahead of us in dangerous waters.'

Christmas 1944 in Poona included a children's party and on New

Eva (right) & Esther in Poona

Year's Eve dancing around a huge bon-fire to the music of the bagpipes. 'Esther and I cried as we did not know what the next year would bring. It was our last night there.'

Once again hastily bundled onto a train, the wives were taken back to Bombay to board the *City of Paris*. 'On this ship we had nice cabins which Esther and I shared.'

When they left port the next day Ray was ill and spent two days in the sick-bay recovering from what the ship's doctor called sea sickness. This ship, Eva reports was only half full – with some returning soldiers and nurses. 'In the morning the boys would go up to the dining room for breakfast on their own and were looked after by the Indian staff. They loved the boys and the boys were well behaved and happy.'

Next stop, seven days later, was Colombo, in what was then known as Ceylon and is now Sri Lanka. A power boat took them into the port for two hours sightseeing and they departed the next day into very rough weather and a period of sea sickness.

Fourteen days later Eva was able to write: 'At long last we arrived in Australia, to be precise in Fremantle, WA, and had our passports stamped by Immigration.' The welcoming committee from Travellers Aid was there to meet them and lend them prams for the children and provide tickets to Perth.'

Initial impressions? 'To our eyes everything looked so old-fashioned,' writes Eva. 'The whole city looked boring.' Hardly surprising after the bustling cities of India and the vibrant lives they had lived in Palestine.

'That night we left [Fremantle] and continued through the [Great] Australian Bight, and now at last we were in safe and calm waters and could be told that when travelling between Bombay and Fremantle there was still the danger of Japanese submarines, about which, at the time, we had no idea.'

On the morning of Monday 29 January 1945 the *City of Paris* entered Sydney Harbour.

What an unforgettable sight that was to my eyes. Holding Ray in my arms so he could see everything as well, I moved from side to side of the ship so I would not miss any of the lovely little bays coming into view. We saw beautiful houses small and large, green parks in those bays and people standing along the coastline waving flags. There were hundreds of little boats and yachts sailing around, all decorated and sounding sirens, some using water fountains, the whole place was alive and celebrating. First we thought "what, for us?" But no, we found later that it was Australia Day and also it was a welcome to the Governor General the Duke of Gloucester who arrived before us on a great passenger liner.

Eva and Esther were to part in Sydney. Esther's mother-in-law arrived to meet Esther and her son Maxi, but Esther's husband Warren was not there – he had been sent to New Guinea. 'Poor Esther was devastated, which made our parting even harder, but we knew we would stay in touch.' Eva wrote.

Eva and Ray were again met by the ladies from Travellers Aid, taken for a drive, which Eva wrote she was 'too tense' to enjoy, and then for a meal 'which I could not eat. I was not used to a typical Australian meal of those years,' before being put on a night train for Melbourne. Once again penniless, Esther and Ray sat up throughout the night with an elderly woman who shared her fruit with them.

In Melbourne they were taken to a room at the YWCA by the ladies from Travellers Aid. And the following night they boarded another train for Adelaide. Eva still remembers the long journey from Sydney to Adelaide and how she had no idea how long it would take. On this last leg they were given First Class seats and Ray was able to lie down. Now Eva began to feel apprehensive about meeting her husband's family. 'What if no one came to meet us?' she worried. 'What if they did not like us? What sort of people were they? I had corresponded with my in-laws and kept sending them photos since Ray's birth but [had] never had a photo from them. I had no idea what they looked like. Jim was in England and when would I see him again? What got into me to make that long journey with a small child and my husband not even here to help me?'

Eva and Ray arrived in Adelaide on 31 January 1945. 'Such a pretty city, I thought, and everything will be all right, it will be our home from now on, so I will make it all right.'

Eva and Ray were the last to leave the train in Adelaide and sat down on the platform to wait.

'After a while I saw a group of people slowly walking up and down the platform and looking at us. Then the elderly white-haired woman approached and asked quietly, "Are you Mrs Tuckfield?" when I nodded she said, "I am Mum". Relieved I got up and was embraced and kissed as was Ray. It was a warm welcome for us so I felt at peace.'

Eva had sent a telegram which had not yet arrived, but Jim's family knew she was to be on the station because the army had advised them.

For Eva, her new life in Australia began in her husband's family home, without her husband. She found the outdoor toilet very strange and also the lack of hot water in the bathroom. She learnt to wash clothes in a copper when at home she had sent clothes to a laundry to be washed. Eggs, which Eva was used to buying from Bedouin women for a shilling each, were abundant.

Despite her optimistic, bright nature Eva found settling into life with her Australian family without her husband was not easy. 'For the next few weeks I had nightmares. Also Ray would wake up screaming once every night, something he had never done before.' She also found that the husband she called Jim was known as Milton to his family.

Adelaide itself was a culture shock for Eva. 'All the shops closed at 5.30 p.m. and the pubs at 6 p.m. The working men used to race to the pub straight after work to gulp down their beer before closing time and that was called "the 6 o'clock swill". On Sunday the buses and trams only started running after lunch, at about 1.30 p.m, so that families could attend church services in the morning without the noise of traffic.'

The food Eva had to get used to. She describes it as very bland. 'Everything was either boiled in a lot of water or fried in lots of fat. I missed the food that I was used to eating but could not find it any-where. Even the coffee came in bottles as essence.'

And evenings she found boring. 'I was used to going out in the evening when the city of Tel Aviv was just coming alive. But here in Adelaide we returned home for the evening meal which was the main meal of the day and then the city was dead. We used to sit around the radio and listen to different serials. It took me a while to get used to the Australian way of speaking and their plain food, also their sense of humour.' She was also surprised to find the women of Australia dressing in their best clothes to shop in the city – not something the inhabitants of Tel Aviv did. She was a foreigner and the insular nature of the Australians of the time was apparent. Many of the people she met had no idea where Palestine was.

Eva's husband, Milton (Jim) returned to Australia with the last of the Australian and New Zealand troops on the *Andes*. In the middle of October 1945 Eva waited on the front porch of the family home from early morning for her husband's return. 'It had been two years and ten months since we said good bye and Ray had been two months old. In ten days he would be three years old and Milton had missed all his babyhood and saw in front of him a real grown independent boy. Now making Ray speak to his picture every day paid off as he recognised him as Daddy and took to him straight away.'

Once the war was over, news of the concentration camps and the Holocaust reached Australia. 'We had heard about it, and in the newsreel at the pictures we saw the horror of the concentration camps,' writes Eva. 'Now also through letters from home I heard that my father's younger brother and his wife from Kepno (Kempen) were killed, also his youngest sister Rifkah Frankfurter and her husband, a rabbi who lived in Yugoslavia, were killed as soon as the Germans entered that country. Also killed were the husband and little son and daughter of their daughter Ruth who was incarcerated in a prison and suffered greatly. My mother also lost her brothers in the Holocaust.'

Towards the end of the war, Ora Kaminer was walking down a road in Tel Aviv with a friend when two Aussies – 'big mischievous boys!' – came up and started a conversation. 'They picked us up,' reminisces Ora. 'We lived on the top of a hill in Tel Aviv and if anyone wanted you they didn't walk up the hill, they would stand at the bottom and whistle.' Edgar Bert Scutter the Aussie Ora had just met joined the whistlers. At the time Ora worked in a bank and she spoke English because it had been compulsory to learn it when she had been at commercial school.

Ora and Eddie, as she soon came to call him, wanted to get married but while she was under twenty-one her parents refused their permission.

Ora (right), Eddie and friend in Palestine

Ora was an only daughter and her parents did not want her to leave Palestine. When she did turn twenty-one they married immediately. They had only just known each other nine months, and Eddie was about to be sent back to Australia, so it was a hasty marriage. They spent the next three weeks living in a single room and then Eddie left for Australia and Ora moved back with her parents to await her passage to Australia.

Ora was not given any warning of when that would be and was told to have her clothes ready at all times. From Tel Aviv she went by train to the port, Tofic, where she stayed in an army camp until it was time to embark. The *Port Charmer* was a merchant ship and the passengers, three war brides and one child, were given one cabin in the officers' quarters. They sailed directly to Fremantle then onto Port Pirie and to Adelaide by rail.

Ora Scutter's Australian family were not welcoming. Eddie and Ora settled in Renmark. Here Eddie worked for his mother growing grapes and she drank the final product – 'his family were such drunks,' remembers Ora. Life was hard. Soon Eddie was knocked over in a hit-and-run accident and was unable to work. With no social security Ora and Eddie depended on Eddie's mother for board and a weekly two-pound hand-out to buy cigarettes. By this time Ora had given birth to their first child.

Eventually the couple moved to Adelaide to stay with Norm Wilson, a friend of Eddie's. Ora worked, first in Woolworths and then at another department store, providing the only income for the three of them. Ora found the friend an abusive drunk, though she never complained to Eddie because she knew they had nowhere else to live. It was only when her husband heard him calling her a whore and prostitute and the men had a fight that they

Ora & Eddie Scutter

moved. They moved to a little fruit shop that provided one-room accommodation at the back and from there their luck improved.

Switzerland – a neutral sanctuary

In 1939 Switzerland declared itself a neutral country and threatened to blow up the Alpine tunnels if this neutrality was breached. It remained neutral throughout the war, becoming the spy centre of Europe with the Americans basing themselves in Geneva and the Russians centring their operations on Lucerne. It was also a magnet for escapees of all nationalities.

Australians were amongst escapees who, with the help of locals in the surrounding countries, made their way successfully to the safe haven of Switzerland. One researcher has estimated that 420 Australians saw out the war in Switzerland, and that there were fourteen marriages between Australians and Swiss women or women living in Switzerland.[3] Most of these men had escaped from POW camps. They arrived dressed in all manner of clothing but rarely in uniform – if they did they were interned, otherwise they lived in the local communities.

Hedy Schäfli was one Swiss girl who fell in love with an Aussie on the run. Ted Triffett was an Aussie army officer who had escaped from a POW camp in Italy into Switzerland. In 1943 Hedy was helping in her sister's restaurant in the village of Elgg when Ted came in to arrange for twenty-eight soldiers to eat their meals there daily. The restaurant did not have to prepare the meals, just provide a place and utensils. These men were escaped POWs who the little village of Elgg had agreed to accommodate. For almost a year Ted and his men ate in the restaurant

Hedy & Ted on wedding day

and he and Hedy found they were in love. They got engaged but Hedy did not want to marry until the war was over. Then in November 1944 the men were recalled to England. In August 1945 Ted returned to Switzerland and Hedy met him in Geneva. 'I hardly recognised him, he had lost so much weight,' Hedy writes. Ted and Hedy went to stay with Hedy's parents in Aadorf. Once they knew that Ted would be leaving for Australia from England on the *Aquitania* on 15 September, hasty wedding arrangements were made.

Leaving home, writes Hedy, 'was very sad, heart-wrenching. Furthermore, not knowing where I was going had that added element of risk. However it was also exciting to be with my husband, heading for a completely new country where everything would be so different, even the language.' Hedy's brother Jack was not so convinced and as she was leaving whispered in her ear that it was not too late to change her mind – but Hedy's mind was made up.

They took a train from Switzerland to Paris – standing room only and no food available apart from the sandwiches that Hedy had made. In Paris they had to spend their first night in the railway station because accommodation was so scarce. Then the newly-weds decided to see the sights and arranged with a porter to mind their luggage. Hedy tells of incidents which highlight the drastic shortage of everyday goods. She remembers that when they collected their luggage from the porter she gave him a reel of white cotton and the porter thanked her on bended knees. He told her that his wife had not been able to mend anything for years and that she would be delighted. Another time, Ted threw down a cigarette butt at the entrance to a Paris railway line and three men ran to grab it – Ted gave each of them a few cigarettes. Living in neutral Switzerland Hedy had been protected from the damage the war had done and she was shocked by the bombed ruins.

It was when they reached London that they realised that they would not be able to travel to Australia on the same ship. Ted left behind a pregnant Hedy living with a friend in Cornwall. It was not until August 1946, three months after her daughter Susan was born, that Hedy was given passage on the *Stirling Castle*. This was the trip mentioned by some of the English war brides which was notable because of the presence of the English cricket team. Hedy enjoyed the trip, though baby Susan suffered from heat rash and breastfeeding was not easy.

After a brief stopover in Fremantle, Hedy and Susan disembarked in Sydney where they were met by her aunt and sister-in-law as Ted was working very far north on the Gulf of Carpentaria. The trip from Sydney to Brisbane was by steam train. 'Very slow in comparison to what I was used to in Switzerland, where we had electric trains,' remembers Hedy. In Brisbane they were met by Ted's mother and three sisters. Two days later their journey recommenced and they flew from Brisbane to Townsville, followed by a two-day train journey on another steam train to Julia Creek. At Julia Creek they were met by Hedy's father-in-law who said, 'I will look after you my girl'. 'The most wonderful words of welcome,' Hedy remembers. It was not until the next day that Ted arrived from the bush. 'I hardly recognised him in his bush uniform. I almost felt like a stranger at first,' said Hedy.

Ahead of her was the task of learning to live in the hot outback of Australia with few luxuries or even conveniences after the totally different climate and culture of her native Switzerland. Hedy coped extremely well until five years later when after the death of a baby and her own severe illness Ted moved his family to a house in Toowoomba. He continued to work in the far north for eight months of the year and the family spent holidays together.

Japan

The first soldiers who arrived to occupy Japan at the end of August 1945 were Americans – 430 000 of them. Australian servicemen began to arrive in February 1946 as part of the British Commonwealth Occupation Forces (BCOF). There were around 11 000 and they were stationed around Kure, about forty kilometres from Hiroshima. They stayed for nearly ten years both as part of the BCOF and the British Commonwealth Forces, Korea (BCFK). From the very beginning the Commonwealth authorities had an anti-fraternisation policy that instructed soldiers that they should be formal and correct in their dealings with Japanese people and not enter their homes.[4]

Cherry, whose Japanese name is Nobuko Sakuramoto, met her husband Gordon Parker at an ex-Japanese naval camp in 1946. So many Japanese women found it difficult to get employment in their country which had been ravaged by war, they took whatever was available. Many Japanese women found that without their menfolk they had to assume the role of family breadwinner, and part of this break with tradition found many young Japanese women moving away from home in order to earn money to send home. Nobuko had a friend who had a job at the camp and she introduced her to a well-paid job in First Aid. At first she was frightened of the loud, brash Westerners but it was here that she met Gordon, who gave her the name of Cherry.

They married early in 1948, not without going through an enormous amount of red tape with the authorities. Then Gordon returned to Australia to resume his studies – alone. At this time, Australian law did not allow Japanese people to enter the country. In 1948 Arthur Calwell, the Immigration Minister, had ruled that no Japanese women (including 'half-castes') would be allowed to enter Australia. It was not until four years later that Calwell lifted this ban[5] and this was probably largely due to intensive lobbying by Gordon and wide newspaper coverage. Cherry Parker was the first Japanese war bride to arrive in Australia in 1952. Gordon's family was welcoming but they did suffer verbal attacks from outsiders who did not approve.

Michiyo (Mitsy) Iwakuni met Michael Ronald Wintersun at a dance in her hometown of Yanai, two hours from Hiroshima in 1950. Michael had come to Yanai to look around and stayed at Mitsy's grandmother's hotel. While he was there he went to the dance which was to change his and Mitsy's life. Mitsy spoke a little English, which she now describes as 'pidgin' and Michael a smattering of Japanese. Despite these communication problems their relationship grew.

Before Michael was sent to Korea in 1952 he proposed. The decision for Mitsy was a difficult one. Her family's reaction was 'horrible, awful', she remembers. She was forced to sneak out to meet him and the family tried to persuade her that this was not a good marriage, saying all her children would be 'half-castes' for a start. Michael's family was in England and Mitsy does not remember any adverse reaction – though this is not to say there wasn't any as many folk still saw these marriages as 'fraternising with the enemy'.

However, roughly two years later when Michael returned to Japan, he and Mitsy married.

Being allowed to live in Australia was another matter.

Mitsy remembers that there was a great deal of paperwork to go through. The Australian authorities were 'very helpful, but harsh'. Her papers had to be checked by the police at Yanai before permisssion could be granted.

Michael arrived in Australia before Mitsy who arrived on the *Changi* in 1954. Mitsy knew nothing about Australia and her mother had said to her before she left, 'If you arrive in Sydney and he is not there, stay on the boat!' However Michael was there and they were reunited. Not long after there was a welcome party. 'Everyone was friendly,' remembers Mitsy 'and it was at the RSL!'

Mitsy's first impressions of Australia were of a vast countryside and of people 'wiping flies off themselves'. At first she thought they were waving to her (as did quite a few war brides who arrived at the height of the Australian summer).

When the first Japanese war brides arrived in Australia they were amongst a huge wave of post-war European immigration to Australia. Australians expected them to blend in with Australian society and the Japanese women likewise were expected to be able to adapt to their husband's world. Many of them adopted anglicised or English first names and most of their children were given English-sounding names.

Even though Australia decided to allow Japanese war brides into the country in 1952 it was not as permanent citizens. They were granted five-year temporary visas. By 1956, however, the rules had changed and they could become Australian citizens – which many of them did.

Sadako Kikuchi was a dressmaker in Kure in 1946 when she met John Morris who was a signaller in the army. He asked her while she was at work if she would meet him later, saying he would be at the bridge. 'I didn't want to go so I went to a restaurant with a girlfriend,' said Sadako, who is now known as Jane, 'but he was still on the bridge. I felt sorry

John & Sadako (Jane) Morris

for him so I let him walk me home.' Although at that time a Japanese woman walking with a member of the Occupation forces was not acceptable to either the Japanese or the Australian authorities. In fact it was this which led Jane to take John home to her parents' house. Jane said, 'I told a lie, I told them he had got lost.' From then Jane and John saw each other regularly.

At first Jane's parents were not concerned but after a while they became worried. Jane was only eighteen and her parents did not want her to marry a foreigner and go to live a long way from home.

It was not until 1952, when the ban was lifted on Japanese being allowed into Australia, that John proposed and the couple married in Japan. Jane's parents were still not happy about the relationship. Her father had been very angry when she told him she wanted to marry John.

By the time they left for Australia they had a daughter, June. Jane and June left Kobe on the *Changi* in December 1953 and a week or so later John flew home. He was there to meet her when she arrived. What did she notice first when she arrived in Sydney? 'White people everywhere', was Jane's reply. She had left behind a large loving family and come to Adelaide where there was no Japanese food, not even a fish shop. Her husband's stepmother taught her to cook and shop and she chose to stay with her husband's family for six months so she could learn Australian ways, even though John had saved enough money for them to buy a house.

Mitsuko (Mitsy) Aoyama was working in the house of an American family in Tokyo – where the daughter had married an Australian colonel – when she met her husband, Clyde Hollow. He was the colonel's driver and one day she went with the daughter by car from Tokyo to Kure where most of the Australian troops were stationed. That was the beginning of their relationship. There were not many Australians in Tokyo. It was mainly occupied by American GIs and the colonel had suggested to Mitsy that she might go out with a GI, although his wife was against it.

It was 1951. Mitsy was twenty-one and Clyde was twenty-nine. Not long after they met, Clyde was sent to Korea, where he was stationed for eleven months. Mitsy says she does not remember Clyde asking her to marry him; it was more of an understanding when he left for Korea that they would marry one day. They married in Kure in 1952.

Mitsy's parents were not alive, but her sister and brother were. Her brother who had been in the Japanese army fighting in China, was not happy about his sister's marriage to an Australian. But her sister's husband told her that it didn't matter who she married as long as she was happy and she worked at a happy marriage.

In 1953 Clyde was ordered back to Australia. By this time the couple had a son who was one year old. They sailed to Australia as a family on the *Taipin* in the same year.

When they arrived they spent two weeks in Sydney then boarded a train to Broken Hill, where Clyde's mother lived. Mitsy remembers the train trip vividly. 'Nothing but paddocks,' she said, 'just like an American cowboy picture! Nothing there!'

Broken Hill in the 1950s would have been quite a culture shock for a Japanese girl from Tokyo – and the residents from Broken Hill would no doubt have found her most exotic. However Mitsy made the best of it and decided that if her son was to talk to his cousin he would have to learn to speak English, not Japanese, so she began to speak to him in 'broken English'. Her husband Clyde said to her, 'Always speak English, doesn't matter if it is broken English it's still English,' so she did. Today she regrets that she did not teach her children Japanese but realises that at the time Australian children did not speak other languages – everyone was expected to speak English.

She was also not as dismayed at the Australian food and the lack of familiar ingredients as many of the other war brides. Her time working for an American family in Tokyo had accustomed her to Western food.

Ayako Wakabayashi was working as an assistant in a gift shop owned by a Japanese. She met Ron Cameron when a friend brought him into the shop. Ron invited Ayako to a movie and, she says, 'I think it was love at first sight but Ron always laughs when I say that'.

Ron & Ayako, 1946

For six months they saw each other regularly before they began to talk about the possibility of getting married. 'There was no "going down on one knee" type of proposal,' said Ayako. 'It was over dinner at a restaurant called Gastronome that Ron asked me to marry him.'

Ayako was the youngest of six children and both her parents had died when she was young, so she lived with one of her brothers. The family already knew Ron and Ayako found she did not have much difficulty talking them around to agreeing to her marriage. 'They told me that they couldn't guarantee me happiness if I married a Japanese man and lived in Japan. I must admit that when talking to each brother I intimated that the other brothers did not object – not quite a fib,' she admitted. 'After much talking it was agreed that it was up to me.' Though one of Ayako's old aunts did advise her to put aside a little money each payday in case she wanted to come home.

Ron & Ayako's wedding

Ayako's friends were happy with her decision. 'I believe that the older people did not approve of these relationships,' said Ayako, 'but we were young, the soldiers were young, these were enlightened days never before seen in Japan.'

Ron and Ayako decided that they would not tell Ron's parents until shortly before the wedding – 'to avoid any upset ... Ron's mother was not happy. His father's attitude was very different and Ron seems to think that was because his father spent four years of World War I in the army in Egypt and saw it from the soldier's point of view.' Her mother-in-law's disapproval did not last, however, once Ayako and her daughter were in Australia.

The authorities were the only real obstacle Ayako and Ron encountered. Once they applied to marry, Ron was sent away from Kure to Tokyo. His absence lasted six weeks, after which there were many forms to fill in and interviews to attend. 'Any criminal record in my family would have put an end to my application,' remembers Ayako. Ron's religion was Catholic and Ayako decided that she would take instruction in his religion before they were married. She joined the church before the wedding and it was celebrated with a nuptial mass in October 1954.

In July 1955 Ayako gave birth to the couple's first child and later that year they decided that is was time the family moved to Australia. Ron flew ahead and Ayako and baby Janet arrived in Australia on the SS *Taipin* in January 1956. They were met by Ron and his family.

As with other Japanese brides, Ayako found the change of diet and the unavailability of Japanese food one of the most difficult things to get used to.

These women have positive stories to tell of their marriages to Australian servicemen, but they were not all like that. In her book *Michi's Memories: The Story of a Japanese War Bride*, Keiko Tamura tells the story of Michi, whose marriage to an Australian was a struggle from the time she set foot on Australian soil. Michi's Australian husband was not the caring family man that so many Aussies who married Japanese women were, and her life in this strange country was an uphill battle – it was ten years before she learnt English. It is nonetheless an uplifting story and gives a great insight into a time when the arrival of a Japanese war bride into Australian society was unusual – and often not welcomed by other Australians.

THE
VIETNAM
WAR

CHAPTER 11
Three Love Stories of the Vietnam War

A time for us some day there'll be.
When chains are torn by courage born of a love that's free.
A time when dreams so long denied
can flourish as we unveil the love we now must hide.
At time for us at last to see
a life worthwhile for you and me.

By the outbreak of the Vietnam War, Vietnam had been a country in turmoil for many years. In the nineteenth century it was part of the French empire in South-East Asia and during the Second World War it was invaded by the Japanese. When the Vietnamese leader Ho Chi Minh declared Vietnam an independent country at the end of the war the French returned to reclaim their colony. The French fight against Vietnamese guerillas lasted ten years – until the French were defeated in 1954 at the battle of Dien Bien Phu. From then on Vietnam was divided into North and South with Ho Chi Minh ruling a communist regime from the northern capital of Hanoi and President Diem, the leader in the democratic south.

The decision to divide Vietnam into North and South was taken at an international conference in Geneva, Switzerland. At the same time the conference decided that elections should be held with the aim of uniting the two Vietnams. These elections did not take place. The United States, which was backing the government of Diem in the south, was afraid that Ho Chi Minh would win the elections and unify the country under a communist regime. For this reason they sent in aid and advisers.

At the beginning of the 1960s civil war broke out between North and South. Diem's government did little for the people of South Vietnam and opposition to his government, in the form of the National Liberation Front (Vietcong), grew. US President Kennedy increased American support by sending 700 advisers to South Vietnam in 1961 to try to fight the political troubles in the country and the Vietcong. In 1963 Diem was shot when his government was overthrown and by this time there were 16 000 American troops in the country. In 1964 the new American president, Lyndon B. Johnson, increased the American presence to 22 000 troops.

In 1962 Australia began sending troops to Vietnam in support of the USA, an ally since the Japanese attack on Pearl Harbor and the subsequent surrender of Singapore to the Japanese in 1942. Conscription (known as National Service) was introduced in 1964. Between 1962 and 1972 over 46 000 Australians – men and women – served in the Vietnam War, and over 17 000 of the men were conscripts.

Democracy was the ideal that the USA and its allies claimed to be fighting for in Vietnam, and the Vietcong (a word coined for Vietnamese communists) and communists invading from the North were the enemies. But the coverage given to the events of the war by the Western press and television reports did not justify the claims of the US and its allies, including Australia. It also became clear that the longer the war continued the more likely it was that the US would end up at war with China, a country the Americans suspected was supporting the North Vietnamese. When Richard Nixon became President of the USA in 1969 he set about extricating the USA from the Vietnam War.

By the early '70s many Australians objected not only to the war but also to the conscription of young men to fight in it. In 1971 Australia began to withdraw from the conflict. The

Tuyet in traditional dress

war was not won, but international and domestic opinion was against further involvement.

Phil Coen first arrived in Vietnam in 1968 as part of the regular army. He worked as an interpreter, having done a year's course in Vietnamese in Australia in 1967. While based in Saigon (now Ho Chi Minh City), Phil met Tuyet, a telephone operator. 'I had a [Vietnamese] girlfriend who was one of the clerical assistants in the headquarters. She came from North Vietnam and was a 1954 refugee. [The other girls] used to dislike this young lady intensely. She had a gammy leg but it was mainly her voice that used to drive them up the wall. Whenever these girls heard me talking to my girlfriend on the phone they would find any excuse to interrupt me.' Then Phil was asked to be an interpreter of a different kind. 'A friend sent Tuyet a copy of John O'Grady's book, *Aussie English*, and the girls on the switchboard pored over this but couldn't understand a word of it. Eventually they got to thinking they'd ask that interpreter bloke upstairs because it was a waste of time asking another Vietnamese – and that's how Tuyet and I met.'

Phil and Tuyet found they enjoyed each other's company and spent more and more time together until Tuyet's father told her to keep away from foreigners. This had the opposite effect and Tuyet and Phil con-

tinued to meet and to go for rides on Phil's motorbike. Phil has fond memories of his little Honda PC49, which he left to his prospective father-in-law when they left Vietnam, and was disappointed when he heard it had been sold.

Wanting to spend more time with Tuyet, Phil asked for an extension of his stay in Vietnam. However, when he was told the only position open for him was in Nui Dat, two hours drive away from Tuyet, he was not happy. 'I thought, well, that's the sharp end and that's the end of any romantic illusions one might have, so I said no.' The authorities were not happy about Phil's relationship with a

Phil & Tuyet's wedding day

Vietnamese woman and in the end he decided to return to Australia and sponsor Tuyet as his fiancée to join him. 'If I had applied to get married in Vietnam it would have been extremely difficult. Within a couple of months she was here and we had three months to get married.'

This was 1969. Meanwhile Phil had signed a document in which he agreed that he would help Tuyet to stay if they decided not to marry once she had arrived in Australia. 'She was just like any other fiancée, this was part of the immigration process,' Phil remembered.

Having been involved with other Australians who had wanted to marry Vietnamese, Phil was sure that his approach was the easy way. 'I had had quite a bit to do with some of these girls who were marrying Australians, because of my role as interpreter, and some of them I quite disapproved of!' he said. 'These girls had made up their minds and I felt sorry for the husband, they had no idea what they were getting themselves into. The men spoke next to no Vietnamese, the brides spoke what we used to call "servants' language".'

Phil remembers one case which he felt was a mistake: 'It was the first interpreting job I did in Vietnam. This fellow was all over the TV trying to get his Vietnamese wife to Australia. He accused everyone and everybody of putting barriers in his way. She was in her late thirties and he was about twenty-two, all she was looking for was a better life.'

He does not blame the Vietnamese women for taking this path. 'They saw Australians and Americans as very similar. In the back of their minds they thought Australia must be like America, land of John Wayne...land of opportunity,' he said. Most of the girls the Aussies met were prostitutes or bar girls, not many were in respectable employment.

Ralph Schwer was also an army interpreter in Vietnam. In May 1970 he found himself on an American airforce base getting drunk. Said Ralph, 'About two weeks earlier I had received a letter from a brother in Sydney saying that my father had lung cancer and was dying. My father was old already when I was young, but this letter was completely out of the blue.' His unit commander arranged for Ralph to go home for five days and it was on his return from this visit that Ralph ended up on the American airforce base on the outskirts of Saigon. Here he was to spend the night so after being allocated a bed, he went off the the Airmen's Club – 'a hanger-sized concrete block building that had no windows and was dimly lit inside, something Americans seem to prefer in their bars.

'The huge, surly black sergeant managing the club didn't seem to want me to drink at the bar, so I found an empty table. There were a lot of pretty Vietnamese waitresses...when an attractive waitress asked if I wanted another beer I said yes. We had a short chat in Vietnamese and she astonished me by speaking in the clearest, most perfect Hanoi dialect I had heard since leaving language school. Hanoi dialect,' Ralph explained, 'is to Vietnamese what BBC English is to English.'

Ralph found the waitress appealing and this, together with the emotional roller coaster he was experiencing over his father's illness, led to one beer following another. Before he left the bar he asked the waitress to write down her name. The next day Ralph and his hangover went back to base at Nui Dat, two hours by road from the base in Saigon. Ralph now had to work out how he was going to get back to Saigon to see the enchanting waitress. It was not long before he had worked out a strategy for weekend leave which had the approval of his commanding officer.

His tent mate, Andy, was the unit clerk and he arranged to book Ralph on the Wallaby Flight. This was a Caribou transport plane which flew a circular route twice a day from Nui Dat to Saigon to Vung Tau and back to Nui Dat. So on his weekends off Ralph could fly to Saigon on Saturday afternoon and be back in Nui Dat by Monday morning. Said Ralph, 'So began my courtship of Nguyen thi Thuy.'

Ralph's memories of the young Thuy are vivid: 'She was nineteen years old and beautiful. She stood 142 centimetres tall, had brown eyes, jet black hair worn short in a fashionable hairstyle and fair skin inherited from her French great-grandfather. Her figure was very curvaceous, which was unusual for Vietnamese women. She wore red lipstick and dressed very smartly in miniskirts for work. To go to the local market she wore a casual *bo do bo* or a *bo ba ba*, rather like western pyjamas, sometimes with a conical grass hat. She always looked best of all when she wore her Vietnamese national dress, the beautiful, flowing *ao dai* for going downtown.'

Thuy worked at the American airforce base because it paid well and she needed the income to help support her family – she was the eldest of nine children in a Catholic family.

Thuy was born in Tan Thuong village in North Vietnam. In the first Indo–China war, which lasted from 1947 to 1954, Thuy's father fought with the French against the Viet Minh. The French were defeated. The Viet Minh was formed when nationalist groups united under one banner to fight for the independence of Vietnam from both France and Japan and by 1945 this group was dominated by the communist movement. In 1954 the family joined the huge exodus to the south of Catholics, who opposed the Viet Minh. Ralph recalls that 'the family stayed in Da Nang for around eight years, with the children going to school and the father being called up into the army of the new, American-sponsored, South Vietnamese government. As the [Vietnam] war heated up, the family moved to a Catholic village, Tan Son Nhi, on the edge of Saigon.' Here the family raised pigs and grew vegetables. Thuy's father, after being discharged from the army joined an American road construction crew and was rarely at home.

Thuy and Ralph saw each other every week:

I went up to Saigon on Thuy's day off and we went out somewhere. To the zoo on the edge of the Saigon River where the animals were very, very poorly looked after, though no-one seemed to notice; to the Rex Cinema in the middle of town, where the odd grenade had been tossed in during the period leading up to the Tet Offensive in early 1968; Saigon Central Market, Cho Ben Thanh, was a popular spot both for Thuy to do her shopping, and for us to sit and watch the world go by over iced drinks.

On these excursions Thuy would walk so far behind me sometimes that I couldn't see her. This avoided impolite comments from people who didn't approve of Vietnamese women accompanying Westerners, assuming that any Vietnamese woman with a foreigner must be a prostitute. Thuy would tell me where to stop to catch the bus, she would meet me there, and then we'd get on the bus together. If there were few other passengers it was possible to talk, but if the bus was full we sat quietly and kept an eye out for pickpockets who preyed on passengers in crowded buses.

Ralph and Thuy would also visit Thuy's family:

We would catch a little three-wheel bus, jam-packed with passengers on the bench seats down the sides and hanging off the step at the back

entrance. Then we'd walk a kilometre through alleys and across rice paddies to her village. As we approached the village, the children from the
village would see us and start a chant, '*Ong My, Ong My* – American,
American'. Other children would come and see this sight, so that by the
time we got to Thuy's house there would be 200 children and a dozen
adults following us. Fortunately they were there for the fun of it and
didn't bother us.

Once at the house, Thuy's mother was always so polite, and would
offer me snacks and drinks and treat me royally. Sometimes Thuy's mater-
nal grandmother, *ba ngoai*, would also be visiting. Grandmother lived
two or three kilometres closer to town with one of her sons and his
family. She had come from a wealthy, land owning family in the north,
but did not put on any airs and graces and was always in the best of
good humour. After refreshments Thuy and I would often go for a stroll
with Thuy's younger brothers and sisters from their house along the
unpaved dirt street to the end of the village. There the children would
point across the rice paddies to the distant banana groves and say, "There
are VC there, we can't go any further".'

Thuy lived with a friend in a flat in Lang Cha Ca, just outside the
airforce base. It was easier and safer for Thuy to get to work from here.
Thuy's flatmate was very much in love with an American serviceman
who had returned to the States. Ralph recalls:

She had his letters and his combat jacket, on which she rested her head
to sleep and used to dry her tears, remembering him every day. Her
parents forced her into an arranged marriage to a village boy down in
the Mekong Delta. She went through the Buddhist wedding ceremony,
but returned immediately to Saigon to avoid having to sign the papers
to make the marriage a legal fact. She also avoided her wedding feast,
dam cuoi, without which the villagers would not recognise the marriage
according to custom. So she wasn't legally married, but the Buddhist ceremony was enough to keep her parents off her back.

By September 1971, when the Australian government began to withdraw its troops from Vietnam, Ralph had decided that he wanted to marry
Thuy. However Thuy was not so sure.

She said, 'I like you very much, but I can't leave my family. I work to help my family and they need my income. I can't marry you.' I understood her situation, there was nothing I could do. I spent the next week back at base feeling very sad indeed. I could talk only with my two tent mates and accept their comforting commiserations. When I met Thuy the next weekend, she quietly said that she had spoken to her family and that they had given her permission to marry me. I was so happy, I couldn't believe my ears.

However Ralph's relationship with Thuy was not to continue on its smooth path. He had a new commanding officer who was not happy about his men fraternising with Vietnamese women. He stopped Ralph's regular trips to Saigon until Ralph persuaded him that he needed to mix with the locals in order to practise the language. But there was more trouble to come once Ralph advised his CO that he wanted to marry while overseas:

First the CO referred me to the padre (in accordance with the regulations). Then I asked permission to go to Saigon to discuss with Thuy the issues that the padre had raised, including possible language problems, discrimination, and cultural differences. Thuy still wanted to marry, and I again informed the CO of our intentions. He instantly withdrew my security clearance and informed me not to come to work again. I knew he wasn't kidding, but what was I to do with myself in the middle of a rubber plantation in Vietnam? 'Just wait in your tent,' he said.

What happened a few days later was totally unexpected. To try and prevent me from marrying, the CO arranged to have me posted to an infantry battalion which was returning to Australia in three weeks time. He informed me of my impending posting at ten o'clock at night. At one o'clock in the morning I showed him my response, which was a letter to the Minister of Defence stating the simple facts of the situation and asking that he intercede on my behalf so that I could stay in Vietnam long enough to marry the woman I loved. The CO looked uncomfortable and asked me not to send the letter yet. Three days later I was posted to Australian Headquarters, Saigon, where the Administration Officer kindly offered, 'If anyone bothers you about getting married, just come and see me.' I had no problems after that.

Ralph and Thuy were now free to organise with the Migration Consul at the Australian Embassy to witness the marriage and to arrange Thuy's passport and exit visa from Vietnam. Thuy's uncle, who was deputising for her absent father, also wanted Ralph to become a Catholic. Ralph visited a local priest

Ralph & Thuy in Australia, 1972

who accepted that since Ralph was Church of England and prepared to raise any children as Catholics that was enough. The marriage went ahead with 'what looked like the whole village of Tan Son Nhi' at the wedding party and a few of Ralph's friends from the base.

Ralph and Thuy moved into a flat not far from Australian headquarters until they decided to move to Australia. Ralph remembers one incident where he nearly frightened the life out of his landlady who 'almost fainted on me the first day when I appeared with my SLR rifle in my hand'. She recovered enough to cook the newlyweds a curry for Christmas lunch. On 28 February 1972 Ralph and Thuy left Saigon together bound for Australia. An incident at the airport as they left has stayed with Ralph. 'Because it was the last flight the officer in command of Australian forces in Vietnam came to the airport to farewell us. He walked along a long line of 200-odd troops shaking hands and wishing each of them well until he got to us three Australian soldiers with our Vietnamese wives. He then turned his back on us and walked away.'

When they reached Australia Ralph's family was there to greet them, including Ralph's mother who had suffered a stroke and was unable to speak. She hugged Thuy and the entire family welcomed the couple with a party.

John H was conscripted into the Australian army in 1966. He describes himself as 'a rather too doctrinal Catholic, not a little influenced by the DLP' (the Catholic Democratic Labor Party).[1] John remembers the DLP as running 'crude propaganda commercials depicting Australia being descended upon and devoured by Asian Communism'.

Vung Tau bar girls, 1971

He enjoyed the army training and when he had finished, volunteered for a language aptitude test. In January 1967 he found himself in the army's one-year intensive language course learning Vietnamese. In April 1968 he was placed in a secret unit located on the edge of Luscombe airstrip in Nui Dat, Vietnam. There were four in the team. However, John found the army intimidating. He had only been in Vietnam for two days when, he says, 'I was told by a soldier in the unit how one of my predecessors allegedly took off in a chopper carrying two tight-lipped VC prisoners and landed with only one who had a lot to say. I hoped this would not happen during our tour...'

Every fortnight or so John joined others on a trip to Vung Tau:

Ostensibly this was to take the unit's clothing for cleaning [but also] to have a few beers, perhaps a swim, or to visit local brothels. Often on these trips we went to the Beachcomber, a Hawaiian-style US services recreation spot where you could sip beers, play the US jukebox, eat and be waited on by local Vietnamese female employees. This was a legitimate club as opposed to the Back Beach bars and their hookers. I got to know two of the workers, Mui and Mai. It was a chance to practise my Vietnamese and to talk to female company between their serving customers.

John fell in love with Vietnam 'for its beauty, its climate, the simplicity of life, the language, and the people. The facts of the war, as opposed to the DLP propaganda, ground me down. There were stories of torture and massacres involving US, Australian, and communist (VC and NVA) forces. I found it increasingly difficult to defend our involvement and found it even more disturbing when everyone else considered this irrelevant.' He found Vung Tau to be a place where he could observe the Vietnamese and forget about the war. He also found he was constantly drawn to the Beachcomber and to Mai, one of the workers:

She was lovely. She had an inner stillness and we enjoyed each other's company.

One long afternoon, keeping the beers up just enough to hold my nerve, I eventually spoke at length to Mai about marriage and Australia. It was a subtle conversation, hypothetical, full of 'ifs'. Basically, what would Mai feel if I were to ask her to marry me? How would she feel about coming to Australia where reactions to Vietnamese people may be prejudiced and racist? As long as she was with me it would be all OK, she said. I did not propose; I had to think hard about what I would be asking a young Vietnamese woman, the oldest daughter whose father was permanently disabled and bed-ridden from war injuries: to leave her family. She understood that the conversation would go on.

That evening John waited for Mai and together they took a crowded Vespa taxi to Mai's family home.

There was a lot of chatter and giggling about an Australian going home with a Vietnamese. I hoped they did not misconstrue the relationship and damage Mai's reputation.

Mai took me to an old, French colonial mansion that housed numbers of sick and disabled people. We went in to where her father lay. 'A sniper's shot. Up on the border,' he said, smiling, shaking my hand and accepting me as a fellow soldier. Mai's mother and brother were there having brought the evening meal. I was made very welcome. Mai's mother apologised that another daughter was not present and suggested disapprovingly that her daughter may have been 'playing up'. Mai looked shame-faced when her sister arrived later full of 'Hi, GI' patter.

We spoke of life, the war, the suffering. But there was no pessimism in all this, despite the electric lamp which yellowed each time the local supply faltered, the crowding, the prospect of Mai's father being a permanent victim of the war at age thirty. Eventually, the family took their leave to make their way home and I said goodbye and headed back to the Badcoe Club for sleep.

John's pleasure in his relationship with Mai was not shared by his superior officers however and soon John found himself in trouble. It was not long before he discovered that his captain had his own agenda. What followed next completely changed John's attitude to the army – and his relationship with Mai.

I was working in the office when the captain entered, fixed me with an uncharacteristically grave look and told me he wanted a word in an adjoining room. He proceeded to accuse me of being engaged to a Vietnamese national who was probably a Viet Cong spy along with her family. He said that intelligence sources had been contacted and US intelligence had no record of Mai being employed by the American Army which ran the Beachcomber. There was no security clearance for her. He expressed concern that I could be compromised. In the space of a minute or so, the captain had portrayed me as a potential spy and traitor and Mai and her family as a lie and as the enemy.

I tried to explain we were not engaged and that Mai and her family were not VC and that I would never reveal what we did. But the captain was adamant. He claimed to be citing US and local police intelligence. The exchange became louder as I desperately fought to defend my integrity, my loyalty to the unit, and the fact I had revealed nothing of our highly secret work. The captain became more intense and led me away from the work hut out to the tent inside the compound where I slept.

Alone, the captain spoke as someone completely in charge. This was someone I had admired and trusted. He pursued the line that I might be a spy. He told me quietly with a gleam in his eye that if he wanted to, he could take me out to the perimeter and shoot me with his pistol. His hand rested on the butt of his side-arm. [The captain didn't stop there. The next thing he said to John made him feel particularly scared and helpless.] 'No one would ask any questions, we're in a war zone,' were his words. [He then went on to tell John that no one would ever find out what had happened to him.] The captain convinced me he had absolute power over me. I believed he could kill me if he wanted to. I was shattered too. I could never quite hate the enemy. I was, in fact, on the way to discovering I was a pacifist. But to paint me a collaborator with the VC was so unjust. After all, I had come to Vietnam believing the government's lie that we had been sent to help the Vietnamese.

John was so stunned he admits 'I don't know how this incident ended. The choice was clearly give up Mai or die. I had to let my feelings for Mai go.'

Now John found himself avoiding Mai, worried that the captain might make trouble for her. 'In South Vietnam, being reported as a suspect communist was sufficient to have you arrested, detained, tortured, jailed and end up dead. I was frightened attention of any kind could have disastrous consequences for Mai and her family.' But John never told Mai what had happened and she was left wondering why his attitude had changed so abruptly.

John's remaining time in Vietnam was not happy. He began to drink more and more. His sadness at the breakup with Mai was worsened by his own doubts about Australia's reasons for being in Vietnam. What his captain had to say when he spoke to him about his doubts was astonishing.

'We're not here to help the Vietnamese,' he had said. 'The only reason we're here is because it's good, cheap guerilla training and that's the only way we could defend Australia if we were ever taken over.'

'I gave up the ghost then,' said John. 'I hoped it would never happen that my mates would ever need to rely on me to defend them.'

John left Vietnam in May 1969.

Back in Australia he met Ralph Schwer who had just completed his language course and was going to Nui Dat to take over John's role. Then some months later he received a letter from Mai. She was puzzled about the way he left. John was confused, he was still unsure about whether Mai was the communist spy his captain had accused her of being. He was also puzzled about how she had got his address. When one of his mates at the boarding house where he was living suggested that Mai might be looking for an easy entry into Australia that was where he left it. At this time he was still in the army.

Eventually he received a letter from Ralph telling him that he was marrying a Vietnamese woman and also telling him that it was he who had given Mai the address in Australia.

John's experience in Vietnam made a lasting impression on him and affected the rest of his life – both personal and professional. It took a very long time for this relationship to be laid to rest in his mind and he would still like to know what happened to Mai.

APPENDICES

APPENDIX
What Happened After

Gonna take a sentimental journey
Gonna set my heart at ease
Gonna make a sentimental journey
To renew old memories

Adams   Mary and John Adams were reunited when the *Athlone Castle* docked in Melbourne in 1946. They first lived in Griffith, then moved to Eugowra where they raised two sons. Mary said what she missed most about England was 'the way of life. There was nothing to gain over here except John!' They have retired to the central coast of New South Wales.

Adcock   All I know about Garnett Adcock and his Belgian bride Marguerite is included in this account from material held by the Australian War Memorial, except that I did discover that they had one son.

Arnold   Barbara and Cedric Arnold now live in Western Australia. They had five children. Cedric stayed with the RAAF and the family followed him, living in places like Melbourne and at the Butterworth airforce base in Malaysia. Barbara has been home to Devon five times, on three occasions staying for twelve months.

Ashdown   Molly Barton met Brian Ashdown who was serving with the RAAF towards the end of the war when she went to London to 'chaperone' a friend who was going out with another Aussie. It was a whirlwind romance of six weeks at the end of which Brian proposed before he left to return home. Molly was unsure until she received Brian's first letter. She arrived on the *Asturias* at the end of 1946. Molly and Brian returned to the UK to live for three years. Brian died in 1967 at the age of forty-three, leaving Molly and two children.

Badcock Bill Badcock stayed in England to learn a trade in Farming and Saddlery. In 1920 after the birth of their first child, also called Bill, Bill and Violet Badcock left England on the *Bahia-Castilo* for Australia. They settled in Yuleba, north Queensland. They had seven children and later moved to Warwick Queensland. Violet died in August 1973. Her son, Bill, who wrote and talked about his mother's story, died in April 2001, before this book was completed.

Baker Rosa Baker, according to her daughter Coralie Welch, 'Grew to be more Australian than any of us with her delightful drawl and sunny smile. But it came as something of a shock to her some fifty-five years later when she applied for a passport to go back to London with her eldest daughter, to be handed a DP passport, and to find she was a Displaced Person – there was no Bohemia any more.' Rosa and Leo had five children and Rosa lived until she was 88.

Baulch Dorothy Willmer and her husband Wal Baulch met when he was stationed in Dorothy's home town of Eastbourne to assist repatriation of Australian prisoners of war from Europe and Dorothy was home on leave from the ATS. They married in the UK in June 1945. They have five children, nine grandchildren and one great-grandchild. Dorothy says she would not want to live in England again.

Bell Phyllis and Philip Bell married in Sydney in 1946. They had two children and now have three grandchildren. Phyllis admits to awful homesickness for Canada in the early years. 'After I had been here seven years and I had my children my husband sensed I was homesick so he saved enough money so I could go and see my parents with our children. I thought it was great. After about six weeks I realised it wasn't home and I couldn't get back quick enough.' Philip died in 1994.

Boyd Beryl and Trevior Boyd continued to move around the countryside with their young son, following work. They had two more children and eventually settled in Brisbane where they still live. Beryl often travels back to the UK, via other countries, but Trevior prefers to stay home. 'Sometimes I have felt that I would like to live in England, I still love the place,' writes Beryl, 'but as I have never been there for a winter since leaving in 1946, and having lived in Queensland for so long, I do not know if I could tolerate the cold.'

Bridgford Estelle and Keith had a second daughter, Jacqueline in 1947. Estelle has been a widow since 1973, 'Keith was a sick man due to war injuries for many years.' She has come to love Australia, though it took a while. 'I

must admit that when I first arrived I hated the areas my husband showed
me with such pride. The ground always looked dirty with little green showing. It took a trip back to England in 1956 to make me realise Australia
was a brown country.'

Bruton Daisy sailed to Australia on the *Otranto* and married Frederick Lance
Bruton in Brisbane in January 1947. They spent the years 1948 to 1950 in
Japan and had one child. Daisy has never been back to England because
her family, mother, father and two brothers migrated to Australia in 1948.
Daisy died in November 2000, before this book was completed.

Butterfield Hilary and Earle Butterfield settled in Wattle Park, Victoria where
they built their first house. They had two daughters and five grandsons.
Hilary says, 'On the whole I have been very happy in Australia but I do
absolutely hate the heat'.

Cameron Ayako and Ron Cameron have three children and four grandchildren
and live on the south coast of New South Wales. Ayako has been back to
Japan twice, the first time in 1964. Ayako has always felt welcome in
Australia. Ron admits that 'it is only of late that I too realised that I had to
do some changing in my behaviour in order to make a success of mixed
marriage. Strange how when we are young we do things with such confidence'.

Campion After the death of her husband, Eva Campion worked in Sydney
until 1922 when she met John Jackson, an Englishman from Cumbria, and
married him. Eva never returned to London. 'Although she always referred
to it as "home", [she] lived to a day short of her eighty-first birthday and
always kept her "Londoner's" accent,' writes daughter Ruth Reynolds.

Chard Yvonne and George Chard had three children in their home in
Adamstown near Newcastle, with the third born in 1950. Then George met
another woman and left his wife from Greece and their three children –
Yvonne and George divorced not long after and Yvonne brought up the
children alone. She worked with migrants and as an interpreter. Yvonne
died in January, 2001, aged seventy-five years.

Coen Phil and Tuyet Coen married in Sydney and have one daughter. They
went back to Vietnam in 1971 to visit Tuyet's parents and so she could see
how Vietnam had changed since she had left. 'And to show her father that
I wasn't mistreating her!' said Phil. Because the war was still on and Phil
was still in the army he found it 'a bit strange visiting a war-torn country.
My comrades were serving and I was on holiday'. When they left, Tuyet
said 'I am not coming back to Vietnam', and she has never returned. Since
then her family has migrated to Australia.

Coleman I have no further details on Oliver Coleman and his bride Dolly, though I would be delighted to know what happened to this couple.

Cornwell Elizabeth Brown and Henry Cornwell married in March 1944. They had one daughter and now have twin grandchildren and lived in Roseville, NSW, where Henry worked as an accountant. Elizabeth died in 1992 and Henry in 2000.

Crane Joan and Russell moved to Western Australia in 1969. Russell died in December 1987. They have one son and two grandchildren. It was Joan's son Bruce who mended the bridges with her family in the UK when as part of his naval training he was stationed there. Joan is an active member of the British War Brides Club in WA and has never regretted moving 12 000 miles away from home.

Darby Pat and Max Darby had five children – three boys and two girls. Max worked for thirty years for a commercial airline and in 1950 the family moved to Melbourne. 'I have never regretted one moment,' says Pat, 'and still keep in touch with the girls I met in Perth who were also war brides who came out on the *Rangitaki*. Pat and Max now have eight grandchildren.

David Arvona and Hedley settled in Perth where they built their own house – literally. Hedley, an auditor, built the three-bedroom house on evenings and weekends. They had three children and now have seven grandchildren. Hedley died in January 1999 and Arvona still lives in Perth where she goes to the British WAAF lunches and the War Brides lunches regularly.

Dover Enid met wireless air gunner Jim Dover in Chipping Norton in 1944. She sailed to Australia in May 1946 with Joyce Berrill on *SS Atlantis* and settled in Brisbane. They have three children and six grandchildren.

Dowell Esther Dowell, Eva Tuckfield's friend, was married to Warren Dowell. She died in 1994. Esther had three children and she kept in touch with Eva for many years by letter and occasionally visited.

Ellsworth Norman Ellsworth was born in Creswick, Victoria, and joined the AIF on 19 August 1914. He wrote regular interesting and informative letters to his mother – and was as much at ease telling her about women and his relationships with others as he was about the war. Norman never married and died on 31 July 1917 of wounds received at Zillebeke. His letters, which his mother saved, can be found in the Australian War Memorial.

Fethers June and Willard Fethers, the author's parents, lived in Melbourne for the first fifteen years of their married life. They moved to Sydney in the 1960s and now live in country New South Wales. They have three daughters and eight grandchildren.

Fitzgerald   Olive's Johnny became a builder. 'I think his main object in life was to build me bigger and better houses to live in, to make up for that dreadful first year,' said Olive. They had another child, nine years later, a son. Johnny died in 1994 and Olive still lives in the house he built her by the sea.

Foster   Jose Foster and her husband Laurie settled in Melbourne. They had two children. Jose went back to England in 1978 'but couldn't wait to get back to Laurie and family. I love England but couldn't live there again – the climate would get me down'.

Gehrig   Betty and Con Gehrig settled in Toronto in NSW because Con was stationed there in 1942. They had four children and have ten grand children. Con died of cancer in 1986 just after a visit to England to see Betty's mother. 'I love Australia,' writes Betty, 'and am forever grateful that such an ugly event as World War II brought to my homeland such a good man.'

H   John H married and divorced and went through 'feelings of worthlessness [and] depression' after he left Vietnam and his relationship with Mai. He attended counselling and in so doing sorted out his relationship with his ex-wife and his children. In writing out his story for this book he wrote, 'I came home partly unhinged. In writing this, I have found some of the reasons'.

Harper   Ina and Leo Harper lived and worked in Queensland, firstly in Kempsey and later as publicans in the town of Aramac. 'I knew nothing about pubs and trembled at the knees when I first walked into the bar,' writes Ina. 'The people were friendly – not as bad as they looked.' They ran another three pubs and raised four children. Leo died in May 1989 and Ina 'still misses him terribly at times'. She has been back to Canada twice but doesn't think she will be going back again.

Heath   Patricia and Athol Heath lived in Sydney and had a daughter and three grandsons. Athol died in1990. Patricia has been 'back home' six times. She says, 'I consider myself very fortunate but I must admit as much as I love Australia my heart remains in England'.

Henderson   Kate and Gordon Henderson made their home in Sydney, although initially they had planned to stay in England. Kate was welcomed by Gordon's family. They lived in a house in the suburb of Gordon and raised three daughters. Kate visited England in the early twenties but died before she was able to take her third daughter, Sheila, home before the Second World War ended.

Henderson   Sheila and Vic Henderson settled in Brisbane and had two daughters. 'I have been happy here,' says Sheila, 'but still miss my family in England, especially my twin brother and my sister. We have been lucky though as they have all been to Brisbane and I have been home several times.'

Holden Dorothy and John Holden first made their home in Melbourne, then moved to Adelaide. They had two children and three grandchildren. John died in an accident in 1998 but before then they had travelled back to England a number of times. Dorothy considers both England and Australia to be 'home'.

Hollow Mitsuko (Mitsy) and her husband Clyde eventually moved to Adelaide, where she meets regularly with other Japanese war brides. They had six children and there are now nine grandchildren and two great-grandchildren. Clyde died in 1991. Mitsy has been back to Japan a number of times, the first time being ten years after she first arrived in Australia.

Howard Mary and Bill Howard settled in country New South Wales and ran a dairy farm. They had two daughters. Bill died in 1960 at the age of forty-five and Mary has not remarried. She returned to England three times in the 1970s.

Johnson Mary and Harold Johnson settled in Mittagong where Harold ran a garage. They built their own home and Mary still lives there. They had five children and there are ten grandchildren. Harold died in 1984. Mary has been active member of the local community and has received a British Empire Medal for her services to Youth and Community. She says, 'I have loved my life in Australia and have only once been told to go home, I should not have married one of their menfolk!'

Kindred Edith Kindred's diary from her 1919 voyage to Australia was not found until the family home in Scotland was sold in 1977, when it was sent out to Edith who was still alive – Arthur had died in 1969. A story about Edith and her diary appeared in *The Newcastle Herald*. Edith died in October, 1981 – and her daughter Trish Westbury kept the diary.

Lumby Pola and Noel have retired to Queensland. They have two daughters and a grandchild. Their friend Helen visits them often from Melbourne. Pola has very fond memories of her mother-in-law whom she describes as 'absolutely wonderful'.

McDonald Vittorina (Vicki) and George had five children. George passed away in November 1984, and at time of writing Vicki had fourteen grandchildren and nine great-grandchildren. She still lives in Queensland with her eldest daughter Margherita.

Morris Jane (Sadako) and her husband lived in Adelaide. They had three children and there are now four grandchildren. John was killed in an accident in 1985 and Jane continues to live in the town where she first arrived in 1954. She has been back to Japan many times, though the first trip took her ten years to save for. Her children have also visited their mother's homeland.

Muirhead   Evelyn and John Muirhead still live in Cairns where they have raised three children and at time of writing have four grandchildren and five great-grandchildren. Evelyn has been back to the US but home is Cairns.

Procter   Violet and Chris Procter lived on the edge of the Mallee in Victoria, where they had three children. Chris was a builder and in 1928 they moved to Frankston, Victoria where another daughter was born. Violet's parents and sisters migrated to Australia in 1926. Violet suffered from a heart condition as a result of rheumatic fever as a child and died in 1940 at the age of forty-two. Chris Procter married again and died in 1981 at the age of ninety.

Neely   Audrey Neely sailed for Australia on the *Empire Grace* in August 1945 and with husband Aubrey Vincent (known to everyone as Joe), settled in Eugowra, New South Wales. 'The flies, the heat, no water laid on, no electricity, no neighbours for two miles. Loneliness wasn't the word to describe Australia and how I felt about this country... Now I love Australia.' Audrey and Joe had five children. Joe died in 1985.

Parker   Cherry and Gordon Parker led the way for other Japanese/Australian couples to come to Australia in the 1950s. They settled in Melbourne where they received quite a bit of media attention. They had eight children and numerous grandchildren.

Perry   Marie and Ray Perry had two children and lived in the outback until 1962 when they travelled to Canada to visit Marie's brother and then onto England. Marie counts herself very lucky to have a husband who understood how homesick she was and arranged for her to return to 'go home' quite often, the first time in 1951. Ray died in 1997.

Robinson   Robbie Robinson and his wife Meg began their life together on a farm at Perwillowen west of Nambour in Queensland. They had four children and Meg found 'preparing meals for her husband and three workmen was a tremendous challenge. Her efforts at making scones were disastrous...' She boiled clothes in a copper in the backyard and made all her own and her children's clothes. Meg's greatest sadness was the absence of extended family – her own and her husband's. Meg returned home for her first visit in 1949. She died at the age of ninety-six, in 1991. Robbie died in 1967.

Schwer   Ralph and Thuy Schwer moved to Adelaide where in the early years Thuy struggled to learn English until Migrant English classes were made available by the government. They had two children. In 1979 Thuy's family migrated to Australia. However the marriage did not survive and Ralph and

Thuy divorced. Thuy still lives in Australia and has never been back to Vietnam.

Scutter Ora and Eddie Scutter had three children and Ora now has seven grandchildren. She lives on her own in Adelaide where she keeps in touch with fellow war brides Eva Tuckfield and Malka Mocktyre, who she sailed to Australia with, and they reminisce about their youth in Tel Aviv. Eddie Scutter died in 1979.

Smith Brenda Morton worked in telecommunications research when she met Stewart Smith, a Mosquito navigator. They married on the Isle of Wight in 1945 and Brenda came to Australia on the aircraft carrier *Indefatigable*. She now lives in Queensland, Stewart died in 1987. She has one child and two grandchildren.

Sunderland 'When I came to Australia I hadn't made a bed, I hadn't boiled an egg, I hadn't made a pot of tea – when Ted said to my mother we would like to get married, she said "Ted you couldn't have chosen anyone as a wife more useless than Queenie".' were Queenie's own words. Queenie and Ted made their home on the family farm in Dubbo, NSW and had two daughters. Ted died in 1976 and Queenie wrote her life story, first simply for the family, in her '100th year'. This book has since been published as *Bride of Anzac. My Life Story* (published by Gary Allen, Sydney, 2000). I interviewed Queenie in February 2000 when she was 103 years old.

Taylor H.G. Taylor's account in the Australian War Memorial reveals nothing about H.G. himself, except that he was very young, served with the 17th Battalion and lived to tell his tale. We do not even know his Christian names. Maybe he married his Lil.

Thomson Sheila and Johnnie Thomson lived in Sydney. They had three children and there are now seven grandchildren. Johnnie died in 1990. Sheila went back to the UK after eighteen years for her parents' Diamond Wedding anniversary. 'I thought the family was absolutely fabulous, but I was glad to come back to Australia,' Sheila said.

Triffett Hedy and Ted Triffett lived in Toowoomba with their two daughters, running a nursing home until Ted died in 1989. Hedy continued to run the home as a hostel until 1994 when she moved to Surfers Paradise. Ted was one of the famous Rats of Tobruk[1] and was decorated at Buckingham Palace with a DCM. Hedy died in June 2001 before this book was completed.

Tuckfield Eva and Milton (Jim) Tuckfield lived with his family until November 1946 when they moved into their first home – a rented maisonette and two weeks later had a daughter. They also had a second son. Eva kept in touch with her friend Esther and they would meet up at times. In 1970 Eva's father died and she and Milton went back to Israel to visit her family. Milton died in September 1979. Her friend Esther died in 1994. Eva continues to travel and enjoy her family both in Adelaide and Israel.

Turner   Constance Turner lives in Melbourne and at the time of writing this was almost 103 years old. JJ died in July 1953. They had two children and there are now two grandchildren and two great-grandchildren.

W   Kathleen and her husband had five children and spent many of the children's early years moving about. They now have thirteen grandchildren and a number of great-grandchildren, but Kathleen says that although she feels she has been lucky she would never leave her home country if she had to do it all again. She feels that war was responsible for her husband not reaching his full potential.

Webster   Phyllis Webster and her husband Alan raised their three children in Western Australia. They have five grandchildren. Phyllis returns to the UK every two or three years.

West   Doris' unhappy marriage ended when she died in 1969, her husband died in 1981. Their daughter Claire discovered that her father, who often left them, told others that he had never married. He left a small amount of money to the Salvation Army. Doris returned home once in 1952 for the coronation of Queen Elizabeth II when her sister's husband left her money to cover a trip home on the SS *Oriana*.

Wintersun   Mitsy Wintersun missed her family in Japan and for the first two years she did not speak to another Japanese person. She and Michael worked hard at buying their first home and they had three daughters. After thirteen years Mitsy was able to go home to see her family; she was terribly homesick. Since then Mitsy, the children and grandchildren, have been back many times. 'I have a close-knit family and my brother thought he would never see me again,' she said.

Endnotes

Introduction

1 Lloyd, Clem & Rees, Jacqui, *The Last Shilling. A History of Repatriation in Australia*, Melbourne University Press, Melbourne, 1994, p. 294
2 The initials GI stand for Government Issue. A term which came from the US which came about because the American soldier was only distinguishable by the number on the dog tag around his neck.
3 Shukert, Elfrieda Berthiaume & Scibetta, Barbara Smith, *War Brides of World War II*, Presidio Press, Novato, CA, 1988, p. 1
4 Bean, C.E.W., *Anzac to Amiens*, Australian War Memorial, Canberra, 1946, p. 516
5 Bean, p. 516
6 Bean, p. 519
7 Mason, K.J., *Experience of Nationhood: Australia and the World Since 1900*, Second Edition, McGraw-Hill, Sydney, 1990, p. 199

Chapter 1 Sex, War and the Role of Women

1 Gabor, Mark, *The Pin-Up: A Modest History*, Pan Books, Fulham, England, 1973, p. 17
2 Gabor, p. 109
3 Holmes, Katie, 'Day Mothers and Night Sisters: World War I Nurses and Sexuality', in *Gender and War: Australians at War in the Twentieth Century*, edited by Joy Damousi & Marilyn Lake, Cambridge University Press, Cambridge UK, 1995, pp. 43–59
4 *Argus*, 23 June 1917, p. 18 as cited in Bassett, Jan, *The Home Front, 1914–1918 Inquiring into Australian History*, general editor: Barbara Vance Wilson, Oxford University Press, Melbourne,1983, p. 22
5 Quoted in Turner, E.S., *Dear Old Blighty*, Michael Joseph, London, 1980, p. 202

6   From Montague, C.E., *Disenchantment*, quoted in Turner, E.S., *Dear Old Blighty*, Michael Joseph, London, 1980, p.202

7   Letters 1914–1917 of Sergeant N.G. Ellsworth, 102nd Howitzer Battery, AIF. AWM file 12/11/1146

8   Letters from 3330 Gnr F. B. Oldfield, 8th Aust. Fld Artillery Bde., 1/1/1917–9/1/1921, Australian War Memorial

9   Tolerton, Jane *Ettie: The Life of Ettie Rout*, Penguin (New Zealand) Auckland, 1992, p. 146

10 McKernan, Michael, *The Australian People and the Great War*, Collins, Sydney 1984, p. 132–3 quoting letters of W. D. Gallwey 21 September 1917 and 2 January 1917 AWM 12/11/4802

11 Taylor, H.G., 'The Mob That Shot the Camel', MSS 0863, AWM

12 McKernan, Michael, *All In! Fighting the War at Home*, Allen & Unwin, St Leonards NSW, 1995, p. 239

13 Tolerton, p. 172

14 Kent, David, *From Trench and Troopship. The Experience of the Australian Imperial Force, 1914–1919*, Hale & Iremonger, Sydney, 1999, p. 127

15 Orpen, Sir William, *An Onlooker in France 1917–1919*, Williams and Norgate, London, 1924, p. 16–17

16 From: In Flanders Fields – website: www.inflandersfields.be/

17 Adam-Smith, Patsy, *The Anzacs*, Penguin, Ringwood Vic, 1978 p. 283

18 McKernan, *The Australian People and the Great War*, p. 134

19 Adam-Smith, p. 289

20 Tolerton, p. 93

21 Adam-Smith, Patsy *Australian Women at War*, Thomas Nelson, Melbourne, 1984 p. 341–2

22 *The World at Arms: The Reader's Digest Illustrated History of World War II*, Reader's Digest Association, London, 1989, p. 157

23 McKernan, *All In! Fighting the War at Home*, p. 254

24 McKernan, Michael, *All In! Fighting the War at Home*, p. 247

25 Adam-Smith, Patsy, *The Anzacs*, pp. 71–2

26 Dower, John. W., *Embracing Defeat. Japan in the Wake of World War II*, Allen Lane, The Penguin Press, London, 1999, p. 124

27 monpe pantaloons are the baggy pants generally worn by peasants

28 Dower, p. 126

29 Tamura, Keiko, *Michi's Memories. The Story of a Japanese War Bride*, Pandanus Books, Research School of Pacific and Asian Studies, Australian National University, Canberra, 2001, p. 7

30 Gerster, Robin & Bassett, Jan, *Seizures of Youth: 'The Sixties' and Australia*, Hyland House, Melbourne, 1991, p. 21

31 Gerster, Robin, 'A Bit of the Other: Touring Vietnam' in *Gender and War: Australians at War in the Twentieth Century*, p. 230

32 McHugh, Siobhan, *Minefields and Miniskirts: Australian Women and the Vietnam War*, Doubleday, Sydney, 1973, p. 60

Chapter 2 The Great War: Meetings

1 Soldier's account quoted in Stewart, David, et al, *The Great War. Sources and Evidence*, Thomas Nelson, South Melbourne, 2nd edition, 1997, p. 150, from Dawes, J.N.I. & Robson, LL. *Citizen to Soldier*, Melbourne University Press, Melbourne, 1977

2 WWI letters from Oliver Coleman to his family, circa 1916–1917 from the Manuscripts collection of the State Library of Victoria MS 10141. MSB 172

3 Mant, Gilbert (Ed.) *Soldier Boy: The letters of Gunner W. J. Duffell, 1915–18*, Kangaroo Press, Kenthurst NSW 1992, p. 85

4 7/8/17, Mant p. 90

5 Mant, p. 128

6 Mant, p. 132

7 Mant, p. 134

8 Adam-Smith, Patsy, *The Anzacs*, p. 476, Appendix II: Battle casualty admissions to field ambulances from the AIF in France from April 1916 to March 1919.

9 Enteric fever was the term used then for typhoid fever or paratyphoid fever. Now preventable by vaccine, typhoid is an infection caused by a salmonella bacterium and is a serious illness. Paratyphoid fever resembles typhoid.

10 Letters 1914–1917 of Sergeant Major N.G. Ellsworth, 102nd Howitzer Battery, AIF, World War 1914–1918, AWM File 12/11/1146

11 McKernan, Michael, *The Australian People and the Great War*, p. 139

12 Letters 1914–1917 of Sergeant Major N.G. Ellsworth, 102nd Howitzer Battery, AIF, World War 1914–1918, AWM File 12/11/1146

13 *The News of the World*, 13 January 1918, page 4.

14 Interview with the author, 1 February 2000

15 Sutherland, Queenie, *Bride of an Anzac. Queenie Sunderland's Story as Written in Her 100th Year*. First published in 1996 by Queenie Sunderland. Rosebery, NSW

16 Blighty, according to one veteran is either a corruption of the Hindustani 'biliak' meaning a foreign country, especially England, or from 'Vilyat, Persian from strange or foreign. From this arose an Urdu corruption *Bvelait*, which soldiers distorted to *Belati* and eventually to *Blighty*'. (From Brophy & Partridge, p. 86.)

17 Brophy, John & Partridge, Eric, *The Long Trail: What the British Soldier Sang and Said in the Great War of 1914–18*, Andre Deutch, London 1965, p.220

18 Simmelhaig, Helen & Spenceley, G.F.R, *For Australia's Sake: A History of Australia's Involvement in Nine Wars*, Thomas Nelson, Melbourne, 1984, p. 48

19 From: In Flanders Fields – website: www.inflandersfields.be/

20 In collection of letters of Stanley Roland Mills, State Library of Victoria, MS10016 MSB 129A

21 boko = beaucoup

22 From *Tommy's Tunes*, compiled by F. Nettleingham, Erskine McDonald, London, 1973, p. 35

23 Kent, p. 194
24 Brophy & Partridge, p. 49 (Brophy used a dash instead of the word 'fucked')
25 Extracts from 'Letters from the Front' by Major G. I. Adcock, 2nd Aust. Tunnelling Co. World War 1914–1918. AWM File No. L/12/11/2122
26 It is possible that Garnett Adcock deliberately omitted this letter as the collection was typed up and edited by Adcock with a note, written in 1930, which says 'The completeness of the picture presented by these letters has of course been marred to a certain extent by the censorship, which prevented any mention of many details of our daily life. Some slight attempt has been made to remedy this by the interpolation of notes…'

Chapter 3 The Great War: Marriage

1 McKernan, Michael, *The Australian People and the Great War*, p. 135
2 Sunderland, p. 30
3 Adcock, G.I, AWM File No. L/12/11/2122
4 McKernan, Michael, *The Australian People and the Great War*, p. 137
5 'Imperial and Foreign News Items', *The Times*, London, 31 October 1919, p. 11
6 As quoted in Kent, p.197

Chapter 4 The Great War: The Bride Ships

1 Kent, p. 165 (Historians differ on this number, David Stewart & James Fitzgerald in *The Great War. Using Evidence*, Thomas Nelson, Melbourne, 1987, p. 142, report that 'In November 1918 there were 167 000 Australians in France, Belgium, England, Egypt and Syria, including a number of wounded and convalescent soldiers'.)
2 Tolerton, p. 193
3 News item, *The Times* (London), 31 May 1919, p. 11
4 Kent, p. 165
5 Lloyd & Rees, p. 129
6 Harding, Stephen, *Great Liners at War*, Motorbooks International,Osceoala, USA, 1997, pp. 85–6
7 Lloyd & Rees p.129
8 Lloyd & Rees p. 128
9 Bean, p. 519
10 Fifth Annual Report of the Australian Red Cross Society, year ended August 7 1919
11 Lloyd & Rees, p. 129
12 A Warrant Officer is a Regimental Sergeant Major, a rank and status between commissioned and non-commissioned officer. Non-commissioned officers include sergeants and corporals.
13 'Free Passages to Australia' *The Times*, 6 January 1919, p. 9; 'Repatriation Ship Scandal', *The Times*, 1 November 1919, p. 12
14 'Troopship Scandal', *The Times*, 3 November 1919, p. 12
15 Sunderland, p. 54

16   *Author's note*: Violet's writing is sometimes hard to read and this looks like 10 p.m. but she obviously had trouble with p.m. and a.m. and in the scheme of things it should probably have been a.m.

17   Sunderland, p. 35

18   Sunderland, p. 39

19   A dixie is a large iron pot which the troops used to make stews and tea 'with an iron lid and a thin white metal handle devised to bite into the hands carrying it', write veterans John Brophy and Eric Partridge in *The Long Trail: What the British Soldier Sang and Said in 1914-1918*. At this stage Arthur was waiting in France for transfer to a camp in England.

20   'From War Zone to Australia: Nearing Port Said' (from our Special Correspondent) *The Times*, 29 January 1919, p. 11

21   Sunderland, p. 36

22   House was a favourite gambling game using discs and cards marked with a variety of numbers. A banker calls out the numbers on the discs he takes from a bag and each player marks the numbers on his card. The first player with a full card of numbers marked off is the winner. Now known more commonly as housie or bingo, this game is still played in many clubs.

23   Australian War Memorial collection

24   Free. Usually used to describe something which came as a surprise such as Edith and Arthur's tram ride. Regular soldiers before 1914 learnt the word from Hindustani (Brophy & Partridge)

25   Sunderland, p. 40

Chapter 5 The Great War: Arriving in Australia

1   cwt = 1 hundred weight or 112 lb (51 kg)

2   As reported in Lloyd & Rees, p. 130

3   19 July, 1915

4   McKernan, *The Australian People and the Great War*, p. 137

5   *The Digger*, vol.1, no. 4, Sunday 25 August 1918. Held in the Australian War Memorial.

6   'Soldiers' Brides Disembark from a Transport', *The Sydney Morning Herald*, 11 January 1919, p. 14

7   Roland, Betty, *The Touch of Silk*, *Granite Peak*, revised edition introduced by Philip Parsons, Currency Press, Sydney, 1988

8   'Soldiers' Wives', *The Sydney Morning Herald*, 10 January 1919, p. 5

9   *Repatriation*, 25 September 1919, as reported in Lloyd & Rees, p. 130

10   Scates, Bruce & Frances, Raelene, *Women and the Great War*, Cambridge, UK, 1997, p. 156

Chapter 6 The Second World War: Meetings

1   Stanley, Peter, 'Air Battle, Europe, 1939–1945, *Australians at War*, Time-Life, Sydney, 1987, pp. 22–3

2   Lloyd & Rees, p. 294

3   A servicewoman assigned to officers as a servant

4 McBryde, Brenda, *Quiet Heroines: Nurses of the Second World War*, Chatto & Windus, The Hogarth Press, London, 1985, p. 2
5 Adam-Smith, Patsy, *Prisoners of War*, Penguin, Ringwood, Vic, 1997, pp. 102,104
6 *The World at Arms: The Reader's Digest Illustrated History of World War II*, Reader's Digest Association Limited, London, 1989, p. 84
7 V-weapon was the name the British gave to the German Vergeltungswaffen (retaliation weapons).

Chapter 8 The Second World War: The Bride Ships

1 Lloyd & Rees, pp.294–5
2 ' English Wives in Desperate Straits', *The Argus*, 28 February 1946, p. 5
3 'Bride Ship Delays', *Sydney Morning Herald*, 1 March 1946, p. 3
4 Robert G. Maguglin, *The Official Pictorial History: The Queen Mary*, RMS Foundation, Long Beach, California. Asiaprint and Albion Publishing Group, 1993, pp. 70–71
5 Maguglin, p. 89
6 'Passages for Brides', *The Argus*, 2 March 1946, p. 1
7 *Sydney Morning Herald*, 16 April 1946, p. 1
8 'Brides to Picket Australia House' *The Argus* 17 April 1946, p. 7
9 'Luxury Ship for Canadian Brides', *The Argus,* 17 April 1946, p. 7
10 It continues 'but of this total not more than £10 may be in Sterling Bank Notes, and Bank of England Notes of £5 denomination may not be taken out of the United Kingdom or accepted on board.' There were allowances made for passengers who wished to take more money, but they were complicated.
11 It was a two-berth cabin with six bunks, two each on three of the walls. A wash basin and door were on the fourth wall.
12 'Brides and babies arrive in aircraft-carrier', Betty Nesbit, *The Australian Women's Weekly*, 22 September 1945, p. 26
13 'Arrived on American "Slum Ship"', *Daily Telegraph*, 24 August 1946, p. 3
14 'Passengers tell of Hell Voyage', *The Sun*, 23 August 1946
15 *The Argus*, 31st July, 1946, p. 13 'Conditions on Bride Ship Criticised'.
16 Unidentified newspaper article, from Betty Cornwell's scrapbook
17 'Bride Ship Conditions Criticised', *The Argus*, 6 August 1946, p. 3
18 'Australian Brides Complain of Transport Conditions', *The Argus*, 5 August 1946, p. 5
19 'Remember Me? I'm Your Wife', *The Argus*, 27 May 1946, p. 25

Chapter 9 The Second World War: Arriving in Australia in the 1940s

1 Oppenheimer, Melanie, *Red Cross VAs: A History of the VAD Movement in New South Wales,* Ohio Productions, Walcha NSW, 1999, pp. 116–7
2 VAD *News Sheet* No. 12, 15 February 1946, as quoted in Oppenheimer, p.122

3 'Canadian and USA Brides Arrive', *The Argus,* 14 February 1946, p. 8
4 'Chilly Welcome for Brides', *The Argus,* 23 April 1946, p. 20
5 Oppenheimer, p. 121-122
6 Re-establishment and Re-employment Act (no. 11 of 1945, 28 June) as described in *The Australian Encyclopaedia,* 1963
7 'Living in Sydney as seen by English and Canadian Brides', *Sydney Morning Herald,* 23 October 1946, p. 6
8 'Overseas Brides in Sydney', *Sydney Morning Herald,* 19 July 1946, p. 8

Chapter 10 The Second World War: Against the Odds

1 A derogatory slang term mostly used by Australians to refer to people of Latin or Mediterranean race and no longer commonly used.
2 Eva Hava Tuckfield, *Recollections of My Life.* An Autobiography, self-published, Adelaide, Australia, c. 2000, p. 1
3 Author's interview with Spr Bill Rudd who is researching Australians in Switzerland during the Second World War.
4 Tamura, Keiko, pp. 5–6
5 Sissons, D.C.S., 'Japanese' in *The Australian People: an Encyclopedia of the Nation, Its People and Their Origins,* edited by James Jupp, Angus & Robertson, North Ryde, NSW p. 637

Chapter 11 Three Love Stories of the Vietnam war

1 The Democratic Labor Party was a Catholic splinter group of the Australian Labor Party, which held the balance of power in the Senate in Australia when Menzies was Prime Minister.

Appendix: What Happened After

1 The 'rats of Tobruk' was a name given to the Australian troops by German General Rommel who led the attack on this seaport. The 'rats' inflicted the first major defeat on the Germans in the Second World War.

Acknowledgements

This book would not have been possible without the co-operation and support of the many people who happily gave up their own time to answer my questions and write down their stories. A special thank you to everyone who answered my requests for stories, family histories and photos. I am naturally an optimist and this book took much longer to research and write than I had anticipated. I would therefore also like to thank all my contributors for being so patient and for continuing to maintain an interest in this project.

It was extremely difficult deciding what to include and what to leave out. In the end it came down to making the stories and the historical background fit together. Every account I received provided valuable context for the whole story though unfortunately I was not able to use all the accounts that were sent to me. Thank you to:

Mary Adams; Marion Allen; Ron Anderson and his cousin Jocelyn Sussman for the story of Loulou Anderson; Barbara Arnold; Molly Ashdown; Bill Badcock and his widow Barbara; Doreen Balderstone; Marcia and Genevieve Bassin, who told the story of their mother and grandmother, Yvonne Chard; Dorothy Baulch; Phyllis Bell; Joyce Berrill; Phil Bidwell; Joyce Boas; Beryl Boyd; Mary Brand; Estelle Bridgford; Daisy Bruton; Hilary Butterfield; Ayako and Ron Cameron; Nancy Campbell; Eve Campion; Phil and Tuyet Coen; Daphne Collins; Diana Cumming Cornwell; Joan Crane; Betty Cunningham; Pat Darby; Arvona David; Enid Dover; Joan Durham; Rosemary Evans; Olive Fitzgerald; Jose Foster; Betty Gehrig; Edith Gibbons; Grace Grigg; Bill Grainger; John H; Ina Harper; Patricia Heath; Sheila Henderson; Rita Henry; Iris Hogan; Dorothy Holden; Mitsy Hollow; Mary Howard; Mary Johnson; Audrey Lawrence; Pola Lumby; Ellen McFadden; Betty MacKinnon; Wendy Macklan; Sara McCarthy; Vicki MacDonald and her son-in-law, Neil Bauer; Ellen McFadden; Pearl McKeenan; Gwladys Mason; Patricia Miller; Joan Morgan; Jane Morris and her daughter June Hammond; Evelyn Muirhead; Claire Murphy; Audrey Neely; Elizabeth Nation; Vera Northeast; Cherry Parker; Jean Parker who lent me her mother Violet Procter's diary; Marie Perry; Ruth Reynolds; Betty Reynolds; Daphne Robbins; Marjorie Roseneder and her daughter Jan; Audrey S; Dorothy Scanlon; Ralph Schwer; Ora Scutter; Margaret Small; Brenda Smith; Ann Paton Smythe; George Stirzaker; Gwladys Strong; Queenie Sunderland; C.F. Thiely; Sheila Thomson; Hedy Triffett and Vren Hunniford; Eva Tuckfield; Constance Turner and Margaret Dickson; Lilian Turner; Richard Voss; Kathleen W who already had a collection of war brides stories in her possession and who was a valuable contact; Ann Waterhouse; Patricia Watts; Phyllis Webster; Coralie Welch; Trish Westbury for lending the diaries of her mother Edith Kindred and her father, Arthur; Frances Whishaw; Mitsy Wintersun; Margaret Wright; Sheila Yeatman; Mary Yewell.

I would also like to thank the editors of the RSL and Legacy newsletters who willingly published my requests for interviews, not once but a number of times; Val Lakeman and the other war brides from the Overseas War Brides Association for their help with contacts for brides from the Great War; Elizabeth Smith, Welfare Officer at the Legacy Club of Adelaide whose wonderful exhibition 'War Brides—Our Stories' at the Migration Museum, Adelaide, was an inspiration; the staff at the Australian Red Cross office in Sydney and Dr. Melanie Oppenheimer; Bill Rudd for giving of some of his extensive research into Australians in Switzerland during World War II; Keiko Tamura, author of *Mitsy's Memories* and a number of articles about Japanese war brides in Australia.

I would also like to thank Mrs G. Mant for permission to use extracts from *Soldier Boy. The Letters of Gunner J. Duffell. 1915–1918*. Kangaroo Press, 1992.

Sources of songs
The words to songs are used with the following permissions:

'Is 'E An Aussie Is 'E Lizzie' (Our Share 100%) B. Hilliam. © 1963 Lawrence Wright Music Co. Limited. Used by permission of EMI Music Publishing Australia Pty Limited. All rights reserved.

'Hello! Hello! Who's Your Lady Friend?' (Worton/Fragson/Stodden). © Lyrics reproduced with kind permission of J Albert & Son Pty Ltd

'You Found Me and I Found You' Kern/Wodehouse, © Copyright Universal Music Publishing Pty Ltd.

'Who's Taking You Home Tonight' (Sherwin/Connor). © Lyrics reproduced with kind permission of J Albert & Son Pty Ltd

'Love is the Sweetest Thing' (Noble). © Lyrics reproduced with kind permission of J Albert & Son Pty Ltd

'Wish Me Luck (As You Wave Me Goodbye)' by Phil Park/Harry Parr-Davies (W/C 100%). © 1939 Chappell Music Ltd. For Australia And New Zealand:

Warner/Chappell Music Australia, Pty Ltd. (ABN63 000 876 068) 3 Talavera Rd, North Ryde NSW 2113. International Copyright Secured. All Rights Reserved. Unauthorised Reproduction Is Illegal.

'Que Sera Sera' Words & Music: Ray Evans/Jay Livingston. © Universal Music Publishing Pty Ltd. Reproduced by kind permission of Universal Music Publishing Group.

'The Clouds Will Soon Roll By' by George Brown/Harry Woods (W/C 100%). © 1932 Shapiro, Bernstein & Co, Inc. For Australia and New Zealand: Warner/Chappell Music Australia, Pty Ltd. (ABN63 000 876 068), 3 Talavera Rd, North Ryde NSW 2113. International Copyright Secured. All Rights Reserved. Unauthorised Reproduction Is Illegal.

'A Time For Us' (Love Theme) from the Paramount Picture ROMEO AND JULIET. Words by Larry Kusik and Eddie Snyder. Music by Nino Rota. Copyright ©1968 (Renewed 1996) by Famous Music Corporation. International Copyright Secured. All Rights Reserved.

'Sentimental Journey' (Green/Brown/Homer). © Lyrics reproduced with kind permission of J Albert & Son Pty Ltd.

Sources of photographs

I found the illustrations from the Australian War Memorial, Mitchell Library, and State Library of New South Wales mostly on their internet sites.

The photo on page 57 is AWM H18659; the photo on page 66 of SS *Zealandic* is courtesy of Claire Murphy; on page 129 the photo is of Enid and Jim Dover; on page 137 the photo is of Beryl Boyd and Pamela Garrett on the *Asturias*; the photo on page 161 is of Mary Johnson (second from left) and other war brides from the *Atlantis*; the photo on page 213 is AWM EKN/70/0441/VN; Christine Pearson provided the photo on page 215.

Various photos came from newspapers of the First and Second World Wars, including *The Sydney Mail*:pages ix, 36, 96, 97, 98, 99, 106 and 107; *The Sun*: pages 152, 153 and 160; and *The Sun News Pictorial*: page 156.

Every effort has been made to contact the copyright holders of material used in this book. If any thing has been overlooked please contact the publisher.

This book would not have come together without the patience and skills of my editor Katie Stackhouse and the support of Transworld publisher Fiona Henderson. I thank them both. Also Sue Tsoromokos, who patiently processed many of my taped interviews, and Tricia Waters for another great index and her help with the research.

Lastly I would like to thank Martin, my husband and partner, who did an amazing job as critic, proofreader, courier and emotional support—without him I would never have started, let alone finished.

Bibliography

Books

Adam-Smith, Patsy, *The Anzacs*, Penguin Books, Melbourne, 1978

Adam-Smith, Patsy, *Australian Women at War*, Thomas Nelson Australia, Melbourne, 1984

Bassett, Jan, *The Home Front, 1914–1918 Inquiring into Australian History*, General editor: Barbara Vance Wilson, Oxford University Press, Melbourne,1983

Bean, C.E.W., *Anzac to Amiens*, Australian War Memorial, Canberra, 1983

Bolt, Andrew (ed.) *Our Home Front: 1939–1945*, Wilkinson Books, Melbourne, c.1995

Brophy, John & Partridge, Eric, *The Long Trail: What the British Soldier Sang and Said in 1914–1918,* Andre Deutsch, London, 1965

Carlyon, Les, *Gallipolli*, Pan Macmillan, Sydney, 2001

Costello, John, *Love Sex and War: Changing Values 1939–45*, Pan Books, London, 1986

Dear, Ian, *Oxford Companion to the Second World War*, Oxford University Press, Oxford, 1995

Dennis, Peter, *Oxford Companion to Australian Military History*, Oxford University Press, Melbourne, 1995

Dower, John, *Embracing Defeat: Japan in the Wake of World War II*, Allen Lane, Penguin Press, London, 1999

Harding, Stephen, *Great Liners at War*, Osceola, WI Motorbooks International, 1997

Harpur, James, *War Without End: Conflict in Indo-China*, Longman Cheshire, Melbourne, 1990

Haythornthwaite, Philip, *The World War One Source Book*, Arms and Armour Press, London, 1992

Johnston, Susan, *Experiences of the Great War, 1914–1918: A Documentary Resource Book for Senior Students*, Longman Cheshire, Sydney 1987

Jones, Barbara & Howell, Bill, *Popular Arts of the First World War,* Studio Vista, London, 1972

Jupp, James, *The Australian People: An Encyclopaedia of the Nation, Its People and Their Origins*, Angus & Robertson, Sydney, 1988

Keesing, Nancy (ed.), *The Home Front Family Album*, Weldon, Sydney, 1991

Kent, David, *From Trench and Troopship: The Experience of the Australian Imperial Force, 1914–1919*, Hale & Iremonger, Sydney, 1999

Lewis, Robert, *A Nation at War: The Australian Home Front in the Second World War. Documents & Commentary*, Longman Cheshire, Melbourne, 1984

Lloyd, Clem & Rees, Jacqui, *The Last Shilling: A History of Repatriation in Australia*, Melbourne University Press, Melbourne, 1994

Lumley, Joanna, *Forces Sweethearts*, Bloomsbury, London, 1993

McHugh, Siobhan, *Minefields and Miniskirts*, Doubleday, Sydney, 1993

McKernan, Michael, *All In! Fighting the War at Home*, Allen & Unwin, Sydney, 1995

McKernan, Michael, *The Australian People and the Great War*, William Collins Sydney, 1984

Mant, Gilbert (ed.), *Soldier Boy: The letters of Gunner W.J. Duffell, 1915–18*

Kangaroo Press, Kenthurst NSW 1992

Plowman, Peter, *Passenger Ships to Australia and New Zealand 1945–1990: Emigrant Ships to Luxury Liners*, New South Wales University Press, Sydney, 1992

Reader's Digest, *The World at Arms: The Reader's Digest Illustrated History of World War II*, Reader's Digest Association Limited, London, 1989

Reader's Digest, *Life on the Home Front*, Reader's Digest Association Limited, London, 1993.

Sir William Orpen, *An Onlooker in France 1917–1919*, Williams & Norgate, London, 1924

Scates, Bruce & Frances, Raelene, *Women and the Great War*, Cambridge University Press, Cambridge, 1997

Simmelhaig, Helen & Spenceley, G.F.R., *For Australia's Sake: A History of Australia's Involvement in Nine Wars*, Thomas Nelson, Melbourne, 1984

Shukert, Elfrieda Berthiaume & Scibetta, Barbara Smith, *War Brides of World War II*, Presidio Press, Novato, CA, 1988

Stanley, Peter & McKernan, Michael, *Australians at War 1885–1972: Photographs from the Collection of the Australian War Memorial*, Collins, Sydney, 1984

Tamura, Keiko, *Michi's Memories: The Story of a Japanese War Bride*, Pandanus Books, Canberra, 2001

Taylor, Eric, *Forces Sweethearts: Service Romances in World War II*, Robert Hale Limited, London, 1990

Tolerton, Jane, *Ettie:A Life of Ettie Rout*, Penguin Books, Auckland, 1992

Turner, E.S., *Dear Old Blighty*, Michael Joseph, London, 1980

Walsh, Colin, *Mud, Songs and Blighty. A Scrapbook of the First World War*, Hutchison of London, 1975

World War Songs, Albert Publications, Sydney, 1983

Magazines, newspapers

Advertiser (Adelaide), *Age* (Melbourne), *Argus* (Melbourne), *Australian Womens Weekly* (Sydney), *Daily Express* (London), *Daily Mirror* (London), *Daily Telegraph* (Sydney), *Illustrated London News, News of the World* (London), *People* (London), *Repatriation, Sun* (Sydney), *Sydney Mail* (Sydney), *Sydney Morning Herald, Times* (London)

Websites

The Australian War Memorial at www.awm.gov.au

Index

Iwakuni, Michiyo *see* Wintersun, Michiyo (Iwakuni)

Japan, allied forces in 22, 205
Johnson, Harold 236
Johnson, Mary 178, 236
Johnson, Olive *see* Fitzgerald, Olive (Johnson)
Jungwirth, Barbara 141

Kaminer, Ora *see* Scutter, Ora (Kaminer)
Kangaroo Club 141
Kikuchi, Sadako *see* Morris, Sadako (Kikuchi)
Kindred, Arthur 59, 75–9, 83–4, 86–7, 90–91, 100–3, 236
Kindred, Edith 59, 75–84, 86–7, 90–91, 100–3, 236
knitting 9, 17–18

Leperere, Helen 188, 189, 191
Locke, Betty 139–40
Locke, Harry 139–40
Lumby, Noel 188–91, 236
Lumby, Pola (Brafman) 188–91, 236

marriage 57–64, 129–36
McDonald, George 184–6, 236
McDonald, Vicki (Pellegrini) 183–6, 236
men, shortage of 12, 95
Middle East, Australian troops in 21, 67, 187, 192
Monash, General Sir John 66, 69
morality 20
Morris, John 207–8, 236–7
Morris, Sadako (Kikuchi) 207–8, 236–7
movies 3, 6–8
Mowberry, Mary *see* Howard, Mary (Mowberry)
Muirhead, Evelyn (Stephens) 116, 155, 175–6, 237
Muirhead, John 116, 155, 237
Mullins, Patricia 139–40
Mullins, Reg 139–40
Mydat, Estelle *see* Bridgford, Estelle (Mydat)

Neely, Audrey 149, 178–9, 237
nurses 9, 34, 122

Oldfield, Fred 12–13
Orpen, Sir William 15

Palestine 191
Parker, Cherry (Sakuramoto) 206, 237
Parker, Gordon 206, 237

Parker, Jean 43
Pellegrini, Vicki *see* McDonald, Vicki (Pellegrini)
Perry, Marie 172, 237
Perry, Ray 172, 237
pin-ups 1–5
poems *see* songs and poems
Poland 188–90
Port Said 87, 157
postcards 2–3
prisoners of war xv, 126, 127, 184, 188–9, 203
Procter, Christopher 43, 70–3, 87–8, 237
Procter, Violet (Apkins) 43, 70–3, 76, 82, 87–8, 103–4, 237
prostitution 13–15, 21, 22

rationing
  clothing 129
  food 57, 60, 103, 129, 177
recruiting campaigns 10
Red Cross, Australian 64, 69, 95, 162, 163
repatriation of Australian soldiers 66–70
resettlement schemes 108–9, 170
Reynolds, Ruth 73
Robinson, Meg (Woollen) 46–7, 59, 76, 82–3, 87, 103, 237
Robinson, Robbie 47, 59, 76, 87, 103, 237
Rock of Gibraltar 89–90
Rodrigues, Eva *see* Campion, Eva (Rodrigues)
Roland, Betty 99
Roseneder, Marjorie 181–2
Roseneder, Robert 181–2

Sakuramoto, Cherry *see* Parker, Cherry (Sakuramoto)
Schäfli, Hedy *see* Triffet, Hedy (Schäfli)
Schwer, Ralph 218–23, 237–8
Schwer, Thuy 219–23, 237–8
Scutter, Eddie 201–3, 238
Scutter, Ora (Kaminer) 201–3, 238
sea sickness 80, 148–9
Seidel, Rosa *see* Baker, Rosa (Seidel)
sexual behaviour 1
  Great War 12–17
  Second World War 21–2
  Vietnam War 23–4
ships
  aircraft carriers 142, 150
  Amerika, MV 138–9
  Andes 201
  Aquitania 68, 204